Essential Steps to College Success

Review this list, and work to complete each of these tasks in your first few weeks of college. These are important first steps to assure that you will get off to a good start in college.

☐ Meet your academic adviser. Make sure you feel comfortable with him or her.

☐ Figure out how to access your campus e-mail, learning management system, and any other technology tools that you'll be expected to use in your classes or across campus.

☐ Be sure you know important deadlines such as those for dropping or adding courses and due dates for upcoming quizzes, papers, and exams. Write them down in your planner or add them to your electronic calendar.

☐ Create a weekly schedule that includes time for study, recreation, and sleep.

☐ Purchase all your textbooks and keep up with reading assignments.

☐ Find an upper-level student you can talk to and ask for advice.

☐ Make an appointment to talk to one or more of your instructors outside of class.

☐ Find a quiet place to study. You might need to negotiate with a roommate for dedicated study space and time.

☐ Find a club or organization you would be interested in joining.

☐ Learn about academic support available on your campus, and make an appointment to visit the academic support center.

☐ Create a budget, and monitor it regularly to make sure you're sticking to it.

☐ Join or form a study group, especially for your most challenging courses.

☐ Get some exercise every day.

☐ Check back over this list weekly, and knowing yourself as you do, add other items that are necessary for your success.

Step by Step

to College and Career Success

Seventh Edition

Step by Step
to College and Career Success

Seventh Edition

John N. Gardner

President, John N. Gardner Institute for Excellence in Undergraduate Education
Brevard, North Carolina
Distinguished Professor Emeritus, Library and Information Science
Senior Fellow, National Resource Center for The First-Year Experience
 and Students in Transition
University of South Carolina, Columbia

Betsy O. Barefoot

Senior Scholar
John N. Gardner Institute for Excellence in Undergraduate Education
Brevard, North Carolina

bedford/st.martin's
Macmillan Learning
Boston | New York

For Bedford/St. Martin's

Vice President, Editorial, Macmillan Higher Education Humanities: Edwin Hill
Publisher for College Success: Erika Gutierrez
Senior Executive Editor for College Success: Simon Glick
Development Manager: Susan McLaughlin
Developmental Editor: Jennifer Jacobson, Ohlinger Publishing Services
Senior Production Editor: Kerri A. Cardone
Media Producer: Sarah O'Connor
Senior Production Supervisor: Lisa McDowell
Production Supervisor: Victoria Anzalone
Marketing Manager: Kayti Corfield
Editorial Assistant: Mary Jane Chen
Copyeditor: Jennifer Greenstein
Indexer: Jake Kawatski, Live Oaks Indexing
Photo Researcher: Krystyna Borgen
Photo Editor: Angela Boehler
Director of Rights and Permissions: Hilary Newman
Senior Art Director: Anna Palchik
Text Design: Jerilyn Bockorick, Cenveo Publisher Services
Cover Design: William Boardman
Cover Photo: David Schaffer/Getty Images
Composition: Cenveo Publisher Services
Printing and Binding: LSC Communications, Willard

Manufactured in the United States of America.

11 10 9 8 7
f e d c b

For information, write: Bedford/St. Martin's, 75 Arlington Street, Boston, MA 02116 (617-399-4000)

ISBN 978-1-319-02917-3

Brief Contents

01 Starting Out on the Right Foot *1*

02 Cultivating Motivation, Resilience, and Emotional Intelligence *17*

03 Managing Your Time *33*

04 Understanding How You Learn *53*

05 Getting the Most Out of Class *71*

06 Reading for Success *89*

07 Taking Exams & Tests *107*

08 Thinking in College *127*

09 Developing Information Literacy and Communication Skills *143*

10 Connecting with Others in a Diverse World *161*

11 Managing Money *179*

12 Staying Healthy *197*

13 Considering Majors & Careers *215*

Contents

Preface   *xvii*

01 Starting Out on the Right Foot *1*

The College Experience   3

Did You Make the Right Choice to Attend College?   *3*

What Opportunities Does College Provide?   *3*

What Is Your Purpose for Attending College?   *4*

How Is Your College Committed to Helping You Succeed?   *4*

The College Success Course and This Textbook—Making a Difference!   *5*

Making the Transition by Connecting with Others   6

How Is College Different?   *6*

Building Relationships with Your Instructors   *6*

TRY IT! Feeling Connected ▷ Get to Know Your Instructors   *7*

Setting Goals   8

TRY IT! Managing Time ▷ How Will You Get Where You Want to GO?   *8*

Consider Your Strengths   *8*

Get Started with Goals   *8*

TRY IT! Making Decisions ▷ This Way or That Way?   *9*

Follow the SMART Goal-Setting Guidelines   *9*

Academic Planning   11

Majors   *11*

Connecting Majors with Careers   *11*

TRY IT! Setting Goals ▷ Get to the Career Center   *12*

Working with an Academic Adviser   *14*

Chapter Review   15

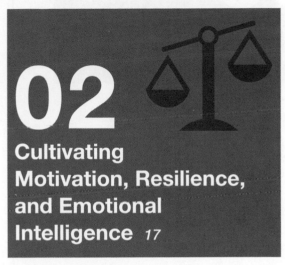

02 Cultivating Motivation, Resilience, and Emotional Intelligence *17*

Motivation, Attitude, and Mindset   19

Motivation   *19*

TRY IT! Setting Goals ▷ Extrinsic or Intrinsic?   *19*

Attitude   *20*

Mindsets   *21*

The Case of Amber   *22*

Resilience   23

TRY IT! Feeling Connected ▷ Get Inspired from Those around You   *24*

From Rejection to Success   *24*

Understanding Emotional Intelligence   25

Understanding and Managing Emotions   *25*

TRY IT! Managing Time ▷ Fussing and Fuming: Time Wasted   *26*

Emotional Intelligence Questionnaire   *26*

Improving Emotional Intelligence   *27*

Identifying Your EI Skills and Competencies   *27*

TRY IT! Making Decisions ▷ Commit to Improving Your EI   *28*

EI = College and Career Success   *30*

Chapter Review   31

03 Managing Your Time 33

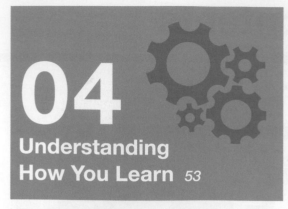

04 Understanding How You Learn 53

Time—Your Most Valuable Resource 35

Setting Goals 35

Prioritizing 36

Finding Balance 36

TRY IT! Setting Goals ▷ **"I've Got to Get My Priorities in Order!"** 36

Time in College and in Career 36

R-E-S-P-E-C-T 37

Managing Your Energy 38

Time-Management Pitfalls 40

Procrastination 40

Is Procrastination a Problem for You? 40

Being "Spread Too Thin" 41

Distractions 42

TRY IT! Managing Time ▷ **About to Lose It!** 42

Motivation Problems 42

Ask Yourself the Tough Questions 43

Get Smart about Organizing Your Days, Weeks, Tasks, and More 44

Using a Daily or Weekly Planner 44

Scheduling Your Time Week by Week 44

At the Top of My To-Do List Is "Make a To-Do List"! 46

Thinking about Your Class Schedule 47

TRY IT! Feeling Connected ▷ **Compare Your Class Schedules** 47

Maximizing Study and Review Time 48

Getting from Here to There—Using Travel Time Wisely 49

Chapter Review 50

Why Be an Engaged Learner? 55

TRY IT! Setting Goals ▷ **Engage in Learning** 55

Collaborative Learning Teams 56

TRY IT! Making Decisions ▷ **Group Study—Give It a Chance** 57

How People Learn 58

Learning Theories 58

Learning Styles 59

The VARK Learning Styles Invertory 60

The VARK Questionnaire 60

Scoring the VARK 62

TRY IT! Feeling Connected ▷ **Connect with VARK "Buddies"** 63

Using VARK Results for Success 64

TRY IT! Setting Goals ▷ **Developing Study Strategies That Match How You Learn** 64

When Learning Styles Clash with Teaching Styles 65

Learning with a Learning Disability 66

Attention Disorders 66

Cognitive Learning Disabilities 67

TRY IT! Feeling Connected ▷ **Prepare for a Learning Disability to Touch Your Life** 67

Exploring Resources 68

Chapter Review 69

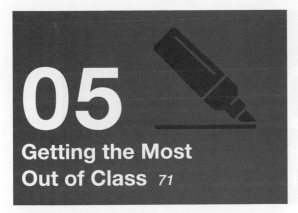

05
Getting the Most Out of Class 71

06
Reading for Success 89

Preparing for Class 73

TRY IT! Setting Goals ▷ Do All of Your Assigned Reading before Class 73

Pay Attention! Listening, Participating, and Note Taking 74

Listening Critically 74

Becoming an Active Class Participant 75

TRY IT! Feeling Connected ▷ Work Up the Nerve 75

Taking Notes 76

Learning Online 76

Approaches to Note Taking 77

Cornell Format 77

Outline Format 78

Paragraph Format 79

List Format 80

Taking Notes in Class 81

Make Adjustments for Different Classes 81

Use Specific Strategies for Note Taking in Quantitative Courses 82

Take Better Notes in Better Ways 83

Keep It Fresh by Reviewing Your Notes 84

Compare Notes 85

Class Notes and Homework 85

TRY IT! Managing Time ▷ Review Your Notes before Class 86

Chapter Review 87

Four-Step Plan for Active Reading 91

Step 1: Previewing 91

TRY IT! Setting Goals ▷ Be Motivated to Do All Your Required Reading 91

Map It! 91

Step 2: Reading and Marking 93

TRY IT! Setting Goals ▷ Pratice Marking a Chapter 94

Step 3: Reading with Concentration 94

Make the Most of Your Textbook 95

Step 4: Reviewing 96

Reading Online 96

Different Courses — Different Kinds of Textbooks 97

Reading Math Textbooks 97

Reading Science Textbooks 98

Reading Social Science and Humanities Textbooks 98

The Value of Primary Source Material 99

TRY IT! Managing Time ▷ Plan Your Reading Assignments 100

Improving Your Reading 101

Developing Your Vocabulary 101

What to Do When You Fall Behind in Your Reading 102

TRY IT! Feeling Connected ▷ Two (or More) Are Better than One 103

If English Is Not Your First Language 103

Chapter Review 104

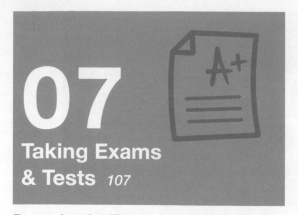

07 Taking Exams & Tests *107*

08 Thinking in College *127*

Preparing for Tests *109*

Work with Instructors, Peers, and Tutors *109*

TRY IT! Feeling Connected ▷ Tutoring and Study Groups *110*

Prepare Properly for Math and Science Exams *110*

Prepare Physically and Emotionally *111*

TRY IT! Setting Goals ▷ Be at Your Best for the Next Test *113*

Study to Make It Stick *114*

Help Your Memory Help You *114*

Use Review Sheets, Mind Maps, and Flash Cards *115*

Create Summaries *115*

Taking Tests and Exams *117*

Be Ready for Every Kind of Pitch *117*

TRY IT! Managing Time ▷ Time Flies—Even during an Essay Test *118*

You Bombed a Test—Now What? *119*

Online Tests *120*

Academic Honesty and Misconduct *121*

Cheating *121*

Plagiarism *122*

TRY IT! Making Decisions ▷ Ignorance Is No Excuse *122*

Consequences of Cheating and Plagiarism *122*

Reducing the Likelihood of Academic Dishonesty *122*

Chapter Review *124*

College-Level Thinking *129*

TRY IT! Feeling Connected ▷ Reflecting on How You Think *129*

Developing Strong Thinking Skills *130*

Challenge Assumptions and Beliefs *130*

Ask Questions *130*

Consider Multiple Points of View and Draw Conclusions *131*

Make Arguments *131*

TRY IT! Setting Goals ▷ Make Up Your Own Mind *131*

Examine Evidence *132*

Recognize and Avoid Faulty Reasoning *132*

Applying Your Critical-Thinking Skills *134*

Collaborate *134*

TRY IT! Making Decisions ▷ Study Groups: Pros and Cons *134*

Be Creative *134*

Learn to Problem-Solve *134*

Role Models in Creativity *136*

Think—and Find What You're Looking For *137*

Bloom's Taxonomy and Your First Year of College *138*

Chapter Review *140*

09
Developing Information Literacy and Communication Skills *143*

Information Literacy *145*

Learning to Be Information Literate *145*

Research—Information Literacy in Action *145*

Choosing, Narrowing, and Researching a Topic *146*

Using the Library *147*

Library Resources *148*

TRY IT! Feeling Connected ▷ Is the Library a Thing of the Past? *148*

Evaluating Sources *149*

Relevance *149*

Authority *149*

Bias *150*

Synthesis and Sharing *150*

The Writing Process *151*

Steps to Good Writing *151*

Knowing Your Audience *153*

Time and the Writing Process *153*

TRY IT! Managing Time ▷ Is It Worth Some Extra Time to Improve Your Writing? *153*

Citing Your Sources *154*

TRY IT! Making Decisions ▷ Which Way Will You Go? *154*

At the Podium: Speaking in Public *155*

TRY IT! Setting Goals ▷ Developing Confidence in Public Speaking *157*

Chapter Review *158*

10
Connecting with Others in a Diverse World *161*

Personal Relationships *163*

Roommates *163*

Romantic Relationships *164*

Breakups *164*

The Ties That Bind: Family *165*

Marriage and Parenting during College *165*

Relationships with Parents *166*

Connecting with Others in a Digital Age *167*

TRY IT! Feeling Connected ▷ Gone but Not Forgotten *168*

Thriving in Diverse Environments *169*

Stereotyping: Why We Believe What We Believe *169*

TRY IT! Making Decisions ▷ Resist Prejudice *170*

Other Differences You Will Encounter in College *170*

Creating a Welcoming Environment on Your Campus *171*

TRY IT! Setting Goals ▷ Make a New and Different Friend *172*

Connecting through Involvement *173*

TRY IT! Managing Time ▷ How Involved Is Too Involved? *173*

Connecting by Working *174*

Connecting through Community Service *174*

Connecting the College Experience to Career Success *175*

Chapter Review *176*

11
Managing Money 179

Living on a Budget *181*

Creating a Budget *181*

TRY IT! Making Decisions ▷ Miscellaneous Expenses *182*

Cutting Costs *182*

TRY IT! Setting Goals ▷ Your Personal Budget: There's an App for That *184*

Unexpected Benefits of Being Good with Money *184*

Understanding Financial Aid *185*

Types of Aid *185*

Navigating and Qualifying for Financial Aid *186*

How to Keep Your Funding *187*

Steps to Qualify for Financial Aid *187*

TRY IT! Setting Goals ▷ Exhaust All Avenues *188*

Achieving a Balance between Working and Borrowing *189*

Advantages and Disadvantages of Working *189*

TRY IT! Managing Time ▷ Be Realistic *189*

Student Loans *189*

TRY IT! Feeling Connected ▷ Search Party *190*

Plan for the Future *190*

Managing Credit Wisely *191*

Understanding Credit *191*

Debit Cards *192*

Frequently Asked Questions about Credit Cards and Identity Theft *193*

Chapter Review *194*

12
Staying Healthy 197

Understanding Wellness *199*

Managing Stress to Maintain Wellness *200*

TRY IT! Making Decisions ▷ Are You About to Lose It? *200*

The Importance of Good Nutrition *201*

TRY IT! Setting Goals ▷ Use Stress to Your Advantage *201*

Risky Eating Habits *203*

Exercising to Maintain Wellness *203*

TRY IT! Managing Time ▷ Scheduling to Stay Fit *204*

Use Technology to Stay Fit *204*

Getting Enough Sleep to Maintain Wellness *205*

Emotional Health *206*

Maintaining Sexual Health *208*

Communicating about Safe Sex *208*

Avoiding Sexually Transmitted Infections *208*

Using Birth Control *209*

Protecting Yourself and Others against Sexual Assault and Violence *209*

Alcohol and Other Substances *210*

The Use and Abuse of Alcohol *210*

TRY IT! Feeling Connected ▷ Sharing and Comparing Experiences *211*

Tobacco and Marijuana *211*

Chapter Review *212*

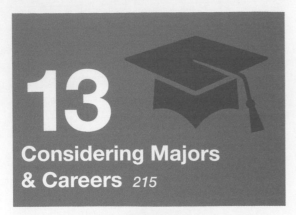

13 Considering Majors & Careers 215

Careers and the New Economy 217

Characteristics of Today's Economy 217

Building the Right Mindset for the Future 218

Self-Exploration in Career Planning 219

Values 219

Skills 219

Aptitude 219

Personality 219

Life Goals and Work Satisfaction 220

Interests 220

Exploring Your Interests 221

TRY IT! Feeling Connected ▷ Where Do You Fit in the Holland Model? 222

Diving into Career Research 223

Planning for Your Career 225

Getting Experience 226

Experiential Learning Opportunities 226

Working in College 227

TRY IT! Making Decisions ▷ College Jobs and Your Career 228

Job Search Strategies 229

Market Yourself 229

Build a Résumé 229

Write a Cover Letter 230

Know How to Interview 230

TRY IT! Setting Goals ▷ Planning an Exciting Future 231

Skills Employers Seek 232

Content Skills 232

Transferable Skills 232

Top-Ranked Skills and Qualities 232

Chapter Review 235

Index 239

Preface

Anyone who teaches beginning college students knows how much they have changed in recent years. Today's students are increasingly job-focused, skilled in using technology, and concerned about the future. And, more than ever, students worry about how they will pay for college. Recently, popular media sources such as the *Wall Street Journal* and *USA Today* have raised doubts about the value of college, concerns about how student debt delays millennials from starting families and businesses,[1] and questions about whether money spent on a college degree would be better invested in a start-up business or travel.[2] While it is tempting to focus on the few individuals who can find an alternate path to a successful future, we know that for the overwhelming majority of individuals, a college degree is more essential than ever before.

Today, we are seeing diverse students of all ages and backgrounds enrolling in both two- and four-year institutions, bringing with them the hopes and dreams that a college education can help fulfill. This textbook is written for students of any age at any type of college—we present comprehensive and helpful information on every aspect of the college experience for a variety of student audiences, from students straight out of high school to returning adult learners, from commuters to residents at all higher education institutions. We provide examples that are relevant to students and do not make assumptions about the realities of their lives.

Step by Step to College and Career Success is designed specifically to give *all* students the practical help they need to set goals, succeed, and stay in college. As our briefest text, it is written to be to the point, yet comprehensive in coverage. We've pared away extras to focus on the most crucial skills and the most important choices that students make in order to succeed in college and beyond. The seventh edition covers pressing topics that affect students' lives and how they learn, such as active learning, time management, test taking, career preparation, relationships, and technology, and we have expanded on the book's themes of motivation, persistence, resilience, and decision-making.

We also want to ensure that students think about long- and short-term goals so that they're able to take the steps necessary to do well in this course, their other courses, and their careers. In addition, this text covers a broad range of academic and life skills, including time management, learning styles, critical thinking, listening and taking notes, reading, communication, testing, money management, diversity, health, and majors and careers.

We aim to convey respect and admiration for our students in our writing while recognizing their continued need for challenge and support. Our text is grounded in the growing body of research on student success and retention. Simply put, we do not like to see students fail. We are confident that if students both read and heed the information herein, they will become engaged in the college experience, learn, and persist to graduation.

Whether you are considering this textbook for use in your first-year seminar or have already made a decision to adopt it, we thank you for your interest, and trust that you will find it to be a valuable teaching aid. We also hope that this book will guide you and your campus in understanding the broad range of issues that can affect student success.

Key Chapter Changes

- **A heavily revised introductory chapter** has been expanded and reorganized to serve as a roadmap to get students off on the right foot, as the title suggests. It offers new sections, "What Opportunities Does College Provide?" and "How is College Committed to Helping You Succeed?" Coverage of goal setting has been expanded to reflect research on the

---

[1] "Recent Grads Doubt College's Worth." The Wall Street Journal online, September 29, 2015, Douglas Belkin (author).

[2] "Kids skip college–not worth the money." USA Today online, April 22, 2013, Oliver St. John (author).

strengths perspective and includes an expanded student activity. Coverage of academic planning (formerly in Chapter 13) has been moved to Chapter 1 and expanded with a new article, "Working with an Academic Adviser."

- **A new Chapter 2, "Cultivating Motivation, Resilience, and Emotional Intelligence,"** offers coverage of extrinsic and intrinsic motivation, resilience, and coverage of emotional intelligence expanded from similar material offered in the learning styles chapter of the sixth edition. Chapter 2 includes a subsection on attitude with a related student activity. The subsection on mindsets explores fixed and growth mindsets and includes a student activity as well as a short case study about a real student—"The Case of Amber." The section devoted to emotional intelligence includes self-assessments so that students can identify their own EI skills and competencies, better understand the role of EI in everyday life (e.g., priority management, anger management), and develop strategies for improving EI.

- **Chapter 4, "Understanding How You Learn,"** offers a new and approachable section on learning theories that introduces students to learning theorists Maslow, Bandura, and Schlossberg. The chapter features a new figure of Maslow's, "Hierarchy of Needs Pyramid." The section, "Learning with a Learning Disability," has also been updated to reflect recent research in the field.

- **Heavily revised and reorganized, Chapter 8, "Thinking in College,"** gives students a better understanding of what is involved in college-level thinking and practical strategies on how to achieve it. Students are clearly shown how concepts like fast and slow thinking, problem solving, creativity, and collaboration all relate to critical thinking.

- **Chapter 9, "Developing Information Literacy and Communication Skills,"** combines what had been two separate chapters in the sixth edition. The chapter now covers information literacy and using the library (formerly Chapter 8 "Developing Information Literacy") and writing and speaking (formerly Chapter 9 "Communicating Clearly"). Content is streamlined and logically organized. The authors have broadened the presentation of the "library" to heighten awareness of how central the library or learning commons is to student life now.

- **Chapter 12, "Staying Healthy,"** now takes a holistic view of wellness including coverage of mental, physical, and spiritual health. The chapter includes expanded coverage of topics such as stress management, cyberbullying, maintaining sexual health, and protecting against sexual assault.

FEATURES OF THIS EDITION

Powerful LaunchPad course space. Available with the seventh edition, LaunchPad Solo for College Success is home to dozens of pre-built assignable and assessable digital resources designed to help students engage with key course concepts and prepare for class, including LearningCurve adaptive quizzing, video activities, self-assessments, case study quizzes, and links to further online resources such as apps and podcasts. Easy-to-use and easy-to-assign modules based on essential college success topics prompt students to apply the strategies discussed in class and are easily adaptable to your own course material, such as readings, videos, quizzes, discussion groups, and more.

A stronger connection between college success and career success through new coverage in the narrative and new articles like "Time in College and in Career" (Chapter 2); "Connecting the College Experience to Career Success" (Chapter 10); "Unexpected Benefits of Being Good with Money," which touches on how money management affects one's overall life including one's job prospects (Chapter 11); and "Diving into Career Research" (Chapter 13).

A narrative that reflects how today's students and instructors use technology and other ways they could use it to achieve educational and career goals. Chapter content incorporates coverage of technological tools and skills, digital examples and models, and more in-text examples that incorporate social media and apps in an effort to reflect the role of these tools in students' lives.

A carefully executed design and art program keeps students focused and engaged with the content by including images that reflect the experiences of all students in the course so that they will feel comfortable and connected. Captions invite students to think critically about the content.

A fun and compelling approach. The text is streamlined, focused, and readable. Inviting "pullout articles" address important, real-world topics of pressing concern to students. New articles in the seventh edition cover topics such as how the college success course and this textbook make a positive difference in student success (Chapter 1), mindsets (Chapter 2), making and using to-do lists (Chapter 3), using commuting time wisely (Chapter 3), improving emotional intelligence (Chapter 4), learning online (Chapter 5), reading online (Chapter 6), the value of primary source material (Chapter 6), knowing and following guidelines for academic honesty (Chapter 6), the importance of being resilient after "bombing" a test (Chapter 7), role models in creativity (Chapter 8), applying critical thinking to research (Chapter 9), risky eating habits (Ch 12), using technology to stay fit (Ch 12), and protecting against sexual assault (Ch 12).

Features and teaching techniques that engage students:

- **Quizzes that open and close each chapter.** Chapter-opening "How Do You Measure Up?" quizzes get students thinking about how key topics in the chapter relate to them. A "Now ... How Do You Measure Up?" quiz at the end of the chapter prompts students to consider what they have learned after reading the chapter and learning new ways of thinking.

- **Try It! boxes encourage students to interact with what they are learning.** Focusing on four themes—managing time, feeling connected, setting goals, and making decisions—each Try It! box explains a specific action for students to try, the benefit of doing so, and first steps to get started. The Try It! boxes that reinforce setting goals also carry an emphasis on motivation. These boxes can be used for student self-direction or as assignments inside or outside the classroom. Examples include Feeling Connected: Get Inspired from those around You (Chapter 2); Setting Goals: Extrinsic or Intrinsic (Chapter 2); Setting Goals: I've Got to Get My Priorities in Order! (Chapter 3); Making Decisions: Group Study—Give It a Chance (Chapter 4); Feeling Connected: Two (or More) Are Better than One (Chapter 6); Making Decisions: I Can't Believe I Fell for That! (Chapter 7); Managing Time: Is It Worth Some Extra Time to Improve Your Writing? (Chapter 9); Setting Goals: Your Personal Budget: There's an App for That (Chapter 11); Feeling Connected: Sharing and Comparing Experiences

(Chapter 12); and Making Decisions: College Jobs and Careers (Chapter 13).

- **Streamlined chapter-ending sections.** These include a Steps to Success checklist that reviews the key action steps in the chapter; an Applying What You've Learned section with application opportunities; and a Use Your Resources section that encourages students to seek out peers (online or in person), use social media, take advantage of instructors' use office hours, study groups, campus resources, and references like books, and Web sites. These features encourage students to take initiative in answering different kinds of common questions and solving different kinds of problems.

Resources for Instructors

To help you meet the challenges of engaging and retaining today's students, we have created a complete package of support materials:

- **LaunchPad Solo for College Success.** LaunchPad Solo for College Success is home to dozens of pre-built assignable and assessable digital resources designed to help students engage with key course concepts and prepare for class, including LearningCurve adaptive quizzing and video activities. Pre-built units are easy to assign or adapt with your own material, such as readings, videos, quizzes, discussion groups, and more. LaunchPad Solo also provides access to a grade book that provides a clear window on performance for your whole class, for individual students and individual assignments.

- **Unique to LaunchPad Solo: *LearningCurve for College Success*.** *LearningCurve for College Success* is an online, adaptive, self-quizzing program that quickly learns what students already know and helps them practice what they haven't yet mastered. LearningCurve motivates students to engage with key concepts before they come to class so that they are ready to participate; it also offers reporting tools to help you discern your student's needs. An updated version of LearningCurve available with *LaunchPad Solo for College Success* features a larger question pool with new multiple-choice questions.

- **Ordering information.** LaunchPad Solo is available to package at a significant discount with select College Success titles. Please contact your Macmillan Learning representative for more information. To order *LaunchPad Solo for College Success* standalone, use ISBN 978-1-319-06478-5.

- **ACES (The Academic and Career Excellence System).** This instrument measures student strengths in twelve critical areas and prompts students to reflect on their habits, behaviors, attitudes, and skills. Norm-referenced reports indicate whether students are at a high, moderate, or low skill level in particular areas. For more information, go to **macmillanlearning .com/ ACES**.

- **Instructor's Manual.** The Instructor's Manual includes chapter objectives, teaching suggestions, an introduction to the first-year experience course, a sample lesson plan for each chapter, sample syllabi, final projects for the end of the course, and various case studies that are relevant to the topics covered in the text. The Instructor's Manual is available online.

- **Computerized Test Bank.** The Computerized Test Bank contains more than 700 multiple-choice, true/false, short-answer, and essay questions designed to assess students' understanding of key concepts. This edition features more challenging scenario-based questions that ask students to apply their understanding to concepts in the text. An answer key is included. A digital text file is also available.

- **Lecture Slides.** Available online for download, lecture slides accompany each chapter of the book and include key concepts and art from the text. Use the slides as provided to structure your lectures, or customize them as desired to fit your course's needs.

- *French Fries Are Not Vegetables.* This comprehensive instructional DVD features multiple resources for class and professional use. This video is also available with our *LaunchPad Solo for College Success.* ISBN 978-0-312-65073-5.

- *Curriculum Solutions.* Our new Curriculum Solutions group brings together the quality and reputation of Bedford/St. Martin's content with Hayden-McNeil's expertise in publishing original custom print and digital products. With our new capabilities, we are excited to deliver customized course solutions at an affordable price. Make *Step by Step to College and Career Success,* Seventh Edition fit your course and goals by integrating your own institutional materials, including only the parts of the text you intend to use in your course, or both. Please contact your local Macmillan Learning sales representative for more information and to see samples.

- The **CS Select custom database** allows you to create a textbook for your College Success course that reflects your course objectives and uses just the content you need. Start with one of our core texts, and then rearrange chapters, delete chapters, and add additional content—including your own original content—to create just the book you're looking for. Get started by visiting **macmillanlearning.com/csSelect**.

- **TradeUp.** Bring more value and choice to your students' first-year experience by packaging *Step by Step to College and Career Success,* Seventh Edition with one of a thousand titles from Macmillan publishers at a 50 percent discount from the regular price. Contact your Macmillan Learning sales representative for more information.

Resources for Students and Packaging Options

- **LaunchPad Solo for College Success.** LaunchPad Solo is an online course solution that offers our acclaimed content including videos, LearningCurve adaptive quizzes, and more. For more information, see the Resources for Instructors section.

  - **Unique to LaunchPad Solo:** *LearningCurve for College Success. LearningCurve for College Success* is an online, adaptive, self-quizzing program that quickly learns what students already know and helps them practice what they haven't yet mastered.

  - **Ordering information.** LaunchPad Solo is available to package at a significant discount with select College Success titles. Please contact your Macmillan Learning sales representative for more information. To order *LaunchPad Solo for College Success* standalone, use ISBN 978-1-319-06478-5.

- **E-book Options.** E-books offer an affordable alternative for students. You can find PDF versions of our books when you shop online at our publishing partners' sites. Learn more at **macmillanlearning.com/ebooks**.

- **Bedford/St. Martin's Insider's Guides.** These concise and student-friendly booklets on topics that are critical to college success are a perfect complement to your textbook and course. One Insider Guide can be packaged with *any* Bedford/St. Martin's textbook. Additional Insider's Guides can also be packaged for additional cost. Topics include:

- **New!** *Insider's Guide for Adult Learners*
- **New!** *Insider's Guide to College Etiquette,* Second Edition
- **New!** *Insider's Guide for Returning Veterans*
- **New!** *Insider's Guide to Transferring*
- *Insider's Guide to Academic Planning*
- *Insider's Guide to Beating Test Anxiety*
- *Insider's Guide to Building Confidence*
- *Insider's Guide to Career Services*
- *Insider's Guide to College Ethics and Personal Responsibility*
- *Insider's Guide to Community College*
- *Insider's Guide to Credit Cards,* Second Edition
- *Insider's Guide to Getting Involved on Campus*
- *Insider's Guide to Global Citizenship*
- *Insider's Guide to Time Management,* Second Edition

For more information on ordering one of these guides free with the text, go to **macmillanhighered.com/collegesuccess.**

The Bedford/St. Martin's Planner. *Everything that students need to plan and use their time effectively is included, along with* advice on preparing schedules and to-do lists, and blank schedules and calendars (monthly and weekly) for planning. Integrated into the planner are tips and advice on fixing common grammar errors, note taking, and succeeding on tests; an address book; and an annotated list of useful Web sites. The planner fits easily into a backpack or purse, so students can take it anywhere. To order the planner standalone, use ISBN 978-0-312-57447-5. To package the planner, please contact your local Macmillan Learning sales rep.

Journal Writing: A Beginning. Designed to give students an opportunity to use writing as a way to explore their thoughts and feelings, this writing journal includes a generous supply of inspirational quotes placed throughout the pages, tips for journaling, and suggested journal topics. To order the journal standalone, use ISBN 978-0-312-59027-7.

About the Authors

John N. Gardner brings unparalleled experience to this authoritative text for first-year seminar courses. His first college teaching experience was at a two-year public college in a small, rural town in South Carolina. That experience was so inspiring that he made a lifetime commitment to continue serving such students. John is the recipient of the University of South Carolina's highest award for teaching excellence. He has twenty-five years of experience directing and teaching in the most respected and most widely emulated first-year seminar in the country, the University 101 course at the University of South Carolina. John is universally recognized as one of the country's leading educators for his role in initiating and orchestrating an international reform movement to improve the beginning college experience. He is also the founding leader of two influential higher education centers that support campuses in their efforts to improve the learning and retention of beginning college students: the National Resource Center for The First-Year Experience and Students in Transition at the University of South Carolina (**www.sc.edu/fye**), and the John N. Gardner Institute for Excellence in Undergraduate Education (**www .jngi.org**), based in Brevard, North Carolina. The experiential basis for all of John Gardner's work is his own miserable first year of college on academic probation, an experience he hopes to prevent for this book's readers. Today, as a much happier adult, John is married to fellow author of this book, Betsy Barefoot.

Betsy O. Barefoot is a writer, researcher, and teacher whose special area of scholarship is the first year of college. During her tenure at the University of South Carolina from 1988 to 1999, she served as co-director for research and publications at the National Resource Center for The First-Year Experience and Students in Transition. She taught University 101, in addition to special-topics graduate courses on the first-year experience and the principles of college teaching.

She conducts first-year seminar faculty training workshops around the United States and in other countries, and she is frequently called on to evaluate first-year seminar outcomes. Betsy currently serves as senior scholar at the John N. Gardner Institute for Excellence in Undergraduate Education. In her Institute role, she led a major national research project to identify institutions of excellence in the first college year. She currently works with both two- and four-year campuses in evaluating all components of the first year.

Acknowledgments

Although this text speaks with the voices of its two authors, it represents contributions from many others. We gratefully acknowledge these contributions and thank these individuals, whose special expertise has made it possible to introduce new college students to their college experience through the holistic approach we deeply believe in.

We are indebted to the following reviewers who offered us thoughtful and constructive feedback on this edition:

Christine Deacons

Kathleen Fitzpatrick

Linda Gannon

Christopher Lau

Kristina Leonard

Von McGriff

Keron Ward-Myles

Brandi Neal

Eric-Gene-Shrewsbury

Chris Strouthopoulos

Jacques Surrency

Michelle Van de Sande

Mike Wood

Andrea Zick

We would also like to acknowledge and thank the numerous colleagues who have contributed to this book in its previous editions: Catherine Andersen, Gallaudet University; Kathryn

Arrington, Baton Rouge Community College; Erin Barnett, Eastern Kentucky University; Elaine Barry, Central Maine Technical College; Michelle Murphy Burcin, University of South Carolina at Columbia; Tom Carskadon, Mississippi State University; Audra Cooke, Rock Valley College; Michael Dunn, Radford University; Peggy Dunn, New River Community College; Jerry Eddy, Sinclair Community College; Juan Flores, Folsom Lake College; Gina Floyd, Shorter University; Philip Gardner, Michigan State University; Britta Gibson, University of Pikeville; Chris Gurrie, University of Tampa; Jeanne L. Higbee, University of Minnesota, Twin Cities; Nancy Hunter, Maysville Community College; Darby Johnsen, Oklahoma City Community College; Tony Jones, Milligan College; Natala Kleather (Tally) Hart, Ohio State University; Christopher Lau, Hutchinson Community College; Jonathan Long, Central Missouri State University; Tawana Mattox, Athens Area Technical Institute; Eileen McDonough, Barry University; Mary Ellen O'Leary, University of South Carolina at Columbia; Stacey Murray, Sonoma State University; Adenike Oloyede, Lake Michigan College; Richard Robers, Virginia Western Community College; Rajon Shore, Blue Ridge Community College; Kate Trombitas, Ohio State University; Lenora White, Baton Rouge Community College; Michelle Van de Sande, Arapahoe Community College; Peggy Whaley, Murray State University; Michael Wood, Missouri State University; and Edward Zlotkowski, Bentley College.

As we look to the future, we are excited about the numerous improvements to this text that our creative Bedford/St. Martin's team has made and will continue to make. Special thanks to Edwin Hill, Vice President of Editorial, Humanities; Erika Gutierrez, Publisher for College Success; Simon Glick, Senior Executive Editor for College Success; Jennifer Jacobson, Development Editor at Ohlinger Publishing Services; Bethany Gordon, Associate Editor; Mary Jane Chen, Editorial Assistant; Kayti Corfield, Marketing Manager; and Kerri Cardone, Senior Production Editor.

Most of all, we thank you, the users of our book, for you are the true inspiration for this work.

Step by Step

to College and Career Success

Seventh Edition

3
The College Experience

6
Making the Transition by Connecting with Others

8
Setting Goals

11
Academic Planning

Starting Out on the Right Foot

LaunchPad
macmillan learning

To access the LearningCurve study tool, Video Tools, and more, go to *LaunchPad Solo for College Success*. **macmillanhighered.com/ collegesuccessmedia**

Congratulations! You are going to college—you have made a choice to change your life for the better. You may have been a star student in high school, or you may have struggled in some of your classes. Your parents may be paying your tuition and giving you spending money, or you may have a job or loans. No matter your age, background, academic skills, or economic circumstances, whether you succeed will depend on your motivation, commitment, and willingness to take advantage of all that your college or university has to offer.

This book is a step-by-step guide to college success. Reading, remembering, and practicing the information and strategies in each chapter will help you accomplish your goals and avoid the kinds of problems that sometimes trip up even the best students in their first year in college. What you learn from this book will also be valuable to you throughout your college experience and in life.

Don't forget that college life is more than just academic work. It is also about making the most of new and continuing relationships and finding your niche on campus. During your first term, look for opportunities to become involved in a campus group or organization. Meeting others who share your talents or interests will help you feel at home in this new environment.

You're on an exciting journey, and this book can be your roadmap. This road will take you to new places and introduce you to new ideas and new people. You will also learn about how to harness your own strengths to achieve the goals you have always had and those you may discover.

How do you measure up?

1. I am excited to be in this college success course because I know I will learn strategies for succeeding in college.
   ○ Agree
   ○ Don't Know
   ○ Disagree

2. To help control the uncertainties of life, long-term goal setting is a must.
   ○ Agree
   ○ Don't Know
   ○ Disagree

3. I know how important it is to begin creating an academic plan for my college experience immediately.
   ○ Agree
   ○ Don't Know
   ○ Disagree

4. I have thought about how my college experience will relate to what I want to do after I graduate.
   ○ Agree
   ○ Don't Know
   ○ Disagree

Review the items you marked "Don't Know" or "Disagree." Pay special attention to these topics in this chapter—you will develop a better understanding of why they are important to your success in college. A follow-up quiz at the end of the chapter will prompt you to consider what you have learned.

The "Aha!" Moment—Linking What You Enjoy to a Major

△ Shawn Mosley

solominviktor/Shutterstock.

"Here's the thing: I'm not planning to stay in college," I tell my academic adviser, Dr. Beene, at our first meeting. "I'm just here for a year to get my parents off my back. College is a big deal for them: They were the first ones in their families to go, and my dad's always regretted dropping out before he got his degree. So, it really doesn't matter to me what I take. Why don't you just pick some courses for me?"

"What are your interests?" Dr. Beene asks. He looks surprised when I say sports—especially rock climbing—and girls and cars, which are pretty typical for an eighteen-year-old, in my opinion. "Well, there's room in your schedule for a humanities elective, so how about a women's studies class?" he says. "And you've got a lab science requirement, so I suggest geology." The fact that I never even took geology in high school doesn't faze him. "You might as well know something about those rocks you're climbing, right?"

Cut to the end of the first term: I'm back in Dr. Beene's office. "Remember how you forced me to take geology?" I say. "Well, our field trips turned out to be pretty cool. The professor was this genius *Man vs. Wild* type and really made me think about the environment in a new way. And I ended up making some good friends."

"So what now?" asks Dr. Beene. "Still planning to drop out?"

"No," I say. "I lined up a work-study position in the geology department next spring, and now I *definitely* want to major in geology. I brought a list of the required courses and a few courses I think would be great electives. Can you help me work these into my schedule?"

What do you think led Shawn to begin college? How do his reasons for being in college compare with yours? What seems to be the motivation behind Shawn's interest in geology? What steps should he take before committing to his decision that geology is the right major for him or even that college makes sense for him right now?

The College Experience

Depending on who you are, your life situation, and your reasons for enrolling, college can mean different things. Some students choose to attend college to learn a specific set of skills or receive training for a particular career. Some attend to explore various fields of study, to experience the social life, or to prepare for graduate or professional school.

College is some students' top priority; for others it can be an additional priority on top of family or work obligations. Some students come to the United States from other countries just to study. College is really far more than any single image you might have about why students attend and what the college experience actually involves.

Whatever your reasons for attending, college will be a time when you take some appropriate risks, learn new things, and meet new and different people—all in a supportive environment.

Did You Make the Right Choice to Attend College?

American society values higher education because receiving a college degree gives you the opportunity to achieve your goals and dreams regardless of your race or ethnic background, national origin, immigration status, family income level, family history, or personal connections. Higher education allows people to improve their lives by obtaining skills, learning to perform different jobs, and establishing successful careers. Making more money isn't the only reason to go to college, but as Figure 1.1 shows, the more education you have, the more likely you are to be employed and the more you will earn.

In addition to increasing your earning power, college is about helping you become a better thinker and a leader in your community, company, or profession. In short, college can change your life for the better.

What Opportunities Does College Provide?

Being in college will provide numerous opportunities for you to develop a variety of social networks, both in person and online. You will enjoy the face-to-face relationships you develop with instructors and fellow students, and social

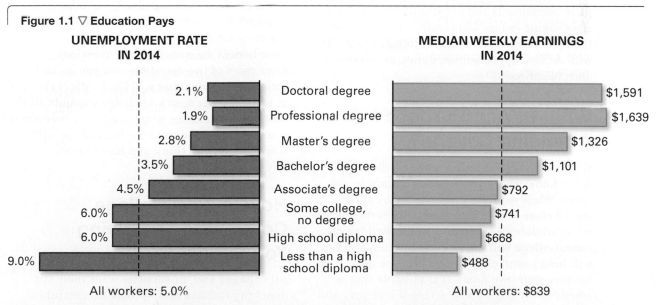

Figure 1.1 ▽ Education Pays

UNEMPLOYMENT RATE IN 2014 | MEDIAN WEEKLY EARNINGS IN 2014

Degree	Unemployment Rate	Median Weekly Earnings
Doctoral degree	2.1%	$1,591
Professional degree	1.9%	$1,639
Master's degree	2.8%	$1,326
Bachelor's degree	3.5%	$1,101
Associate's degree	4.5%	$792
Some college, no degree	6.0%	$741
High school diploma	6.0%	$668
Less than a high school diploma	9.0%	$488

All workers: 5.0% | All workers: $839

Source: U.S. Department of Labor, Bureau of Labor Statistics, *Current Population Survey*, 2015.
Note: Data are for persons age twenty-five and over. Earnings are for full-time wage and salary workers.

media outlets and apps (such as Facebook, Twitter, Snapchat, Instagram, or Viber) will provide ways to expand your interactions with students on your campus and at other campuses as well; most colleges and on-campus organizations have their own Facebook pages where students share different kinds of information.

College can also provide opportunities for you to:

- explore student clubs and organizations, including those that relate to your academic and career interests

- expand your leadership abilities by taking advantage of opportunities in student government and other campus groups

- join intercollegiate or intramural athletic teams

- participate in many activities and traditions that will help you develop a sense of institutional loyalty and belonging

- network for improved employment opportunities with the help of career center professionals and instructors

- meet other people like you who have similar values, life experiences, and plans for the future

While college is an experience you will remember fondly throughout your life, it is also a lot of work. Being in college means studying for hours each week, staying up late or getting up early to complete assignments and prepare for class, going to class, taking exams, and possibly working harder than you ever have. In a sense, college is like a job with defined opportunities, duties, expectations, and obligations.

What Is Your Purpose for Attending College?

Without a purpose for attending college, you won't know where you're going or how to get there. While some students come to college with a clear sense of purpose, others do not. For many students a sense of purpose builds over time. College will be a set of experiences that will help you to clarify your purpose and achieve your own goals. It is possible that as you discover more about yourself and your abilities, your reasons for coming to college will change. In fact, a majority of college students

> **" It is possible that as you discover more about yourself and your abilities, your reasons for coming to college will change. "**

change their academic plans at least once during the college years.

Here are some questions to ask yourself about your purpose for being in college:

- Am I here to study a subject that interests me?

- Am I here to prepare for graduate or professional school?

- Am I here to prepare myself for employment?

- Am I here to meet new people?

- Am I here so I can better serve my community and country?

- Am I here to better understand myself and society?

- Am I here to develop new knowledge and ideas?

Your honest answers to these questions will drive most of the decisions that you make in college, decisions that will likely affect the rest of your life. Because knowledge expands all the time, college classes won't teach you everything you will ever need to know, but college will teach you how to think and how to learn throughout your life.

How Is Your College Committed to Helping You Succeed?

All colleges and universities want their students to graduate and become successful in their future careers. Therefore they provide support services to students at no additional

cost. For example, colleges have academic advisers who provide students with academic information and help them register in the appropriate courses every term. Colleges also have financial aid advisers who are trained to assist students and their families in understanding financial aid options.

Additionally, most colleges have learning centers that provide free tutoring to students and career centers that help students with career planning and job hunting. Remember that the faculty and staff of a college are there to serve students, so do not be shy—ask for help. At the end of each chapter in this book, we provide a list of resources that are typically available at colleges and universities. Students who seek help are the ones who are the most successful, so take advantage of the support available to you. ∎

The College Success Course and This Textbook—Making a Difference!

Research shows that students who take *and complete* a college success course such as this one are more likely to earn better grades, remain in college, and graduate than students who don't. You read that right—just by completing this course and reading this book you greatly improve your chances to earn your college degree. This course will give you information that you need to be successful and will also provide a safe place for you to share your successes and your challenges, get to know other first-year students, build relationships with your instructor and other students, develop your academic plan based on your strengths and interests, and shape your plans after graduation.

As individuals with years of experience working with first-year students, we know that starting college can be challenging. However if you apply the ideas in this book to your everyday life, you are more likely to enjoy your time in college, graduate, and achieve your goals. In this textbook, we cover a lot of topics. For instance, you'll read about managing your time, taking notes, making the most of the way you learn, preparing for tests, building relationships, and planning for your future career. So sit back and take a moment to appreciate that you are enrolled in this course and reading this book—both will make a huge difference in your life.

Making the Transition by Connecting with Others

Colleges can seem like cities, especially if you went to a small high school or grew up in a small town. To feel comfortable in the college environment, you need to find places where you feel that you belong. We know that you have a lot going on, but the time you invest to make this happen now will pay big dividends later.

How Is College Different?

If you just graduated from high school, you will soon find that college is a different kind of experience. For instance, in college you are probably part of a more diverse student body, and you have more potential friends who are from different places.

While you will be able to choose from many more courses, managing your time is sure to be more difficult. In high school you may have had weekly or biweekly tests and quizzes, but tests in college are sometimes given only twice or three times a term. You will probably be required to do more writing in college than in high school, and you will be encouraged to do original research and think critically about different points of view.

You will be expected to read and study out of class to be ready for in-class discussions. Your instructors might rely far less on textbooks and far more on lectures than your high school teachers did. They also might give you fewer rules and allow you more freedom to express views that are different from theirs.

Building Relationships with Your Instructors

An important type of relationship you can develop in college is one with your instructors. Frequent, high-quality interaction with your instructors can have a positive effect on how well you do academically. Your instructors will expect you to be independent and to take the initiative to seek their advice and assistance. In addition, you will enjoy getting to know many of them, especially those who share your interests.

What do instructors expect? Instructors' expectations will be different from course to course. But most of them will expect you to be motivated to do your best, to be in class on time, to do assigned work, to listen and participate in class, and to not give up. Instructors also expect honesty and openness. Many will invite you to express your feelings about the course through anonymous one-minute papers or other forms of class assessment.

To get a clear sense of instructors' expectations, pay close attention to the syllabus for

---

◁ **Don't Be a Lone Ranger**
You can develop learning relationships with other students in a study group, a club or organization related to your major, or even in student activities. It's not wise to be a "lone ranger" as you approach studying; you will learn more deeply by studying with other students. You will also develop friendships that will last through your college experience. The Washington Post.

each course. The syllabus, which you will receive on the first day of class, is both a statement of course requirements and a contract between you and the instructor. The syllabus will give you information and dates for exams or presentations, a grading rubric, the course attendance policy, and other class guidelines or rules. Your syllabus may be in paper or online, but make sure you review and save the syllabus for every course.

In college it is your responsibility to meet your instructors' expectations. In return you can expect your instructors to be organized, prepared, and knowledgeable. They should give you thoughtful feedback on your work and should grade it fairly.

Maximize learning relationships. You can visit your instructors anytime during the term to ask questions, seek help, or discuss a problem. Most of your instructors will have private offices and keep **office hours** when they are available to you. Visiting an instructor may seem a little scary to you, but most instructors welcome the opportunity to get to know their students. The relationships you develop with instructors can be valuable to you both now and in the future—you might find that one or more of them become lifelong mentors and friends. They can also write that all-important letter of recommendation when you are applying for graduate school or a job after college. Many successful college graduates can name a particular instructor who made a positive difference in their lives and influenced their academic and career paths.

Instructors who teach part-time at your college might be called **adjuncts,** and they may not have assigned offices. While adjuncts are not usually required to maintain office hours, they often are available to meet with you before or after class or by appointment.

If you ever have a problem with an instructor, ask for a meeting to discuss your problem. If the instructor refuses, go to a person in a higher position in the department or college. If the problem is a grade, remember that your instructors have the right to assign grades based on your performance, and no one can force them to change those grades. However, you can always speak with your instructor, find out what mistakes you made, and see how you can improve your grade in the future. ■

△ **The Instructor Is In**
Of all the relationships you experience in college, those you have with instructors may be among the most enjoyable and influential. But you must take the initiative to visit your instructors during their office hours. Instructors are available to help you with your coursework, and you may also find one or more to be lifelong mentors and friends. © Hero Images/Corbis.

" Of all the relationships you experience in college, those you have with instructors may be among the most enjoyable and influential. "

TRY IT!

FEELING CONNECTED ▷ **Get to Know Your Instructors**

Developing relationships with your course instructors is important to your college success and to making a successful transition to college. Get to know your instructors each term. Google them. Do any have a biography on the campus Web site, a Facebook page, or a LinkedIn profile? What did you learn about your instructor(s)' motivation to teach and/or conduct research in a particular academic area? Did anything you read pique your interest or your motivation to learn more by talking with them face-to-face? Make an appointment with an instructor whose background interests you, and get in the habit of visiting your instructors during office hours when you have a question, have a problem with a class assignment, or feel like strengthening these important connections.

Setting Goals

We made the point early in this chapter that having a purpose for your college experience is essential. You may be very clear on why you are in college and what you hope to achieve, or you may still be trying to figure this out. Wherever you are, the road to achieving your purpose requires that you set goals along the way.

> " You may be very clear on why you are in college and what you hope to achieve, or you may still be trying to figure this out. "

For most students a central purpose for college is gaining the knowledge and experience that will lead to success. So what does success mean to you? Is it about money, friendship, or power? Is it about achieving excellence in college, employment, or life in general? For most people success is a combination of all of these factors and more. While luck or "who you know" may play a role, first and foremost, your success will be the result of your planning, decisions, and hard work.

TRY IT!

MANAGING TIME ▷ How Will You Get Where You Want to Go?

Ten years from now may seem like a long time, but it will be here before you know it. And the decisions you make today about how you will reach your goals will determine whether you can describe yourself as successful in ten years. List the skills and habits that will make you a successful and competent person. Did you include time management? Consider ways that you can improve your competencies as you prepare for life ten, twenty, or thirty years from now.

Consider Your Strengths

To achieve your purpose and become successful, you can begin by thinking carefully about your strengths. Everyone is good at doing something, and your strengths can help you choose the right path. Your strengths might be

- Intrapersonal: You make friends easily.

- Mechanical: You have always been able to fix things around the house.

- Organizational: You keep your sisters and brothers on track with their duties and chores.

- Leadership and persuasion: You are able to convince others that you are right.

- Persistence: When you want something, you never give up.

All of these characteristics and many others are strengths that you can apply to your college experience. You should also use your strengths for excelling in college while you work on the areas you need to improve. For instance, if you have good interpersonal skills but need to improve your organizational skills, make friends with students who have excellent organizational skills and ask them to help you improve yours.

Get Started with Goals

As you gain an appreciation of your strengths, it makes good sense to establish goals—personal and career goals for today, this week, this month, this term, this year, and beyond. Students who prefer to go with the flow and let life happen to them are more likely to waste their time and less likely to achieve success in college or in a career. So instead of simply reacting to what college and life present to you, you should take more control over the decisions and choices you make now, literally every day, to achieve your goals. While making general plans is easy, you need to determine which short-term goals are necessary if those plans are to become a reality.

MAKING DECISIONS ▷ **This Way or That Way?**

Do you make snap decisions, or is your process of deciding between alternatives difficult and slow? Different people have different ways of decision making, and there is no one right way to go about it. When you're making decisions about your major and your life goals, remember that college gives you lots of opportunities to try out different options. You can decide to explore a major by taking an introductory course in that academic area. If you discover that the major isn't going to be a good fit for you, you'll have plenty of time to make a change. Most colleges won't require you to make a decision about your major right away. But at some point, even if the decision is hard, you'll have to choose. Decide now to use your first year to gather more information about major and career possibilities. Then you'll be ready to choose the best major when you have to make that final decision.

A short-term goal might be to read twenty pages from your history text tonight to prepare for class tomorrow. An intermediate-term goal might be to predict which elective college courses you could choose that would help you attain your career goals. A long-term goal would be to make a final decision about a major and how you will use it after you graduate—you might pursue a career or apply to graduate school, for example.

Follow the SMART Goal-Setting Guidelines

Here are guidelines that break down the aspects of goal setting. We call these the SMART goal-setting guidelines—to set goals that are *Specific, Measurable, Attainable, Relevant,* and *Timely* (**SMART**):

1. Be **specific** about what you want to achieve, why, and when.

2. State your goal in **measurable** terms. That means how many steps you should take to obtain your goal and how you know when each step is complete.

3. Be sure that the goal is **attainable**. If you don't have the necessary skills, strengths, and resources to achieve your goal, change it. Know that you really want to reach the goal. Don't set out to work toward something only because you want to please others. Plan your steps carefully and within a reasonable time frame.

4. Be able to state the **relevance** of the goal to your life—why the goal matters. Make sure your goal helps move you forward.

5. Consider whether the goal is **timely**—achievable within a reasonable time frame considering the difficulties you might face. Plan ways you might deal with problems.

For instance, let's assume that after you graduate you want to get a good job. This goal isn't very specific and doesn't state a particular time period. A more specific goal would be to decide which major will prepare you for the job or position you are interested in. What short-term goals would help you reach this longer-term goal? Once you choose your major, the next goal might be to look through the course catalog to identify courses that you need to take. An even more specific goal would be to prepare your academic plan and identify which courses you should take each term. You can see an academic adviser who can help you create a program plan for your major, specifying which courses you need to take and in what order. Remember that dreaming up long-term goals is the easy part. To reach your goals, you need to be specific and systematic about the steps you will take. Use Figure 1.2 on the next page to set SMART goals for this term. Think through this exercise and then return to it so that you can apply what you learn in the final section, "Academic Planning." ∎

Figure 1.2 ▽ Practice Setting SMART Goals

What are your goals for this term? Using the SMART goal-setting guide, try to set one goal in each of the four areas listed: academic, career, personal, and financial. An example is provided for you.

Type of Goal	S	M	A	R	T
	What is my SPECIFIC goal	What MEASURABLE steps are needed?	Why I can ATTAIN the goal?	How is this RELEVANT to me?	Is the goal TIMELY? What potential difficulties will arise, and how will I deal with them to stay on track?
Academic	Complete my academic plan this term based on my chosen major.	• In the next two weeks, review the college catalog to select a major that interests me and prepare me for my future job/career. • Select my required courses and map every term. • Choose my elective courses. • Meet with an academic adviser to make sure my academic map makes sense.	• I am organized. • I have a manageable range of interests.	• I can't use my time in college well if I don't know where I am headed. • An adviser can give me ideas for how I can apply my interests to a major.	• Meet with an academic and a career adviser by the middle of the term. • Obtain all the necessary signatures to finalize my academic plan. • Have the plan all ready to go by Thanksgiving break. **Potential Difficulties:** • I do not know an academic or career adviser. • I have not made a decision about the major I want to study. **How to Deal with Difficulties:** • Visit the academic and career advising centers to work with advisers. • Discuss my academic and career goals with the advisers and ask for their advice regarding the major I should select.
Career					
Personal					
Financial					

Academic Planning

Some students come to college with clear direction; they know what they want to study, whether they want to go to graduate school, and what career they would like to enter after college. Others enter college as undecided students (sometimes also called undeclared or exploratory). Still others start a major but are uncertain whether or how it can help them find a job later. Each of these situations is normal.

Majors

Even before you have made a final decision about your purpose for college, you might be required to select a major in an area like psychology, engineering, or education. Every major includes required courses and electives. Required courses include courses that are directly related to the major as well as general education courses such as college-level math and English. Electives are courses that you can choose purely because they interest you. Your ultimate career plans might seem unrelated to some of the courses you are required to take in your first year. Sometimes it's hard to see the connection between a math or language course and what you want to do with the rest of your life. But required general education courses will give you a foundation that will help you discover potential areas of interest that you have never considered before, and these areas of interest may lead you to discover new career alternatives.

Many students change their majors as they better understand their strengths and weaknesses, learn more about career options, and become interested in different areas of study. Some colleges allow you to be undecided for a while or to select liberal arts as your major until you make a decision about what to study. It's OK to be undecided as a first-year student, but an early selection does allow you to be more accurate in planning the courses you need to take. An academic adviser can provide you with information and guidance to help you make the right academic decisions.

Even if you are ready to select a major, it's a good idea to keep an open mind and consider your options. You might learn that the career you always dreamed of isn't what you thought it would be at all. Working part-time or participating in co-curricular activities can help you make decisions and learn more about yourself. Students who connect what they learn inside and outside the classroom have a more satisfying college experience and better preparation for choosing a career than students who do not make these connections.

Connecting Majors with Careers

Earlier in the chapter, we asked questions about your reasons for being in college. You might have responded, "I'm in college so I can get a good job or education for a specific career." Yet some majors do not lead directly to a particular career path. You actually can enter most careers from any number of academic majors. Only a few technical or professional fields—such as accounting, nursing, and engineering—are tied to specific majors.

Exploring your interests is the first step to identifying an academic major as well as a career path that is right for you. Here are some helpful strategies:

- **Know your interests, skills, values, and personality.** Assessing your skills and personality is particularly important if you have no idea what you are interested in studying or what career paths are related to your choice of major. For example, if you like science and helping sick people, you may want to consider a career in health care like medicine, nursing, physical therapy, or dentistry. If you like to talk, read, solve problems, and stand up for yourself and others, you may want to consider a career in the legal profession. If you like to work with computers and gaming, you may want to think about computer science or game design. Your campus career center can help you discover your unique strengths—and weaknesses—that

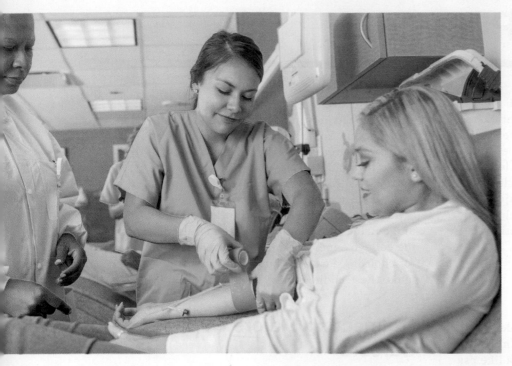

can influence your direction as you explore career choices.

- **Pay attention to grades.** Employers and graduate schools want candidates with good grades. Good grades show that you have the necessary knowledge and skills and a strong work ethic, which are very important to all employers.

- **Explore career paths.** Talking to or observing professionals in your areas of interest is an excellent way to try before you buy. Participation in "job shadowing" or "a day in the life" programs is time well spent. Many college graduates enjoy being career mentors for current students. This is also a great way to

network with those working in your area of interest. Ask your career center about scheduling one of these opportunities.

- **Create a digital footprint.** Have you Googled yourself lately? Do you like what you see? Would an employer? Your online image matters, and it can influence how others see you and what they think of you. If you do not like your online image, improve it by deleting some photos or removing the tags that others have posted.

- **Discover leadership opportunities.** Companies want to hire leaders, so they look for leadership experience when hiring college students for internships or jobs. Be active in a campus club or organization. Volunteer to be a team leader in a group project. Look for campus leadership opportunities, such as becoming an orientation leader, student government officer, or peer leader in the college success course. Active involvement in these opportunities will help you improve your leadership skills.

- **Develop computer skills.** Most of today's college students are comfortable with technology; however, not all technology experience is equal. Become familiar with technologies used in your field. Take advantage of computer courses and workshops at your

TRY IT!

SETTING GOALS ▷ Get to the Career Center

Have you explored your college's career center? If you haven't made a visit, what are you waiting for? How can knowing what's available in the job market motivate you to be successful?

△ **See for Yourself**
In college-level teacher-training programs, future teachers spend time in classroom settings interacting with students in preschool through high school. These experiences help teachers-in-training make decisions about whether they are on the right path. Monkey Business Images/ Shutterstock.

college, or learn by experimenting with different software programs on your own.

- **Build communication skills.** The ability to communicate verbally and in writing is one of the most important skills that employers look for in new graduates. Take every available opportunity to practice communicating, whether through classroom presentations, in group work, or on the job.

- **Take advantage of experiential learning.** Experiential learning is learning by doing and from experience. Internships and service-learning courses are common forms of experiential learning, but they are not the only ways to gain experience in your major. Find opportunities to apply what you learn to what you do outside of the classroom. ∎

> **66** Academic planning is a necessary step in your college career, and it should be an ongoing process that starts early in your first term. **99**

Working with an Academic Adviser

Academic planning is a necessary step in your college career, and it should be an ongoing process that starts early in your first term. An **academic plan** lists the courses you need to complete in your major to graduate with a degree. Before you register for classes next term, sit down with your academic adviser. He or she can map out your degree requirements, help you choose courses that are not required, and weigh career possibilities. Advisers can also recommend instructors and help you simplify the different aspects of your academic life. Here are a few ways to make sure that your first meeting with your adviser is a valuable experience:

- **Prepare by looking at your college course catalog, think about the available majors, and familiarize yourself with campus resources.** If you haven't already decided on a major, ask your adviser about opportunities for taking an aptitude test or a self-assessment to help you narrow down your options.
- **Prepare materials to bring to the meeting. Even if you submitted your high school or other college transcripts with your application, bring a copy of your transcripts to the meeting.** The transcript is your complete academic record to date. It shows your major if you have selected one, your high school courses or those you took at other colleges or universities, and your grades. Your transcript shows your academic adviser your interests and your academic strengths and weaknesses. At some institutions, your adviser may have access to this information online, but even so, it is still a good idea to bring your own copies along to the meeting.
- **If you haven't already selected a major, make a list of ones that appeal to you.** Academic advisers

love it when students come prepared—it shows that they're passionate and are taking their future seriously. Your preparation will encourage them to remember you and invest more time in working with you.

- **Map out your time frame and goals.** When do you plan to graduate, and with what degree? Can you maintain full-time enrollment?
- **Know the right questions to ask.** Once you've chosen a major, you'll need to understand how to move forward in your major to meet the necessary requirements. You will have *prerequisites*—the core courses you need to take before you can enroll in upper-level classes. Your major may also have *co-requisites*—courses you have to take in conjunction with other courses during the same term (a chemistry lab alongside your chemistry class, for instance). So, with this knowledge under your belt, here is what you need to ask your adviser:

  - How many credits must I take each term to graduate on time? (Note: If you are on financial aid, are participating in a work-study program, or are a college athlete, you will have to take a minimum number of credits per term.)
  - What are the prerequisites for my major? What are the co-requisites?
  - Can I use AP (Advance Placement) credits, CLEP (College-Level Examination Program) credits, or placement exams to fulfill some requirements of my major?
  - What career opportunities will I have once I graduate?

- **Know what to take away from your meeting.** When you leave the meeting, take with you a printout of your current course schedule and plans for classes you might take in the next term and beyond.

At many colleges and universities, you and your adviser will set up a four- to eight-term plan online.

- **Know these rules of thumb about selecting your classes:**

  - Most full-time students take four or five courses a term. Decide which classes you want to take, the days and times they meet, and make sure they don't overlap.
  - Be sure to register as early as possible—in person or online.
  - Leave time between courses so that on exam days you can study immediately before the exam.
  - Go for a mix of hard and easy classes. Especially at the beginning, you might not realize how challenging college classes can be or how much outside work they entail. If you load up on two laboratory science courses, a math course, and a course in a new foreign language, your grades and general well-being could suffer.

- **Know what to do if your academic adviser isn't the right match for you.** If you think you and your adviser are not a good match, go to the advising office or academic department office and ask to be assigned to a different adviser. Asking for alternative advising is one of your rights as a student. But whatever you do, don't throw in the towel. Academic planning is so critical to your success in college that it's worth persevering until you find an adviser with whom you feel comfortable. If you don't know where to start in finding a new adviser, talk to your college success instructor.

- **Set up subsequent meetings with your academic adviser.** Check in with your adviser at least once a term, if not more often. It's important to stay connected, especially if you plan to apply to graduate school.

Chapter Review

Steps to Success:
Starting Out on the Right Foot

○ **Be clear about your purpose for being in college.** For many students a sense of purpose builds over time. College will be a set of experiences that will help you clarify your purpose and achieve your goals.

○ **Take advantage of college-sponsored support services.** These services include tutoring, academic advising, financial aid advising, and networking opportunities.

○ **Develop relationships with your instructors.** High-quality interaction with your instructors can have a positive effect on how well you do academically.

○ **Pay close attention to the syllabus for each of your courses.** Here you'll find the requirements for each course as well as each instructor's expectations of you.

○ **Use your own strengths to do well in college.** Knowing your strengths can help you choose the right path for yourself. In this college success course you'll have many opportunities to assess your strengths.

○ **Become an expert in setting and meeting your goals.** Whoever and wherever you are, the road to achieving your purpose requires that you set goals along the way.

○ **Understand the requirements of your major.** Academic planning is critical to achieving your goals. An academic adviser can help you map out when and how to meet your requirements.

○ **Explore your college's career center.** Here you can get help with career planning and job hunting. Remember that the faculty and staff of a college are there to serve students, so do not be shy—ask for help.

Applying what you've learned . . .

Now that you have read and discussed this chapter, consider how you can apply what you have learned to your academic and personal lives. The following prompts will help you reflect on the chapter material and its relevance to you both now and in the future.

1. Review the section "Did I Make the Right Choice to Attend College?" on page 3. While landing a lucrative career is probably high on your list of goals after college, take a look at the other possible advantages of obtaining a college degree. List the three advantages from this section that you relate to the most. If you think of an advantage that is not noted in the chapter, add it to your top three. Why are these advantages important to you?

2. What experience do you already have in setting and achieving goals? Do you have attitudes or behaviors that get in the way of reaching your goals? How can you change any negative attitudes that tend to obstruct your progress?

Use Your Resources

GO TO ▷ Your college success instructor, check your college's directory or Web site, or call or visit student services or student affairs: If you need help finding college support services.

GO TO ▷ The academic advisement center or your assigned academic adviser: If you need help choosing courses and understanding degree requirements.

GO TO ▷ The learning center: If you need help finding tutors and improving your memory and study skills.

GO TO ▷ The career center: If you are interested in learning more about careers, finding job and internship listings, and evaluating your fit with a particular career.

GO TO ▷ Commuter services: If you need help finding off-campus housing options, information about your community, transportation information, or possible roommates.

GO TO ▷ The computer center: If you need help using Word, Excel, PowerPoint, and e-mail or improving your computer skills and are looking for information on campus computer resources.

GO TO ▷ The counseling center: If you need help dealing with personal problems and stress management.

NOW... How do you measure up?

1. I am excited to be in this college success course because I know I will learn strategies for succeeding in college.

   ○ Agree
   ○ Don't Know
   ○ Disagree

2. To help control the uncertainties of life, long-term goal setting is a must.

   ○ Agree
   ○ Don't Know
   ○ Disagree

3. I know how important it is to begin creating an academic plan for my college experience immediately.

   ○ Agree
   ○ Don't Know
   ○ Disagree

4. I have thought about how my college experience will relate to what I want to do after I graduate.

   ○ Agree
   ○ Don't Know
   ○ Disagree

How do your answers here compare to your responses to the quiz you took at the start of the chapter? Which sections of this chapter left a strong impression on you? College can be an amazing, once-in-a-lifetime adventure. In your first year explore your interests and what motivates you to do your best. Take advantage of all that your institution has to offer, and begin creating a life plan by setting goals for this month, this term, and this year.

LaunchPad
macmillan learning

LaunchPad Solo for College Success is a great resource. Go online to master concepts using the LearningCurve study tool and much more. **macmillanhighered.com/collegesuccessmedia**

19
Motivation, Attitude, and Mindset

23
Resilience

25
Understanding Emotional Intelligence

Cultivating Motivation, Resilience, and Emotional Intelligence

IDesign/Shutterstock

LaunchPad
macmillan learning

To access the LearningCurve study tool, Video Tools, and more, go to *LaunchPad Solo for College Success*. **macmillanhighered.com/ collegesuccessmedia**

To be successful in college, you need to do well academically. You need to build on the skills and knowledge you learned in high school and in other life experiences. But doing well academically is only one component of college success. Many students who have the ability to succeed intellectually have other difficulties in nonacademic areas such as maintaining their motivation for college-level work, establishing positive relationships with others, dealing with pressure, or making wise decisions. While some students exude optimism and happiness and seem to adapt to the college environment without any trouble, others struggle with their attitudes, their emotions, and their motivation. The difference between the two types of students lies in their emotional intelligence (EI), or their ability to recognize and manage moods, feelings, and attitudes. A growing body of evidence shows a clear connection between students' EI and whether they succeed in college.

College is like a laboratory where you get to try out new strategies for learning, figure out how to get along with others, and make choices about courses, extracurricular activities, and friendships. One of the most important attributes you can develop is motivation—the ability to consistently and steadily pursue a goal, a course of action that you have chosen freely and "own" because you want to do it. Motivation requires a clear vision, courage, persistence, and a positive attitude. It requires not allowing yourself to get distracted. And it takes resilience—the ability to continue in spite of temporary setbacks.

How do you measure up?

1. I understand what motivates me in different aspects of my life.

- ○ Agree
- ○ Don't Know
- ○ Disagree

2. I have a positive attitude most of the time.

- ○ Agree
- ○ Don't Know
- ○ Disagree

3. When something bad happens, I'm able to bounce back.

- ○ Agree
- ○ Don't Know
- ○ Disagree

4. My emotions do not determine my behavior.

- ○ Agree
- ○ Don't Know
- ○ Disagree

Review the items you marked "Don't Know" or "Disagree." Pay special attention to these topics in this chapter—you will develop a better understanding of why they are important to your success in college. A follow-up quiz at the end of the chapter will prompt you to consider what you have learned.

Powering Through Challenges

△ **Gustavo Meija**

Bedford/St.Martin's

Gustavo Meija grew up in Venezuela and left important parts of his life behind when as a high school junior he moved to the United States to live with his sister and her husband. "My parents had always pounded into me the value of education," he said. After finishing high school, he began college at Wright State University in Dayton, Ohio. During his first term, he was taking five courses and working at his sister's restaurant two days a week. "I missed my parents," he said, "but I learned from my sister how important it is to have a positive attitude and an optimistic spirit even when you're juggling work and school."

In Gustavo's college success class, he learned about emotional intelligence and how stress can set in motion negative emotional reactions to people and situations. Being aware of how his hectic schedule created stress helped him better understand how to deal with his occasional frustration and kept him from reacting negatively around friends and family.

Gustavo had started in engineering, but after taking a public speaking class, he switched to communication. "I lost about 15 credits by switching majors," he said, "and for a while I was really angry about what seemed to me a big waste of time and energy. My academic adviser really helped me—she encouraged me to trust my instincts about the major change and to just 'power through' the extra term."

Gustavo got back on track emotionally. "I'm my usual cheerful self," he noted, "and I'm much more motivated to do well in my new major. I know I will enjoy my college career, even if it's a little longer than I had planned. My dream is a career as a radio or TV personality, and I'm already seeing many opportunities for Latinos in broadcasting. My parents didn't understand my change of major but now they're beginning to come around. More than anything, they want me to be satisfied with my college degree and my future."

Why might Gustavo have started his college career in engineering? What do you think about his new major and career plans? If his dream of being in TV or radio doesn't work out, what else can Gustavo do with a communications major?

Motivation, Attitude, and Mindset

If you're like most students, you will face many challenges every day, from studying for exams to facing money troubles and taking care of family members. At some point in your college career, things *will* go wrong. When you're facing such challenges, how you *think* and especially how you *feel* will have a huge effect on your ability to keep going.

The good news is that you can learn the skills you need to handle tough moments. And remember, you're not alone. Many of your class-mates share your challenges and struggles. In this section we'll go over important habits of mind and we will give you strategies that will help you achieve your goals. These include stay-ing motivated, keeping a good attitude, and developing a growth mindset, all of which we'll explain below.

Motivation

Among the most important factors that will help you achieve college success is your **motivation**—your desire to do well. When you are motivated, you are determined to follow a course of action, and you keep making the effort even when you hit obstacles. Sometimes being motivated involves pledging to yourself and to others to do your best to reach your goal.

People are motivated in different ways and for different reasons. Some of those reasons are "extrinsic"—that is, they are external. If you study only because you want to earn a good grade or because you want to please your parents, you are extrinsically motivated. People are also moti-vated for "intrinsic" reasons—an internal desire to learn or experience the satisfaction that comes from doing well. In actuality, you are motivated by both internal and external factors; there is always a mixture of reasons why you make the decisions you make and do what you do.

TRY IT!

SETTING GOALS ▷ Extrinsic or Intrinsic?

Think about the goals—academic, personal, professional—that you are working toward now. Work through the exercise below. Name a goal in each category. Write what is motivating you to work toward each goal. Circle whether your motivation is extrinsic, intrinsic, or both. You can expand on this exercise in a journal entry or in a group discussion.

My goals	My motivation	Extrinsic, intrinsic or both?
Academic goal: _____	What motivates me to achieve this goal is _____.	extrinsic intrinsic both
Personal goal: _____	What motivates me to achieve this goal is _____.	extrinsic intrinsic both
Career goal: _____	What motivates me to achieve this goal is _____.	extrinsic intrinsic both

Attitude

Attitude is the way you are thinking and feeling in relation to the events around you. Attitude is an important part of staying motivated because your attitude shapes your behavior. For instance, if you have a bad attitude about math because you've had trouble in math in the past, you will be likely to give up on your math courses before you even give yourself a chance to do well.

Whether positive or negative, attitudes often come from our previous environments and experiences with others. Have you ever wondered whether you were "college material"? Has anyone, a family member or teacher, ever questioned your innate abilities? How has a comment like this affected your attitude about starting college? Or maybe friends or family members have told you how proud they are that you are in college and this has made you feel determined to work hard.

A good starting place in developing a more positive attitude is to think honestly about the attitude you're likely to have in certain situations. How would you handle stressful or surprising situations such as the ones listed below?

Situation	Describe your attitude. How you would react?
You ask for time off from your work-study job to study for a final exam, and your supervisor refuses your request.	
Your financial aid check doesn't arrive in time for you to purchase your books.	
You lose a major paper or report because your computer crashes.	
You break up with your girlfriend or boyfriend the night before a major exam.	
As a non-native English speaker, you're struggling in many of your classes.	
Your commute to campus is taking twice as long due to major road construction.	
You fail a pop quiz that caught you entirely by surprise.	
You lose your psychology notebook, and the final exam is next week.	
A group project isn't going well because other members of the group aren't doing their share of the work.	

Any of these things can and do happen to students just like you. When you face these kinds of frustrations, do you get really stressed or mad? Do you expect the worst? Or do you stay relaxed, do your best, and keep going?

If you've been told by people who know you well that you're negative or pessimistic, or you realize that you always expect the worst, maybe it actually is time for an attitude adjustment:

- Spend time thinking about what you can learn from difficult situations you faced and overcame.

- Give yourself credit for good choices that you have made in the past.

- Seek out individuals, both on and off campus, who are positive. Ask them where their optimism comes from.

- Take advantage of the opportunities you will get in your college success course to explore the effect your attitude has on the outcomes you want.

- Be mindful of your attitude as you move through the weeks of this term.

Mindsets

Another way to look at motivation is to examine what are called "mindsets." **Mindsets** refer to what you believe about yourself and about your most basic qualities such as your personality, intelligence, or talents. If you have a fixed mindset, you are likely to believe that your characteristics and abilities—either positive or negative—*are not going to change* through any adjustments to your behavior or effort. A growth mindset, however, means that you are willing to try new approaches and that you believe that *you can change.*[1]

People with a fixed mindset are often trying to prove themselves, and they're very sensitive about being wrong or making mistakes. They also think that having to make an effort means they are not smart or talented. People with a growth mindset believe that their abilities can be improved—that there is no harm in being wrong or making a mistake. They think that the effort they make is what makes them smart or talented. Some of us have a different mindset for different tasks. For instance, you may find that you have a fixed mindset for your athletic abilities but a growth mindset for music. What can you learn about your mindset by walking through the exercise below?

Whether you're in your college classes, your job setting, or your home, your mindset—similar to your attitude—can influence how you think about yourself and others, your opportunities, and your relationships. A fixed mindset will cause you to limit the things you do, the people you meet, and even the classes you take in college. A growth mindset will help you be more willing to explore classes and activities out of your comfort zone. It will help you stay motivated because you will see disappointments or failures as opportunities to learn. ■

[1]Carol S. Dweck, *Mindset: The New Psychology of Success* (New York: Ballantine Books, 2006), 16.

Mindsets: For each pair of statements, select the one that sounds more like you.

a. You believe that your efforts won't change your grades.

b. You believe that with effort you can improve your grades.

a. You believe that a good grade means you have learned everything you need to know.

b. You believe that you can always learn more, even if you have received an A.

a. You tend to blame the world around you when things go wrong.

b. You try to solve the problems when things go wrong.

a. You are often afraid to try new things because you fear you will fail.

b. You believe that failure is an opportunity to learn more.

a. You believe that some jobs are for "women only" or for "men only."

b. You are open to exploring all job opportunities.

a. You believe that leaders are born, not made.

b. You believe that leadership can be developed.

a. You tend to believe negative things that others say about you.

b. You don't allow others to define who you are.

If you selected mostly "a" statements, you likely have a fixed mindset; if you selected mostly "b" statements, you likely have a growth mindset. As mentioned above, our mindset can change depending on the task. Keep in mind that a mindset that is fixed today might not be fixed tomorrow—with some motivation you can challenge yourself, take some risks, and develop a positive attitude about your ability to grow and change.

The Case of Amber

Amber is a second-year university student. She was her high school's valedictorian, and before college she had never earned a grade lower than an A minus. Her high school was pretty small and lacked some advanced courses, but Amber assumed that she was prepared for college. During her first year of college, however, Amber earned Bs, Cs, and even a D in calculus. The extrinsic motivation that had come from good grades was long gone, which turned her fixed-mindset world upside down. For several months Amber was disinterested in almost everything; she completely lost her motivation to study and learn when earning an A had seemingly become impossible.

Slowly, though, Amber turned things around. She began watching how others studied and interacted with instructors. Not all the examples were good ones. Some students would brag about skipping class and pulling all-nighters to study instead of managing their time better. But others had a deliberate plan that included taking really good notes, studying every day, trying to sit close to the front of the classroom, and talking with instructors after class. Amber started adopting these behaviors. Little by little, she practiced new study strategies, began to accept criticism without falling apart, and gained an understanding that sometimes she could learn more from her mistakes than from her successes. It took Amber about a year to regain her positive attitude and a willingness to do her best, no matter what the outcome. She stills likes to see an A at the top of a paper, but she has realized that she is motivated intrinsically more by what she learns than by what grade she earns.

How would you describe how Amber's mindset changed? What did you learn about your own mindset from reading this section?

Resilience

Motivation requires a clear vision, courage, and persistence. And it takes **resilience**—not giving up or quitting when faced with difficulties and challenges. Students who are resilient—who bounce back quickly from difficult situations—will be more successful in college and in life. Learning to keep going when things are hard is one of the most important lessons you'll learn in this class.

There are many other terms that are used to describe resilience and determination. One of these terms is **grit**, a combination of perseverance, passion, and resilience. Psychologist Angela Duckworth has studied grit and has found that people who are "gritty" are more likely to be both academically and personally successful.[2] Another term that encompasses resilience comes from Finland: **Sisu** is a word that dates back hundreds of years and is described as being central to understanding Finnish culture. It means going beyond one's mental or physical ability, taking action even when things are difficult, and displaying courage and determination in the face of challenge and repeated failures.

Resilience is such an important concept in psychological health that the American Psychological Association has developed a list of resilience strategies: "10 Ways to Build Resilience."[3] These are as follows:

1. **Make connections.** Good relationships with close family members, friends, or others are important. Accepting help and support from those who care about you and will listen to you helps you become more resilient. Assisting others in their time of need can also benefit the helper.

2. **Avoid seeing crises as problems that can't be overcome.** You can't change the fact that highly stressful events happen, but you can change how you view and respond to these events.

3. **Accept that change is a part of living.** Accepting situations that cannot be changed can help you focus on those that you can change.

4. **Move toward your goals.** Develop some realistic goals. Do something regularly—even if it seems like a small accomplishment—that enables you to move toward your goals.

5. **Take decisive actions.** Take decisive actions, rather than just wishing that problems and stresses would just go away.

6. **Look for opportunities for self-discovery.** Struggles often make people stronger. Consider what you have learned about yourself from going through tough times.

7. **Develop a positive view of yourself.** Developing confidence in your ability to solve problems and trusting your instincts help build resilience.

8. **Keep things in perspective.** Even when facing very painful events, try to consider the big picture and avoid blowing the event out of proportion.

9. **Maintain a hopeful outlook.** Try visualizing what you want, rather than worrying about what you fear.

10. **Take care of yourself.** Pay attention to your own needs and feelings. Engage in activities that you enjoy and find relaxing. Taking care of yourself helps keep your mind and body ready to deal with situations that require resilience.

Think about your own reactions to frustration and stress. Do you often give up because something is just too hard or because you can't figure it out? Do you take responsibility for what you do, or do you blame others if you fail? For example, how have you reacted to receiving a D or an F on a paper, losing a student government election, or getting rejected for a work-study job?

Negative experiences might cause you to question whether you should even be in college. Resilient students, though, look past negative experiences, learn from them, and try again. For

[2] E. Packard, "Grit: It's What Separates the Best from the Merely Good," *Monitor on Psychology* 38, no. 10 (2007): 10, www.apa.org/monitor/nov07/grit.aspx.

[3] "The Road to Resilience," American Psychological Association, accessed September 4, 2015, www.apa.org/helpcenter/road-resilience.aspx.

instance, what could you do to improve your grade on your next paper? Perhaps you didn't allow yourself enough time to do the necessary research. How can you feel more comfortable in your classes? Maybe it would help to join a study group or go to the academic learning center. You were born with the ability to be resilient.

So far in this chapter we have asked you to consider how thoughts and feelings affect behavior. We've discussed motivation, attitude, and resilience and have asked you to explore what motivates you, to think about your own attitude and how it helps or hurts you, and to reflect on whether you are able to bounce back from difficulty. These topics are part of a broader discussion of emotions, which we turn to next. ∎

TRY IT!

FEELING CONNECTED ▷ Get Inspired from Those around You

Do you know someone who has faced adversity and prevailed? What difficult circumstances did they have to deal with? Make contact with at least two people who have survived hard times and ask them if they will share with you how they did it. Were they lucky enough to have a lot of support from friends and family? What decisive actions did they take? Did they see the challenges as opportunities to learn about themselves? See if you can apply what you learn from others' stories to difficult situations facing you currently.

◁ **Don't Let Anything Stop You**
Show your grit. Have sisu. Be resilient. If your goal is to graduate, overcome the obstacles that get in your way, no matter what they are.
Lucian3D/Shutterstock.

From Rejection to Success

Many well-known and successful people overcame tough circumstances and failure. For instance, J. K. Rowling, the author of the Harry Potter series, was divorced and penniless when she wrote the first Harry Potter book. That book was rejected by twelve publishers before it was finally accepted. Walt Disney's first animation company went bankrupt, and he was fired by a news agency because he "lacked imagination." Michael Jordan was cut by his high school basketball team.

Jordan has been quoted as reporting that he missed nine thousand shots in his career. These people and many others did not let failure get in the way of their ultimate success. Think of other examples of people who didn't let rejection stop them from working toward their goals. What about innovations ranging from vaccinations to spacecraft? Consider all the "failures" that scientists and engineers experience as they work toward their goals.

Understanding Emotional Intelligence

Emotional intelligence (EI) is the ability to recognize, understand, use, and manage your emotions—moods, feelings, and attitudes. As we said earlier in the chapter, how you think and feel will make all the difference in whether you succeed or give up. Developing an awareness of emotions allows you to use your feelings to improve your thinking.

If you are feeling sad, for instance, you might view the world in a negative way, while if you feel happy, you are likely to view the same events differently. Once you start paying attention to emotions, you can learn not only how to cope with life's pressures and demands but also how to use your knowledge of the way you feel for more effective problem solving, decision making, and creativity.

Particularly in the first year of college, many students have difficulty establishing positive relationships with others, dealing with pressure, or making wise decisions. Other students are optimistic and happy and seem to adapt to their new environment without any trouble. Being optimistic doesn't mean that you stick you head in the sand and pretend that your problems will go away, but optimistic people believe in their own abilities to overcome problems successfully.

Emotions, for better or worse, are a big part of who you are. The better the emotional awareness you have about a situation, the more appropriately you can respond to it. Being aware of your own and others' feelings helps you gather correct information about the world around you and allows you to respond in appropriate ways.

Think about the behaviors that help people, including yourself, do well and the behaviors that interfere with success. Get to know yourself better, and take the time to examine your feelings and the impact they have on the way you act. You can't always control the challenges of life, but with practice you *can* control how you respond to them. Remember that emotions are real, can be changed for the better, and significantly affect whether a person is successful.

> " Emotions are real, can be changed for the better, and significantly affect whether a person is successful. "

Understanding and Managing Emotions

If you understand and manage your emotions, you can monitor and identify your feelings correctly (nervous, happy, angry, relieved, and so forth). You can also predict how others might feel in a given situation. Emotions contain information, and the ability to understand and think about that information plays an important role in behavior. Managing emotions is modifying or improving them. Sometimes you need to stay open to your feelings, learn from them, and use them to take appropriate action. At other times it is better to disengage from an emotion and return to it later.

Managing anger. Anger management is an EI skill that is important to develop. Anger can hurt others and can harm your mental and physical health. You may even know someone who uses their anger to manipulate and control those around them. When you're angry, you can act in hostile or even antisocial ways. In spite of the problems it creates, anger does not always result in negative outcomes. Psychologists see anger as a primary and natural emotion that has value for human survival. If you have a good reason to be angry, your anger can help you take a stand against injustice.

MANAGING TIME ▷ Fussing and Fuming: Time Wasted

How much time do you spend on unnecessary "drama," whether "text arguing" with a friend or family member or obsessing about the bad way you were treated years ago by someone you thought you could trust? Time you waste on fuming about things that happened to you in the past or engaging in an ongoing battle with someone in your present life is time you will never recover. Recapture your time; remember the song from the movie *Frozen*, and "Let It Go"!

Managing priorities. Using healthy emotional intelligence to prioritize involves deciding what's most important to you and then allocating your time and energy according to these priorities. For example, if exercise, a healthy diet, friends, and studying are most important to you, then you must make time for them all. When you successfully make time in your days and weeks for what is most important to you, your emotional health benefits. On the other hand, if you cannot keep what is most important to you at the top of your list of priorities, your attitude becomes more negative, you feel stressed out, and you have less patience for other people.

Emotional Intelligence Questionnaire

Your daily life gives you many opportunities to take a hard look at how you handle emotions. Here are some questions that can help you begin thinking about your own EI:

1. What do you do when you are under stress?
   a. I tend to deal with it calmly and rationally.
   b. I get upset, but it usually blows over quickly.
   c. I get upset but keep it to myself.

2. My friends would say that:
   a. I play, but only after I get my work done.
   b. I am ready for fun anytime.
   c. I hardly ever go out.

3. When something changes at the last minute:
   a. I easily adapt.
   b. I get frustrated.
   c. I don't care, since I don't really expect things to happen according to plan.

4. My friends would say that:
   a. I am sensitive to their concerns.
   b. I spend too much time worrying about other people's needs.
   c. I don't like to deal with other people's petty problems.

5. When I have a problem to solve, such as having too many assignments due at the end of the week:
   a. I write down a list of the tasks I must complete, come up with a plan indicating specifically what I can accomplish and what I cannot, and follow my plan.
   b. I am very optimistic about getting things done and just dig right in and get to work.
   c. I get a little overwhelmed. Usually I get a number of things done and then push aside the things I can't do.

Review your responses: "a" responses indicate that you probably have a good basis for strong emotional intelligence; "b" responses indicate you may have some strengths and some challenges in your EI; "c" responses indicate that your EI could negatively affect your future success in school and in life.

Improving Emotional Intelligence

As you reflect more on your own attitudes and behavior and learn why you have the emotions that you do, you'll improve your emotional intelligence. Interacting with new and diverse people in the first year of college will challenge your EI skills and force you to step outside of your comfort zone. Your first year will give you a significant opportunity to grow emotionally as well as intellectually.

Emotional intelligence includes many capabilities and skills that influence a person's ability to cope with life's pressures and demands. Researcher Reuven Bar-On[4] developed the model that is adapted in Figure 2.1. This model shows how categories of emotional intelligence directly affect general mood and lead to effective performance.

△ **Don't Leave It to Chance**
As you learn to identify and manage your emotions, you won't be rolling the dice when it comes to responding to the challenges of everyday life and establishing positive relationships with others. kostasgr/Shutterstock.

Identifying Your EI Skills and Competencies

Table 2.1, based on Bar-On's work, lists skills that influence a person's ability to cope with life's pressures and demands. Which skills do you think you already have? Which ones do you need to improve? Which ones do you lack? Consider the emotional intelligence skills and competencies listed below and rank them accordingly: A = skills I already have; B = skills I need to improve; C = skills I lack. Then go back and rank each one in terms of its usefulness in addressing the challenges of being a successful college student.

Motivation, attitude, and resilience are all linked to emotional intelligence. Students with healthy emotional intelligence are more assertive: they are more likely to ask instructors for feedback on projects, papers, and tests; participate in classroom discussions; and join study groups. Students with

[4] What Is Emotional Intelligence?" from Bar-On EQ-i Technical Manual @ 1997, 1999, 2000 Multi Health Systems Inc. Toronto, Canada. Reproduced with permission from Multi-Health Systems Inc.

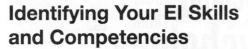

" Motivation, attitude, and resilience are all linked to emotional intelligence. "

unhealthy EI are more likely to struggle academically, panic before taking tests, have trouble concentrating on coursework, and engage in risky behaviors such as alcohol and drug abuse in an effort to cope.

You can do well enough to get by in college without strong EI. However without it, you might miss out on the full range and depth of competencies and skills that can help you succeed in your chosen field and have a fulfilling and meaningful life. ■

MAKING DECISIONS ▷ Commit to Improving Your EI

The benefits of healthy emotional intelligence are many. Review how you ranked the emotional skills and competencies in Table 2.1. What did you learn about yourself? Which skills do you have? Which ones do you need to improve? Which ones do you lack? Explore the resources available at the learning center and counseling center at your institution to help you make the improvements in your emotional intelligence that will propel you forward in college and in your career. Doing so could be one of the best decisions of your life.

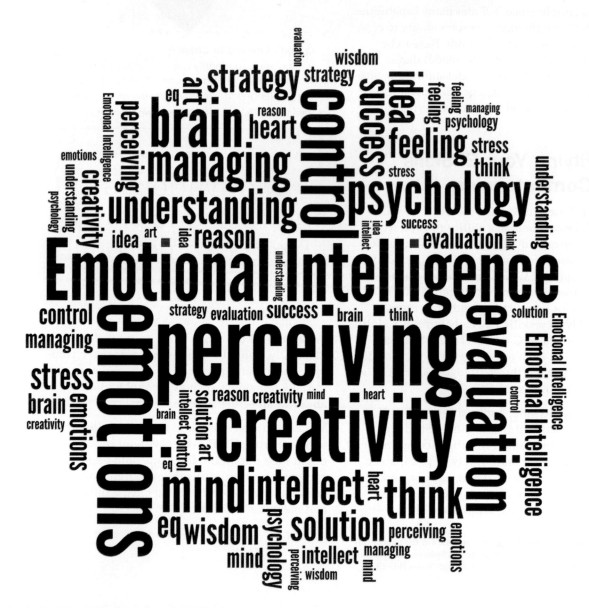

△ **Components of Emotional Intelligence**

Think about how the words used in the word cloud relate to emotional intelligence. And consider how motivation, attitude, mindsets and resilience relate to emotional intelligence. Rob Wilson/Shutterstock.

Table 2.1 ▽ **Emotional Skills and Competencies**

Skills	Competencies	Rank
Intrapersonal	**Emotional self-awareness.** Knowing how and why you feel the way you do.	
	Assertiveness. Standing up for yourself when you need to without being too aggressive.	
	Independence. Making important decisions on your own without having to get everyone's opinion.	
	Self-regard. Liking yourself in spite of your flaws (and we all have them).	
	Self-actualization. Being satisfied and comfortable with what you have achieved in school, work, and your personal life.	
Interpersonal	**Empathy.** Making an effort to understand another person's situation or point of view.	
	Social responsibility. Establishing a personal link with a group or community and cooperating with other members in working toward shared goals.	
	Interpersonal relationships. Seeking out healthy and mutually beneficial relationships—such as friendships, professional networks, family connections, mentoring, and romantic partnerships—and making a persistent effort to maintain them.	
Stress management	**Stress tolerance.** Recognizing the causes of stress and responding in appropriate ways; staying strong under pressure.	
	Impulse control. Thinking carefully about potential consequences before you act and delaying gratification for the sake of achieving long-term goals.	
Adaptability	**Reality testing.** Ensuring that your feelings are appropriate by checking them against external, objective criteria.	
	Flexibility. Adapting and adjusting your emotions, viewpoints, and actions as situations change.	
	Problem solving. Approaching challenges step by step and not giving up in the face of obstacles.	
	Resilience. The ability to bounce back after a setback.	
General mood	**Optimism.** Looking for the bright side of any problem or difficulty and being confident that things will work out for the best.	
	Happiness. Being satisfied with yourself, with others, and with your situation in general.	

EI = College and Career Success

Emotions are strongly tied to physical and psychological well-being. For example, some studies have suggested that cancer patients who have strong EI live longer than those with weak EI. People who are aware of the needs of others tend to be happier than people who are not. An extensive study done at the University of Pennsylvania found that the best athletes succeed in part because they're extremely optimistic. A number of studies link strong EI skills to college success in particular. Here are a few highlights of those studies:

© Randy Glasbergen for RapidBI.com

RAPIDBI

"Any other people skills, besides 400 Facebook friends?"

- **Emotionally intelligent students get higher grades.** Researchers looked at students' grade point averages at the end of their first year of college. Students who had tested high for intrapersonal skills, stress tolerance, and adaptability when they entered in the fall did better academically than those who had lower overall EI test scores.

- **Students who can't manage their emotions struggle academically.** Some students have experienced full-blown panic attacks before tests. Others who are depressed can't concentrate on coursework. And far too many students turn to risky behaviors (drug and alcohol abuse, eating disorders, and worse) in an effort to cope. Dr. Richard Kadison, a former director of mental health services at Harvard University, has noted that "the emotional well-being of students goes hand-in-hand with their academic development. If they're not doing well emotionally, they are not going to reach their academic potential."[5]

- **Students who can delay gratification tend to do better overall.** Impulse control leads to achievement. In the famous "marshmallow study" performed at Stanford University, researchers examined the long-term behaviors of individuals who, as four-year-olds, were tested to see whether they would practice delayed gratification. The children were each given one marshmallow and told that if they didn't eat it right away, they could have another. Fourteen years later, the children who had immediately eaten their marshmallow were more likely to experience significant stress, irritability, and an inability to focus on goals. The children who had waited to eat their marshmallow scored an average of 210 points higher on the SAT; had better confidence, concentration, and reliability; held better-paying jobs; and reported being more satisfied with life.

- **EI skills can be enhanced in a college success course.** Because these skills can be learned, infusing them in a college success course can improve first-year students' emotional intelligence, and thus their ultimate success.[6]

More and more, employers are looking for strong interpersonal skills in job applicants. So, in addition to the greater success you'll find by developing strong EI skills, more career opportunities await as well.

---

[5] Richard Kadison and Theresa Foy DiGeronimo, *College of the Overwhelmed: The Campus Mental Health Crisis and What to Do about It* (San Francisco: Jossey-Bass, 2004), 156.

[6] Schutte, N.S. & Malouff, J.M. (2002). Incorporating emotional skills in a college transition course enhances student retention. *Journal of The First-Year Experience and Students in Transition, 14,* 7–21.

Chapter Review

Steps to Success:
Cultivating Motivation, Resilience, and Emotional Intelligence

○ **Stay motivated.** Consider your own level of motivation to do well in college. If you are lacking motivation, visit a college counselor for strategies to improve it.

○ **If you have a negative attitude** about college or about life in general, work with a counselor to figure out strategies to be more optimistic and realistic at the same time.

○ **Consider the way your mindset affects your attitude about college.** Open yourself to all college has to offer by developing a growth mindset.

○ **Evaluate your own resilience** when you confront obstacles in your life. Look for examples of others who have overcome setbacks by practicing resilience.

○ **Using the questionnaire on page 26, assess your emotional intelligence.** Note areas in which your EI is strong and areas that need improvement.

○ **Be aware of how your emotions affect the way you react to difficult or frustrating situations.** Use your awareness ahead of time to try to control your negative reactions.

○ **If you aren't satisfied with your emotional reactions, make an appointment at the campus counseling center to discuss your feelings and get help.**

Applying what you've learned . . .

Now that you have read and discussed this chapter, consider how you can apply what you have learned to your academic and personal lives. The following prompts will help you reflect on the material and its relevance to you both now and in the future.

1. Select the same show or a movie to watch during the coming week. Take notes on how the characters handle their emotions, especially in stressful situations. How many of the emotional intelligence competencies were represented—either positively or negatively? During next week's class, discuss what you saw and learned.

2. No one has the same mindset in all situations. You may be willing to challenge yourself on the playing field but not in the classroom. In what areas are you the most "fixed" in your self-assessment, and where do you welcome opportunities for challenge and growth?

3. Your emotional reactions, whether positive or negative, affect your interactions with others. Pretend that you are your own therapist. In what kinds of situations have you reacted with defensiveness, anger, sadness, annoyance, resentment, or humiliation? Take a step back and "process" these reactions. Think about what you said or did in response to your feelings, and why. Then consider what you can do to take control and make good choices next time.

Use Your Resources

GO TO ▷ The learning center: If you need help developing strategies for learning and good study skills. Students at all levels use campus learning centers to improve in the skills discussed in this chapter.

GO To ▷ The counseling center: If you need help talking about problems you are having with motivation or managing your emotions. It is normal to seek such assistance. This kind of counseling is strictly confidential (unless you are a threat to yourself or others) and usually is provided at no charge, which is a great benefit.

GO TO ▷ The library: If you need help finding books and articles about motivation, resilience, or emotional intelligence.

GO ONLINE TO ▷ TED (ted.com/talks): If you need help getting motivated and you enjoy inspiring talks. Search TED talks for topics like motivation, failure, and resilience, for instance, Dan Pink's "The Puzzle of Motivation": www.ted.com/talks/dan _pink_on _motivation.

GO ONLINE TO ▷ Mind Tools (mindtools.com/pages/article/ei-quiz.htm): If you need help testing your emotional intelligence skills.

GO ONLINE TO ▷ http://sivers.org/mindset: If you need help finding additional perspectives on mindsets, or to **http://psychology.about.com/od/psychologytopics/tp /theories-of-motivation.htm** to explore theories of motivation.

NOW... How do you measure up?

1. I understand what motivates me in different aspects of my life.
- ○ Agree
- ○ Don't Know
- ○ Disagree

2. I have a positive attitude most of the time.
- ○ Agree
- ○ Don't Know
- ○ Disagree

3. When something bad happens, I'm able to bounce back.
- ○ Agree
- ○ Don't Know
- ○ Disagree

4. My emotions do not determine my behavior.
- ○ Agree
- ○ Don't Know
- ○ Disagree

How do your answers here compare to your responses to the quiz you took at the start of the chapter? Which sections of this chapter left a strong impression on you? Have you thought hard about what motivates you, your attitude about college, and your mindset? What strategies for perceiving and managing emotions have you tried? What other strategies will you commit to trying?

LaunchPad macmillan learning

LaunchPad Solo for College Success is a great resource. Go online to master concepts using the LearningCurve study tool and much more. **macmillanhighered.com/collegesuccessmedia**

03

35
Time—Your Most Valuable Resource

38
Managing Your Energy

40
Time-Management Pitfalls

44
Get Smart about Organizing Your Days, Weeks, Tasks, and More

48
Maximizing Study and Review Time

Managing Your Time

Alexandr III/Shutterstock

How often do you find yourself saying, "I don't have time"? Once a week? Once a day? Several times a day? The next time you find yourself saying it, stop and ask yourself whether it is really true. Do you really not have time, or have you made a choice, consciously or unconsciously, not to make time for that particular task or activity? Once you recognize that you can control and change how you use your time, you'll want to assess your time-management strengths and then set time-management goals and priorities.

The first step in this assessment is to acknowledge that you have control over how you use your time and many of the commitments you choose to make. Every day you make many small decisions that affect your time-management success, such as what time you get up in the morning, how much sleep you get, how much time you spend studying, and whether you allocate any time to exercise. All these small decisions have a big effect on your success in college and in life.

Being in control means that you make your own decisions and take responsibility for your actions. If you're a recent high school graduate, you'll find that two ways in which college differs significantly from high school are students' increased autonomy, or independence, and greater responsibility. If you're a returning student, you most likely have a high level of independence, but coming back to college creates responsibilities above and beyond those you already have, whether they include employment, family, community service, or other commitments. Whichever type of student you are, making the transition into college will create some unanticipated demands on your time, demands that will require new time-management strategies. You'll find these strategies in this chapter as well as tools to help you set time-management goals, get organized, recognize and avoid common time-management problems, and make your schedule work for you.

LaunchPad
macmillan learning

To access the LearningCurve study tool, Video Tools, and more, go to *LaunchPad Solo for College Success.* **macmillanhighered.com/ collegesuccessmedia**

How do you measure up?

1. I set academic and personal goals to guide how I prioritize my time.
   - ○ Agree
   - ○ Don't Know
   - ○ Disagree

2. I am able to focus on the task at hand instead of procrastinating or getting distracted.
   - ○ Agree
   - ○ Don't Know
   - ○ Disagree

3. I use a daily or weekly planner, to-do lists, or other planning devices or apps to keep track of my commitments.
   - ○ Agree
   - ○ Don't Know
   - ○ Disagree

4. I am able to balance my social life and my need for personal time with my academic requirements.
   - ○ Agree
   - ○ Don't Know
   - ○ Disagree

Review the items you marked "Don't Know" or "Disagree." Pay special attention to these topics in this chapter—you will find motivating strategies to develop in these areas. A follow-up quiz at the end of the chapter will prompt you to consider what you have learned.

Getting Out of a Jam

△ **Nicoleta Larsen**

© Hill Street Studios/Blend Images/Corbis.

On the first day of class, my English instructor spent more time talking about deadlines than books. "Review the syllabus and enter all your upcoming tests and papers in your datebook," Professor Hughes said. So, OK, I typed everything into my iPhone. But I was also thinking about my job, my next class, and my quartet's performance on Saturday, and it's sort of hard to think about the future when your here and now is packed.

"Your final research paper should be at least fifteen pages long and will count for 25 percent of your final grade," Professor Hughes added. "Find a topic and start gathering resource materials *now*." I jotted down a couple of ideas and figured I'd go to the library later in the week to get help. As the term went on, I did a pretty good job of keeping up with assignments and tests, but I didn't make much headway on my final paper.

Cut to three weeks before the deadline: I still hadn't made it to the library, and panic was starting to set in. I decided to come clean with Professor Hughes and ask for some help. He referred me to the chapter in my college success textbook on information literacy, and we walked over to the library together so that I could connect with a librarian. I knew that I would have to make some tough choices about my priorities for the rest of the term, but I felt determined to make myself and Professor Hughes proud.

What could Nicoleta have done differently to stay out of this jam? What would you do if you were in her position? What time-management techniques do you hope to get from this chapter that you could apply to a situation like this?

Time—Your Most Valuable Resource

The way you spend your time should align with your most important values. To begin connecting your use of time with your values, first set some goals for the future. What are your goals for the coming decade? If you're like most students reading this book, one of your goals is probably to earn a two-year or four-year degree. Maybe you've already decided on the career that you want to pursue. Or perhaps you plan to go on to graduate or professional school. As you look to the future, you may see yourself buying a new car, owning a home, starting a family, owning a business, or retiring early. Achieving these goals will take a lot of your *time*, and time management is one of the most effective tools to assist you.

When considering all the things you'll need to do and the limited time you have, start with this question: How do you approach time? Because people are innately different and come from many different cultures, they tend to view time in different ways. For example, if you're a natural organizer, you probably enter all due dates for assignments, exams, and quizzes on your calendar as soon as you receive each course syllabus, and you may be good at adhering to a strict schedule. On the other hand, if you are more laid-back, you may prefer to be more flexible, or to "go with the flow," rather than follow a daily or weekly schedule. You may excel at dealing with the unexpected, but you may also be a procrastinator. If this sounds like you, find time-management techniques that feel comfortable but still help you keep on track. You may have to stretch a bit, but your efforts can have a significant payoff.

Setting Goals

More than likely, one goal you will set or have already set is to find a good job when you complete your degree, or a job that is significantly better than the one you have now. You might be working on identifying just what that "good job" looks like—what it pays, where the best opportunities to get that job are, what the

△ **Sold!**
Many people dream of owning their own home. How you spend your time is directly related to how you intend to spend your money. When planning a significant purchase, consider carefully how much money you need to earn and save before you can make the purchase. How much time will it take to make this happen? © Ariel Skelley/Blend Images/Corbis.

hours are likely to be, and so on. You might already be taking steps to make yourself a competitive candidate in a job search or to find an internship in a related field.

In a job search, good grades and a college degree may not be enough to distinguish you. When setting goals and objectives for allocating your time, consider the importance of having a well-rounded résumé when you graduate. What would such a résumé look like? It might show that you participated in extracurricular activities, gained leadership experience, engaged in community service, took advantage of internship or co-op opportunities, developed job-related skills, kept up-to-date on technological advances, or pursued relevant part- or full-time employment while attending classes.

When it is time to look for a permanent job, you want to demonstrate that you have used your college years wisely. Doing so will require planning and effective time-management skills, which are highly valued by employers. Your college or university's career center can help you arrange for an internship, a co-op program, or community service that will give you valuable experience and strengthen your résumé.

Prioritizing

Once you have established goals and objectives, your next step is to prioritize your time. Which goals and objectives are the most important to you? For example, is it more important to study for a test tomorrow or to attend a job fair today? Keep in mind that ignoring long-term goals in order to meet short-term goals isn't always a good idea. In fact, the more time and thought you devote to setting your long-term goals, the easier it becomes to know how to spend your time in the short term. Using good time management, you can study during the week before a test so that you can attend a job fair the day before the test. One way that skilled time managers establish priorities is to create a to-do list (discussed in more detail later in this chapter), rank the items on the list, and then determine a schedule and deadline for each task. These tasks can be related to your long- or short-term planning.

Finding Balance

Another aspect of setting priorities in college is finding an appropriate way to balance an

TRY IT!

SETTING GOALS ▷ **"I've Got to Get My Priorities in Order!"**

How many times have you heard or said this? It's very common to find yourself spending time on the wrong things. Commit to making a list of your priorities for the week. Knowing which obligations and activities are most important helps you manage your time properly. If you are determined to get all the have-tos out of the way, you'll have more time to invest in want-tos and have more balance in your life. Balance helps you maintain your overall motivation for college.

academic schedule, your family life, your social life, and time for yourself. Social activities are an important part of the college experience. Being involved in campus life can enhance your satisfaction with college and thus boost your achievement level and your determination to continue in college. However, if you never have time alone or time to study and think, you might feel overwhelmed. And employment, family, and community obligations are also important and time-consuming and aren't "optional." For many students, the greatest challenge of prioritizing is to balance college with these other valuable dimensions of life.

Many decisions you make today are reversible. You may later decide to change your major, and your career and life goals may shift as well. But the decision to take control of your life—to

Time in College and in Career

If you have a job, you have already learned your supervisor's expectations about time. If you need to start work at 8:00 a.m., it's not OK to come in at 8:15. If you work on projects, you likely have to meet deadlines. You cannot ignore them or make excuses for missing them. If you haven't had a job, you have probably observed someone in your family who works on a set schedule. Unless you work for yourself, you'll find punctuality to be a standard workplace rule, and

even if you are self-employed, your clients will expect you to maintain schedules and do the work you promise. How likely are you to keep your job or earn a promotion if you cannot be depended on to do work on time? College is a lot like the workplace. While no one will "fire" you for being late to class or turning in a paper late, such behavior will have a negative effect on how others, especially instructors, view you, and it will also result in lower grades.

◁ **Practice Makes Perfect**
Most of us don't strive to achieve the level of physical fitness required to be a gymnastics champion, but just as practice makes perfect on the balance beam, so does practice make us better at balancing the many aspects of our busy lives. © Tim Clayton/TIM CLAYTON/Corbis.

establish your own goals for the future, to set your priorities, and to manage your time accordingly—is an important one for the present and the future.

Successful people frequently say that staying focused is a key to their success. To help you stay focused, make a plan. Begin with your priorities, and then think about the necessities of life. Finish what needs to be done before you move from work to pleasure. ■

R-E-S-P-E-C-T

How does time management relate to respect? Think of the last time you made an appointment with someone who either forgot the appointment entirely or was very late. Were you upset or disappointed with the person for wasting your time? In college, if you repeatedly arrive late for class, you are breaking the basic rules of politeness. You are intentionally or unintentionally showing a lack of respect for your instructors and your classmates.

At times what instructors perceive as inappropriate or disrespectful behavior may result from a cultural misunderstanding. All cultures view time differently. In American academic culture, punctuality is a virtue. Being strictly on time may be a difficult adjustment for you if you grew up in a culture that is more flexible in its approach to time, but it is important to recognize the values of the new culture you are encountering.

Here are a few basic guidelines for respectful behavior in class and in other interactions with instructors:

- Be in class on time. Arrive early enough to remove outerwear and have your assignments, notebook or computer, and writing tools ready to go.
- Avoid behavior in class that is disrespectful to the instructor and other students. This includes answering your cell phone, texting, or checking Facebook; doing homework for another class; falling asleep; and whispering or talking.
- Manage your time when participating in class discussions.

Don't "hog the floor"; give others the opportunity to express their ideas.

- Be on time for scheduled appointments with your instructors and advisers, and be prepared with good questions. This will show how much you appreciate their time and the help they can give you.

Time management is a lifelong skill. To secure and succeed at a good job after college, you will have to manage your own time and possibly that of other people you supervise. If you go to graduate or professional school, time management will continue to be essential to your success. Time management is also important as a way in which you show respect for others—your friends, your family, and your college instructors.

Managing Your Energy

Your best plans will not work if you do not have the energy to make them happen. You may plan to spend a couple of hours on your math homework before you go to bed in the evening at the end of a busy day. However, you may find that you are too tired to concentrate and solve the math problems. While learning to manage your time effectively, you must also learn to manage your energy so that you have more control over your life and can achieve success in college.

Along with time, energy is an essential resource, and we have a choice in how we use it. Although energy is renewable, each one of us has a limited amount of it in a twenty-four-hour period. Each person has a daily pattern of physical, emotional, and mental activity. For instance, some people are early risers and have a lot of energy in the morning; others feel the least productive in the morning and can accomplish tasks at the end of the day more effectively, especially tasks that require mental energy and concentration.

The first step to managing your energy is to recognize your daily pattern and establish a routine around it. Use Table 3.1 to record your high, average, and low energy level every day for one week. Use H for high, A for average, and L for low to identify which times of day you feel more or less energetic.

What did you learn about yourself by completing Table 3.1? What are the best and worst times for you to study? Determine whether you are capable of getting up very early in the morning to study or how late you can stay up at night and still get to morning classes on time.

Table 3.1 ▽ Monitoring Your Energy Level

Time	Mon.	Tues.	Wed.	Thurs.	Fri.	Sat.	Sun.
				Energy level			
Early morning							
Late morning							
Early afternoon							
Late afternoon							
Early evening							
Late evening							

Establishing a study routine based on your daily energy pattern will help you develop a schedule that you can maintain and use to your advantage. If you have more energy on the weekend, for example, take advantage of that time to review or catch up on major projects, such as term papers, that can't be completed effectively in short blocks of time.

Schedule some downtime for yourself to regain your energy. Different activities work for different people. For example, you may stream Netflix or use Snapchat for an hour or take a nap before you start doing your homework. Just make sure that you do not go over the amount of time you set aside as your downtime.

Your energy level also depends on your diet and other habits such as exercise or lack of it. If you are juggling many responsibilities across several locations, you can use some very simple strategies to take care of yourself:

- Carry healthy snacks with you, such as fruit, nuts, or yogurt. You'll save time and money by avoiding trips to snack bars and convenience stores, and you'll keep your energy up by eating better.

- Drink plenty of water.

- Take brief naps when possible. Research shows that naps are more effective for regaining your energy than caffeine.[1]

- Try meditation. While meditation takes some time, it will increase your energy level so that you will accomplish more in fewer hours. ▪

[1]Sara C. Mednick, Denise J. Cai, Jennifer Kanady, and Sean P. A. Drummond, "Comparing the Benefits of Caffeine, Naps and Placebo on Verbal, Motor and Perceptual Memory," *Behavioural Brain Research* 193, no. 1 (2008): 79–86v.

△ **Stay Awake**
Like this student, you probably have a lot of demands on your time. Make sure to effectively manage your energy by getting enough rest, eating properly, and pacing yourself, or you might find yourself falling asleep while studying. Ocean Corbis.

Time-Management Pitfalls

If you're human, which of course you are, you likely procrastinate at least occasionally, which makes it harder to manage your time. In fact, procrastination is one of the biggest challenges for college students, so we're going to tackle it right away, along with the other most common time-management pitfalls.

Procrastination

To procrastinate means to put off doing something or to be slow or late about doing a task that should be done. Dr. Piers Steel, a leading researcher and speaker on the science of motivation and procrastination, writes that

Is Procrastination a Problem for You?

Take the following procrastination self-assessment to get a sense of whether procrastination is a problem for you. Place a number from 1 to 5 before each statement. (For example, if you "Agree" with a statement, place a 4 before the statement.)

1 = Strongly Disagree

2 = Disagree

3 = Mildly Disagree

4 = Agree

5 = Strongly Agree

____ I have a habit of putting off important tasks that I don't enjoy doing.

____ My standards are so high that I'm not usually satisfied enough with my work to turn it in on time.

____ I spend more time planning what I'm going to do than actually doing it.

____ The chaos in my study space makes it hard for me to get started.

____ The people I live with distract me from doing my classwork.

____ I have more energy for a task if I wait until the last minute to do it.

____ I enjoy the excitement of living on the edge.

____ I have trouble prioritizing all my responsibilities.

____ Having to meet a deadline makes me really nervous.

____ My biggest problem is that I just don't know how to get started.

If you responded that you "Agree" or "Strongly Agree" with two questions or fewer, then you procrastinate from time to time, but it may not be a major problem for you. Reading this chapter will help you continue to stay focused and avoid procrastination in the future.

If you responded that you "Agree" or "Strongly Agree" with three to five questions, then you are having difficulties with procrastination. Revisit the questions to which you answered "Agree" or "Strongly Agree," and look in the chapter for strategies that specifically address these issues to help you overcome obstacles. You *can* get a handle on your procrastination!

If you responded that you "Agree" or "Strongly Agree" with six or more questions, then you may be having a significant problem with procrastination, and it could interfere with your success in college if you do not make a change. Revisit the questions to which you answered "Agree" or "Strongly Agree," and look in the chapter for strategies that specifically address these issues. Also, if you are concerned about your pattern of procrastination and you aren't having success in dealing with it yourself, consider talking to a professional counselor in your campus counseling center. It's free and confidential, and counselors have extensive experience working with students who have problems with procrastination.

procrastination is on the rise, with 80 to 95 percent of college students spending time procrastinating.[2] According to Steel, half of all college students report that they procrastinate on a daily basis, spending as much as one-third of their time in activities solely related to procrastination. These numbers, plus widespread acknowledgment of the negative effects of procrastination, provide evidence of a serious issue that trips up many otherwise-capable people.

The good news is that, of those people who procrastinate on a regular basis, 95 percent say they want to change their behavior.[3] An important first step toward change is to understand why people procrastinate. According to Steel, people who are highly motivated often fear failure, and some people even fear success, although that might seem counterintuitive. Consequently, some students procrastinate because they are perfectionists; not doing a task might be easier than having to live up to their own very high expectations or those of their parents, teachers, or peers. Many procrastinate because they are easily distracted, they have difficulty organizing and regulating their lives, or they have difficulty following through on long-term goals. They might find an assigned task boring or irrelevant or consider it unimportant "busy work."

Changing how you approach less enjoyable assignments is key to overcoming procrastination and increasing your success in college. For instance, simply disliking an assignment is an *excuse* for putting it off, not a valid *reason*. Life is full of tasks you won't find interesting, and in many cases you won't have the option to ignore them. Whether it is cleaning your house, filing your taxes, completing paperwork, or responding to hundreds of e-mails, tedious tasks will always be there, and you will have to figure out strategies to complete them. When you're in college, procrastinating can signal that it's time to reevaluate your goals and objectives and your readiness for academic work at this point in your life. A counselor or academic adviser can help you sort this out.

[2] Piers Steel, "The Nature of Procrastination: A Meta-analytic and Theoretical Review of Quintessential Self-Regulatory Failure," *Psychological Bulletin* 133, no. 1 (2007): 65–94.

[3] Ibid.

> ❝ Being overextended is a primary source of stress for college students. ❞

Being "Spread Too Thin"

Being overextended is a primary source of stress for college students and another pitfall to managing time. Often, students underestimate how much time it will take to do well in college and overschedule themselves with work and other commitments. The best advice is to prioritize—focus on what you *can* manage. If you do not have enough time to carry your course load and meet your commitments, drop a course before the drop deadline so that you won't have a low grade on your permanent record. Keep in mind, however, that if you receive financial aid, you must be registered for a minimum number of credit hours to maintain your current level of aid. If dropping a course is not feasible and if other activities are not that important, let go of one or more nonacademic commitments. *Learn to say "no."* Saying "no" can be difficult,

△ **Just Give Mommy a Minute . . .**
Anyone who has tried to get work done at home with children around knows that it doesn't usually work out very well. Unless you have a room in your home where you truly will not be disturbed, study at home only when your kids are elsewhere. Trying to focus on kids and work at the same time means neither gets enough attention. © JDC/LWA/Corbis.

especially if you think that you are letting other people down. However, it is far more preferable to respectfully excuse yourself from an activity than to fail to come through at the last minute.

Distractions

Distractions are another common pitfall when it comes to time management. Some students use distractions as excuses to procrastinate. Others don't want to be distracted, and they need coping strategies to help them focus on tasks at hand.

Consider the types of distractions you encounter and when and where you are most often distracted. For instance, where should you study? Some students find it's best to avoid studying in places associated with leisure, such as at the kitchen table, in the living room, or in front of the TV. Similarly, it might not be wise to study on your bed because you might drift off to sleep. Instead, find quiet places, both on campus and at home, where you can concentrate each time you sit down to do your work.

Accurately predicting the distractions you will face is especially important. For instance, if you have children at home, assume that they will always want your attention no matter how much others try to help out. It's a good idea to

TRY IT!

MANAGING TIME ▷ About to Lose It!

Are you trying to do too much, and is your crazy schedule reducing your motivation for college? Are you working too many hours? Are you feeling really stressed out? In a small group, discuss strategies for reducing your stress level and maintaining your motivation for being successful in your academic work.

develop strategies for minimizing distractions while you study. Take a look at the examples and activity in Table 3.2.

Motivation Problems

Motivation is an essential component of setting and achieving your academic and life goals, and the absence of motivation is a major pitfall. Forcing yourself to do something in which you have no interest is almost impossible. If you have lost interest in your academic or career path—if you feel unmotivated—it may be time to consider a change. Talk with an academic adviser or counselor about how to refocus your purpose for being in college and regain your motivation.

Table 3.2 ▽ Strategies for Minimizing Distractions

Distraction	Solution
You're tempted to message your friends or check social media.	Turn off the sound and vibration on all devices; put them in another room or leave them in another location.
Your children want your attention.	Study away from home or after they have gone to bed.
You keep falling asleep when you're studying.	Sit upright at your desk or worktable; avoid studying in bed or on the couch; try to get more rest. Use Table 3.1 to build a new study schedule.

List some distractions that you face, and come up with solutions to avoid them.

Distraction	Solution
_____	_____
_____	_____
_____	_____
_____	_____

Many students of all ages question their decision to attend college and sometimes feel overwhelmed by the additional responsibilities that being in college brings. Prioritizing, rethinking some commitments and letting some things go, and weighing the advantages and disadvantages of attending college part-time versus full-time can help you work through this adjustment period. Make a plan that begins with your priorities: attending classes, studying, working, and spending time with the people who are important to you. Then think about the necessities of life: sleeping, eating, exercising, and relaxing. Leave time for fun things such as talking with friends, tweeting, streaming your favorite show, and going out, but finish what *needs* to be done before you move from work to pleasure. Also, don't forget about personal time. If you live in a residence hall or share an apartment with other students, talk with your roommates about how to coordinate your class schedules so that each of you has some privacy. If you live with your family, particularly if you are a parent, work with family members to create special family times as well as quiet study times.

Don't let the challenges of this early adjustment period into college kill your motivation. Take control of this transition by developing a plan to manage your time. ∎

Ask Yourself the Tough Questions

Why are you in college here and now? Why are you in this course? What is really important to you? Is what you value important enough to forgo some short-term fun or laziness and get down to work? Are your academic goals really your own, or were they imposed on you by family members, your employer, or societal expectations? Think about your answers to these tough questions— are you motivated to get busy? Which of the following strategies for staying focused do you think can help?

- Be more aware of how classes and assignments that you find boring or difficult might be relevant to your interests and goals and therefore worth your time and energy.

- Remind yourself of the possible consequences if you do not begin your work. Then get started.
- Create a to-do list. Check off items when you finish them. Use the list to focus on the tasks that aren't getting done. Move them to the top of the next day's list. Working from a list will give you a feeling of accomplishment.
- Break down big jobs into smaller steps. Tackle short, easy-to-accomplish tasks first.
- Promise yourself a reward for finishing each task, such as watching a new episode of your favorite Netflix show or going out with friends. For more substantial tasks, give yourself bigger and better rewards.

- Find a place to study that's comfortable and that doesn't allow for distractions and interruptions. If you study in your room, close your door.
- Say "no" to friends and family members who want your attention; agree to spend time with them later.
- Stay offline and off your mobile device during planned study sessions.
- If you're taking courses online, find ways to stay engaged and organized. Time management in online courses that have few or no weekly meetings is challenging. Connecting with another student in your courses can help both of you stay on track with deadlines for submitting assignments, completing projects, and posting comments.

Get Smart about Organizing Your Days, Weeks, Tasks, and More

As you begin your first year of college, how far ahead are you in making plans and developing a schedule? Your academic year will be divided into chunks of time or terms—either semesters, which are fourteen to sixteen weeks long, or quarters, which are about twelve weeks long. You will quickly discover the temptation to plan only for today or tomorrow, but begin by taking a long view. Think of the time between now and when you plan to graduate. Do you have a good idea of which courses you will have to take and when? Work with your academic adviser to make sure that you stay on track and get in all your requirements for graduation. If you plan to transfer, make sure that the new institution will accept the credits for the courses you are taking now or planning to take. Seek help from your academic adviser and from an adviser at the college or university to which you plan to transfer.

If you are a parent or are working off campus, the whole idea of planning ahead may seem futile. We all know how often "life gets in the way," and the best-laid plans may have to be adjusted to meet last-minute emergencies. You'll be more likely to manage your life and juggle your responsibilities, though, if you create a term-length calendar as you begin your college experience. Many techniques and tools, both paper and digital, are available to help you manage your time. Which system you use doesn't really matter. What matters is that you select a tool and use it every day.

Using a Daily or Weekly Planner

In college, as in life, you will quickly learn that managing your time is a key not only to survival but also to success. Consider buying a week-at-a-glance organizer for the current year. Your campus bookstore may sell one designed just for your college or university, with important dates and deadlines already provided. Many students today prefer to use an electronic planner; that's fine—your computer, smartphone, or tablet comes equipped with a calendar.

Carry your planner with you at all times and continue to enter all due dates as soon as you know them. Write in meeting times and locations, scheduled social events, study time for each class, and so forth. Add phone numbers and e-mail addresses, too, in case something comes up and you need to cancel plans with someone. Get into the habit of using a planner to help you keep track of commitments and maintain control of your schedule. Choose a specific time each day to check your notes for the current week and the coming week. Making certain that you aren't forgetting something important takes just a moment, and it helps relieve stress!

Scheduling Your Time Week by Week

Use the following steps to schedule your time for each coming week:

- Begin by entering all your commitments for the week—classes, work hours, family commitments, and so on—on your schedule.

- Track your activities for a full week by entering into your schedule everything you do and how much time each task requires. Use this record to help you estimate the time you will need for similar activities in the future.

- Try to reserve at least two hours of study time for each hour spent in class. This 2-for-1 rule reflects many faculty members' expectations for how much work their students should do to master the material in their classes. So, for example, if you are taking a typical full-time class load of fifteen credits, you should plan to study an additional thirty hours each week. Think of this forty-five-hour-per-week commitment as comparable to a full-time job.

Figure 3.1 ▽ **Weekly Timetable**

Using your class schedule for the term and adding other obligations, create your own weekly timetable using an app like iCal or LifeTopix. At the beginning of your term, track all your activities for a full week by entering into your schedule everything you do and how much time each task requires. Use this record to help you estimate the time you will need for similar activities in the future.

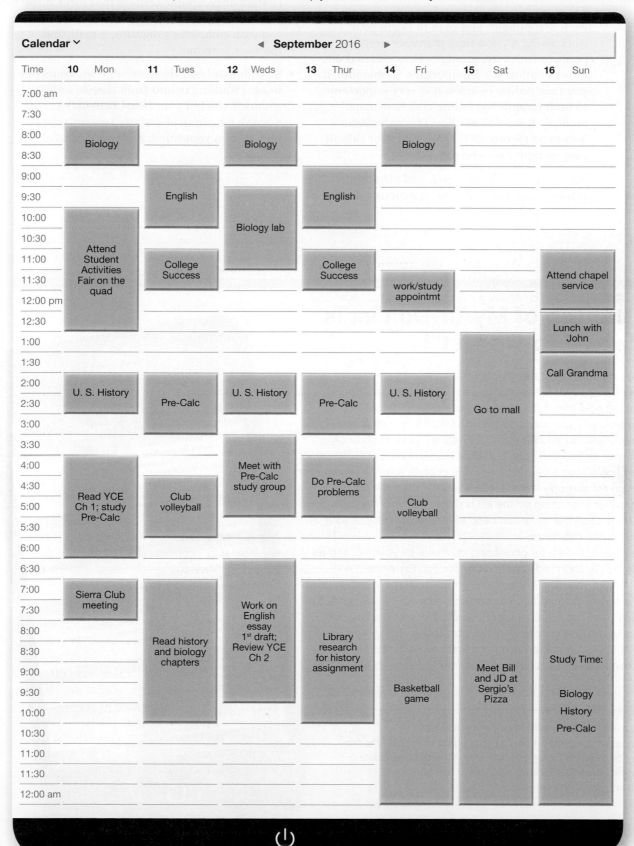

- Establish a study routine that is based on your daily energy pattern (see Table 3.1), obligations, and potential distractions (see Table 3.2).

- Estimate how much time you will need for each assignment, and plan to begin your work early. A good time manager frequently plans to finish assignments before actual due dates to allow for emergencies. Remember, if you take online courses, it is very important to understand that online course management systems do not allow late submissions. You must record all the deadlines for submitting assignments and meet them.

- Set aside time for research and other preparatory tasks. For example, instructors expect you to be computer literate, and they usually don't have time to explain how to use a word processor, spreadsheet, or statistical computer program. Most campuses have learning centers or computer centers that offer tutoring, walk-in assistance, or workshops to assist you with computer programs, e-mail, and Internet searches.

- Schedule at least three aerobic workouts per week. (Walking to and from classes only counts if you get your heart rate up.) Taking a break for physical activity relaxes your body, clears your mind, and is a powerful motivator.

At the Top of My To-Do List Is "Make a To-Do List"!

Keeping a to-do list can help you avoid feeling stressed or out of control. If to-do lists become part of your daily routine, you'll be amazed at how they help you keep up with your activities and responsibilities. You can keep a to-do list on your cell phone—download a to-do list app such as Errands—or in a notebook or memo pad, or you can post it on your bulletin board or refrigerator. Some people start a new list every day or once a week. Others keep a running list and only throw a page away or clear the contents of the list when everything on the list is done. Use your to-do list to keep track of all the tasks you need to remember, not just your academic commitments.

Develop a system for prioritizing the items on your list, and as you complete each task, cross it off your list. Experiment with color—make your lists in black and cross out items in red, or use highlighters or colored ink. You can also rank your to-do items by marking them with one, two, or three stars or with the letters A, B, C, and so on. Use your to-do list in conjunction with your planner. You will feel good about how much you have accomplished, and this positive feeling will help you stay motivated.

Figure 3.2 ▷ Daily and Weekly To-Do Lists
Almost all successful people keep a daily to-do list. The list may be in paper or digital form. Get in the habit of creating and maintaining your own daily list of appointments, obligations, and activities.

Thinking about Your Class Schedule

If you are a first-year student, you may not have had much flexibility in determining your current course schedule; by the time you could register for classes, some sections of your required courses may have been closed. You also may not have known whether you would prefer taking classes back-to-back or having a break between classes.

In building a schedule that is right for you, you have to consider a lot of factors. How early in the morning are you willing to start classes? Do you prefer evening classes? What impact will work or family commitments have on scheduling decisions? What times of day are you more alert? Less alert? How many days a week can you or do you want to attend classes? Over time, have you found that you prefer spreading your classes over five or six days of the week? Or have you discovered that you like to go to class just two or three days a week, or only once a week for a longer class period? Your attention span as well as your other commitments may influence your decisions about your class schedule. Before you register for the next term, think long and hard about how to make your class schedule work for you. ■

> 66 Before you register for the next term, think long and hard about how to make your class schedule work for you. 99

TRY IT!

FEELING CONNECTED ▷ **Compare Your Class Schedules**

Are you happy or unhappy with your class schedule? Do you have enough time to get from one class to another? Are any classes too early or too late for your preference? In a small group, share your current class schedules. Exchange ideas on how to handle time-management problems and the challenges you see in your schedules. Discuss how you would arrange your schedule differently for the next term. Go online and check your college's days and times of classes for next term. See if it's possible for you to get the courses you want within the schedule that you prefer.

Maximizing Study and Review Time

Studying effectively means that you need to consider the time of day or night when you study best, where you can study with the least distractions, and how to actually learn while you study. Here are some strategies you can use to get the most benefit from your study time:

- **Find your space.** Use the same study area regularly, and make sure it is free of distractions and quiet enough so that you can focus. The library is usually the best choice. Try empty classrooms and study halls on campus, too. Bring essential supplies to your study area. Make sure you have everything you need.

- **Stick to a study routine.** The more firmly you have established a specific time and a quiet place to study, the more effective you will be in keeping up with your schedule.

- **Break down large tasks.** By taking on one thing at a time, you will make steady progress toward your academic goals.

- **Set realistic goals for your study time.** Assess how long it takes to read a chapter in different types of textbooks and to review notes in your courses, and then schedule your time accordingly. Allow adequate time to review and then test your knowledge when preparing for exams. Online classes often require online discussions and activities that take the place of face-to-face classroom instruction, so be prepared to spend additional time on these tasks.

- **Review when the material is fresh.** Schedule time to review immediately after class or as soon as possible; you will remember more of what you learned in class. Invest in tools (note cards, digital recorders, flash card apps, etc.) to convert less productive time into study time.

- **Time and attention.** Know your best times of day to study, and routinely assess your attention level. Schedule activities such as doing laundry, checking Facebook or Instagram, and seeing friends or family for those times of day when you have difficulty concentrating. Also, use waiting time (on the bus, before class, before appointments) to review.

- **Study difficult or boring subjects first,** when you are fresh. (Exception: If you are having trouble getting started, it might be easier to begin with your favorite subject.)

- **Divide study time into fifty-minute blocks.** Study for fifty minutes and then take a ten- or fifteen-minute break; then study for another fifty-minute block. Try not to study for more than three fifty-minute blocks in a row, or you will find that you are not accomplishing fifty minutes' worth of work in each block. (In economics, this drop-off in productivity is known as the "law of diminishing returns.") If you have larger blocks of time available on the weekend, take advantage of them to review or to catch up on major projects.

- **Script your study sessions.** Break extended study sessions into a variety of activities, each with a specific objective. For example, begin by reading, then develop flash cards by writing key terms and their definitions or key formulas on note cards, and finally test yourself on what you have read.

- **Avoid multitasking.** Although you may be good at juggling many tasks at once, or at least may *think* that you are, the reality is (and research shows) that you will study more effectively and retain more if you concentrate on one task at a time.

> " You will study more effectively and retain more if you concentrate on one task at a time. "

- **Limit distracting and time-consuming communications.** Check your phone, tablet, or computer for messages or updates at a set time, not whenever you think of it. Constant texting, browsing, or posting can keep you from achieving your academic goals. Particularly if you are taking online courses and need to be connected when studying, turn off all the notifications on your device. The notifications may tempt you to check messages or posts and waste valuable study time. Remember that when time has passed, you cannot get it back.

- **Let others help.** Find an accountability partner to help keep you on track. If you struggle with keeping a regular study schedule, find a friend, relative, or classmate to keep you motivated and on course. If you have children, plan daily family homework times and encourage family members to help you study by taking flash cards wherever you go.

- **Be flexible.** You cannot anticipate every disruption to your plans. Build extra time into your study schedule so that unexpected interruptions do not prevent you from meeting your goals.

- **Reward yourself!** Develop a system of short- and long-term study goals as well as rewards for meeting those goals. Doing so will keep your motivation high. ■

Getting from Here to There—Using Travel Time Wisely

Consider how you might best use travel time, whether going from class to class or commuting to and from your college. If you live on campus, you may want to create a schedule that situates you near a dining hall at mealtimes or allows you to spend breaks between classes at the library. Or you may need breaks in your schedule for relaxation, like spending time in a student lounge or at the campus center. You may want to avoid returning to your residence hall room to take a nap between classes if a nap will make you feel lethargic or make you oversleep and miss later classes. Also, if you attend a large college or university, be sure that you allow adequate time to get from building to building. If you are a commuting student, or you work off campus, you may prefer scheduling your classes together in blocks without breaks. *Block scheduling*, which means enrolling in back-to-back classes, allows you to cut travel time by attending classes one or two days a week, and it may provide more flexibility for scheduling employment or family commitments.

In spite of its advantages, block scheduling can also have drawbacks. If you become ill on a class day, you could fall behind in all your classes. You might also become fatigued from sitting in class after class. Having a last-minute study period immediately before a test will be difficult when one class immediately follows another, because you likely will have no more than a fifteen-minute break between classes. Finally, remember that for back-to-back classes, several exams might be held on the same day. Scheduling classes in blocks might work better if you have the option of attending lectures at alternative times in case you are absent, if you alternate classes with free periods, and if you seek out instructors who are flexible about due dates for assignments.

△ **Getting from Here to There**
College students have the responsibility to get themselves to class on time and must plan transportation carefully, whether walking, driving, bicycling, ridesharing, taking public transportation, or using another method of getting from place to place. If you have an emergency situation that causes you to run late, talk to your instructor. He or she will understand a real emergency and help you make up work you missed. wong yu liang/Shutterstock.

Chapter Review

Steps to Success: Managing Your Time

○ **Make sure that the way you use your time supports your goals for being in college.** All your time doesn't have to be spent studying, but remember the "two hours out of class for each hour in class" rule. Also, plan some intentional out-of-class activities that support your goals.

○ **Manage your energy by recognizing your daily energy pattern and establishing a routine around it.** Decide whether you study more effectively in the morning, afternoon, evening, or some combination.

○ **Identify and address common time-management problems before they spiral out of control.** Be aware of issues with procrastination, distractions, overscheduling, and motivation. If you notice them happening, take stock and make changes. If any of these issues becomes a serious problem, seek help from your campus counseling center.

○ **Get organized by using a calendar or planner.** Use an app or software to generate your calendar or use a paper calendar. Your campus bookstore or Web site will have a campus-specific version that includes exam dates, campus events, and deadlines you will need to know.

○ **Devise a weekly timetable of activities and then stick to it.** Be sure to include special events or responsibilities in addition to recurring activities such as classes, athletic practice, or work shifts.

○ **Create and use day-by-day paper or digital to-do lists.** Crossing off those tasks you have completed will give you a real sense of satisfaction.

○ **Use the tips and strategies in this chapter to meet your time-management goals.** Keep the lists in this chapter handy as reminders of what to do and what to avoid.

Applying what you've learned . . .

Now that you have read and discussed this chapter, consider how you can apply what you have learned to your academic and personal lives. The following prompts will help you reflect on the chapter material and its relevance to you both now and in the future.

1. Review the "Time-Management Pitfalls" section in this chapter. Think of an upcoming assignment in one of your current classes and describe how you can avoid waiting until the last minute to get it done. Break down the assignment, and list each step that you will take to complete the assignment. Give yourself a due date for each step and for completing the assignment.

2. After reading about effective time-management strategies, consider the way in which you manage your own time. If you were grading your current set of time-management skills, what grade (A, B, C, or lower) would you give yourself? Why? Have you overloaded your schedule? Are you working too many hours off campus? Are you being distracted by your roommate or friends? What is your biggest challenge to becoming a more effective time manager?

Use Your Resources

GO TO ▷ The learning center: If you need help with managing your time, studying for exams, reading textbooks, or taking notes.

GO TO ▷ The counseling center: If you need help with difficult emotional issues related to time management.

GO TO ▷ Your academic adviser/counselor: If you need help in finding another person on campus to help you with time-management issues.

GO TO ▷ Fellow students: If you need to commiserate with others who know what it feels like trying to find the time to do all that you need to do as a college student.

NOW... How do you measure up?

1. I have a better understanding of how to set academic and personal goals to guide how I prioritize my time.

   ○ Agree
   ○ Don't Know
   ○ Disagree

2. I have learned some ways to help me focus on the task at hand instead of procrastinating or getting distracted.

   ○ Agree
   ○ Don't Know
   ○ Disagree

3. I am using a daily or weekly planner, to-do lists, or other planning devices or apps to keep track of my commitments.

   ○ Agree
   ○ Don't Know
   ○ Disagree

4. I will keep working on ways to balance my social life and my need for personal time with my academic requirements.

   ○ Agree
   ○ Don't Know
   ○ Disagree

How do your answers here compare to your responses to the quiz you took at the start of the chapter? Which sections of this chapter left a strong impression on you? What time- and energy-management strategies have you begun to use, and are they working? What other strategies will you commit to trying?

LaunchPad Solo for College Success is a great resource. Go online to master concepts using the LearningCurve study tool and much more. **macmillanhighered.com/collegesuccessmedia**

55
Why Be an Engaged Learner?

58
How People Learn

66
Learning with a Learning Disability

Understanding How You Learn

IDesign/Shutterstock

Students who become genuinely engaged in their college experience have a greater chance of success than those who do not. Engagement means participating actively in your academic life, developing a passion for learning, and approaching every challenge with determination to do well. One way to become engaged is to get to know your instructors, especially those who offer you the chance to participate actively in your own learning. As you build relationships with one or more instructors, you can begin to understand how their passion for learning in a particular academic area has become their life's work.

Consider how you learn best: listening in lectures, reading your textbooks, doing experiments in science labs, or working in groups? These "preferences" that you have relate to your learning style. When you understand and use your preferred learning style, it is easier to stay engaged. There is no one best way to learn, and all modes of learning are valuable.

This chapter will help you develop strategies to engage actively with your coursework, classmates, and instructors and will ask you to complete a learning inventory to shed light on how you learn best. It will help you think of ways to meet the expectations of each course and instructor. This chapter will also explore learning disabilities, which are common among college students.

How do you measure up?

1. I would describe myself as an engaged learner.
- ○ Agree
- ○ Don't Know
- ○ Disagree

2. I understand how I learn.
- ○ Agree
- ○ Don't Know
- ○ Disagree

3. I know the benefits of studying in groups.
- ○ Agree
- ○ Don't Know
- ○ Disagree

4. I know where I could get help if I thought I had a learning problem.
- ○ Agree
- ○ Don't Know
- ○ Disagree

Review the items you marked "Don't Know" or "Disagree." Pay special attention to these topics in this chapter—you will find motivating strategies to develop in these areas. A follow-up quiz at the end of the chapter will prompt you to consider what you have learned.

Purestock/Getty Images.

△ **Jalen Washington**

Don't Count Your Grades Before They Hatch

Just as calculus class was ending, Professor Berman dropped the news on us: "I want every student here to participate in a study group," he said. A chorus of groans went up, but after that little moment, everyone started looking at the available times on the sign-up sheet and committing to a group. I sat at my desk and packed up my books. I aced every math course I took in high school, including pre-calc. So what if that was more than ten years ago? I'm good at math. Why would anyone need to show me how to study? A study group would be a waste of my time. I'm juggling school and my family, and living off campus makes my schedule really inflexible.

In the days before the first test, I studied like a crazy man—on my own. I figured I'd get the highest grade in the class even if I had skipped a couple of classes when my kids got sick. If I'd known any of the other students, I would have asked them for notes, but I felt sure I hadn't missed much. Fast-forward a week: When I scanned the test grades posted on Dr. Berman's door, mine was one of the lowest. And after Dr. Berman returned the test, I saw that I had gotten the first two problems right but screwed up the last three. I couldn't believe it. What else had I missed in class?

This was only the first test, so Jalen has the rest of the term to boost his grade in the course. Does Jalen believe that he can do anything to change his performance? How would a study group be helpful to him? What other steps should he take? Does Professor Berman have any further responsibility to help Jalen? Why or why not?

Why Be an Engaged Learner?

No matter how good your academic skills are, you will not get the most out of college unless you become an engaged learner. Engaged students participate in learning activities both in and out of class that help them become excited and even passionate about learning. As a consequence, they learn more and gain more satisfaction from the college experience.

> ❝ You will not get the most out of college unless you become an engaged learner. ❞

Although you might gain knowledge by listening to a lecture, you might not be motivated to think about what that knowledge means to you. When you are actively engaged in learning, you look for what you are learning and your own experience and for more ways to apply your learning in the future. You will go beyond learning basic material in your notes and texts to preparing yourself to:

- work with others
- improve your critical thinking, listening, writing, and speaking skills
- function independently and teach yourself
- manage your time well
- appreciate cultural differences

Engagement in learning is more than simply doing what your instructors or advisers require you to do. As an engaged learner, you will become proactive by taking the initiative to go beyond what is required. For instance, you can do library research to expand your understanding of a concept, make appointments to talk with instructors about their research interests, ask someone to read a paper you have written to see whether you've stated your position clearly, or have a serious discussion with students whose personal backgrounds or values are different from yours. This active and engaged approach to

△ **Engage in Helping**
Most colleges and universities sponsor service projects, from organizing food donations at local food banks to participating in community beautification, mentoring young people through Big Brothers Big Sisters, and serving hot food when natural disasters strike local or nearby communities. Make a difference and make some friends at the same time. © TOM MIHALEK/Reuters/Corbis.

learning will not only make for a richer college experience but also prepare you to stand out in the workplace. In addition, you'll feel more comfortable socially, gain a greater appreciation for the value of education and other viewpoints, and be better able to clarify your academic major and your future career. ■

TRY IT!

SETTING GOALS ▷ **Engage in Learning**

Being an engaged learner not only increases your learning but also builds your enthusiasm for being at your college or university and your desire to get the most out of your experience. Set a short-term goal to learn more about opportunities to engage in learning. Investigate study-abroad programs, many of which have scholarships to help pay for travel and lodging. Find out how you can participate in a service project sponsored by your institution. Stay informed about special events such as concerts or lectures that will expand your knowledge. Check out your instructors' office hours so that you can schedule an appointment to learn about and share mutual interests. By diving deeply into engagement opportunities at your institution, you will build your motivation and find your own passion for learning.

Collaborative Learning Teams

Engage in learning by creating a collaborative learning environment or by joining or establishing a learning team. More than likely, you will be working with others after college, so now is a good time to learn how to collaborate. Students who engage in learning through a team approach not only learn better but also enjoy their learning experiences more. Working in a group, you will be more likely to try new ideas and discover new knowledge by exploring different viewpoints instead of just memorizing facts. Not all learning teams are equal. Sometimes teamwork fails to reach its potential because no thought was given to how the group was formed or how it should function.

Strategies to develop high-quality learning teams that maximize the power of peer collaboration:

- Use learning teams for more than just preparing for exams. Effective student learning teams collaborate regularly for other academic tasks besides test-review sessions. Those tasks can include sharing notes, clarifying textbook reading, and giving feedback on each other's writing.
- Ideally, learning teams will be voluntary—that is, no one will force you to attend. If participants are joining on their own, they will likely be highly motivated instead of being a drag on the group. Seek out team members who will contribute quality and diversity to the group. Look for

△ **Many Heads Are Better than One**
Taking a team approach to learning will help you not only learn better but also have more fun learning. When you're in a group, you benefit from the companionship and you're more likely to be challenged by new techniques and ideas.
Robert Daly/Getty Images.

students who attend class regularly, are attentive, participate actively while in class, and complete assignments.
- Keep the team small (four to six teammates). Small groups allow for more face-to-face interaction and eye contact and less opportunity for any one individual to shirk responsibility to the team.
- Find a quiet place to gather. While the local Starbucks could be appealing, you might not be able to hear or pay attention to what others are saying.

- Find a way to hold individual team members personally accountable for contributing to the learning of their teammates. This can be a challenge; there might be a member who is only participating to receive the benefit of teammates' class attendance and hard work. Make it clear at the outset that every member will be expected to take an occasional leadership role in group meetings by providing specific information or answers to members' questions.

Eight great uses for learning teams:

1. **Note taking.** Team up with other students immediately after class to share and compare notes. Look at the level of detail in each other's notes, and adopt the best styles. Discuss places in the lecture where you got lost. Talk about confusing technical terms and symbols, and ask your instructor about concepts that are confusing to everyone.

2. **Reading.** After completing reading assignments, team up with other students to compare your highlighting and margin notes.

3. **Library research.** Develop a support group for reducing "library anxiety" and for locating and sharing sources of information.

4. **Team/instructor conferences.** Schedule a time for your learning team to meet with the instructor to seek additional assistance as needed.

5. **Preparing for tests.** Divide the job of making a study outline. Team members can discuss and modify the separate outlines before a final version is created for all. Group members can quiz one another or write practice questions, or the group might create an exam and take it together.

6. **Reviewing test results.** After receiving test results, review them together. Help one another identify the sources of mistakes, and share any answers that received high scores.

7. **Teaching each other.** Split up difficult questions or problems, and assign them to various members to prepare and present to the group. The best way to learn something is to explain it to someone else.

8. **Asking questions.** Never criticize a question in your study group; respond positively and express appreciation for all contributions. If you notice someone is lost, give that person an opportunity to ask a question. Above all, come to the group meeting prepared—you don't need to have all the answers, but you should know the specific questions you have.

TRY IT!

MAKING DECISIONS ▷ **Group Study—Give It a Chance**

Most first-year students come to college believing that studying is something they should do alone. Yet research shows and students report that studying in groups is actually more effective and motivational. If you pay attention to the suggestions in this chapter, group learning almost always results in more learning than studying by yourself. Make a decision to find or create at least one study group for a course that you find particularly challenging, even if you're not required to do so. Courses that many students find especially challenging include math and science courses as well as those that require a great deal of reading, such as history, sociology, and psychology. By studying with others, you not only learn more but also are virtually guaranteed to improve your grades.

How People Learn

People learn differently, and understanding how the brain functions helps explain why. An entire field of study called neuroscience focuses on the brain. Neuroscientists and psychologists have developed many theories about how and why people learn differently. Some of the many theories about learning are relevant for college students.

Learning Theories

One of the most well-known learning theories is Maslow's "hierarchy of needs."[1] Abraham Maslow, a psychologist, argued that in order for students to learn, their needs must be met—basic needs such as food, water, and shelter; safety and security needs such as employment and property; needs for love and belonging; needs for self-esteem that comes from achievement; and needs for self-actualization that can be reached through having a purpose and meeting your potential (see Figure 4.1). You probably have found that when you're hungry, fearful, or lonely, it is very hard—nearly impossible—to learn effectively. If your basic needs are met and you develop friendships and experience success, it becomes easier to focus on your courses and continue to learn.

Albert Bandura, a psychological researcher, developed a theory of social learning, that suggests that people learn from each other by observing others' actions and the results of those actions.[2] These observations help them repeat or avoid certain attitudes and behaviors. If you have older brothers and sisters, you probably observed their interactions in the family and learned how to stay out of trouble with your parents. In college you will observe other

Figure 4.1 △ The Hierarchy of Needs Pyramid
This figure illustrates Maslow's theory.

> **"** If your basic needs are met and you develop friendships and experience success, it becomes easier to focus on your courses and continue to learn. **"**

[1]Abraham H. Maslow, *Motivation and Personality*, 2nd ed. (New York: Harper & Row, 1970).

[2] Albert Bandura, *Social Learning Theory* (Englewood Cliffs, NJ: Prentice Hall, 1977).

> **If you pay attention, you can figure out what behaviors actually lead to success.**

students—those who are successful and those who are not. If you pay attention, you can figure out what behaviors actually lead to success. It's not just about "being smart." Successful students come to class, spend time studying, interact with instructors, and take advantage of the academic support available on campus.

In her work on how adult students learn, Nancy Schlossberg, a counseling psychologist, developed a theory of transition.[3] She found that adults learn new roles when they go through change or transition in their lives. As adults we constantly change our roles; for example, we change from being a high school student to a college student and from a college student to an employee. We also experience changes in our personal roles when we get married or divorced or have children. The transition theory states that change actually helps adults grow and learn new ways of thinking and behaving. During the transition process, the more help and support we receive from people around us, the more easily we will adapt to change. For example, college students who ask for help from their instructors, classmates, tutors, advisers, and even their families and friends can make a more successful transition to college life and deal with the challenges of a new environment more effectively than students who do not seek such assistance.

Learning Styles

In addition to looking at theories about learning, we can think about how people learn by focusing on personal learning styles. Simply put, learning styles are ways of learning. Through work and other prior experience, you may have some sense of how you like or don't

[3] Mary L. Anderson, Jane Goodman, and Nancy K. Schlossberg, *Counseling Adults in Transition: Linking Schlossberg's Theory with Practice in a Diverse World,* 4th ed. (New York: Springer, 2012).

△ **Bodies in Motion**
The theater arts have strong appeal for kinesthetic learners, who prefer to learn through experience and practice. Hill Street Studios/Getty Images.

> **It is your responsibility to take charge of your learning in order to be successful in college.**

like to learn. Researchers have developed formal methods and tools—some are simple, and some are complex—to identify, describe, and understand the different learning preferences. These tools help students learn to adapt their learning styles to different classroom situations. Remember, it is your responsibility to take charge of your learning in order to be successful in college, and you will be more likely to succeed in college if you know and use your most effective learning style.

There are many models for thinking about and describing learning styles, such as the VARK Learning Styles Inventory, the Kolb Learning Styles Inventory, and the Myers-Briggs Type Indicator (MBTI). The VARK Inventory investigates how learners prefer to use their senses in learning, while the Kolb Inventory focuses on abilities we need to develop in order to learn. The Myers-Briggs Type Indicator investigates basic personality characteristics and how they relate to human interaction and learning. You can read more about these tools online. In this section we present the VARK Learning Styles Inventory to help you determine your best mode of learning.

As you begin this self-discovery, keep in mind that your learning style cannot be boiled down to one or two defining characteristics. Learning styles are complex and can vary based on what and where you are learning. But the knowledge you will gain about yourself from working through this chapter is a tremendous step in taking responsibility for your learning.

The VARK Learning Styles Inventory

The **VARK Inventory** includes a sixteen-item questionnaire that focuses on how learners prefer to use their senses (hearing, seeing, writing and reading, or experiencing) to learn. The letters in VARK stand for *visual, aural, read/ write,* and *kinesthetic.*

- **Visual learners** prefer to learn information through charts, graphs, symbols, and other visual means.

- **Aural learners** prefer to hear information.

- **Read/write learners** prefer to learn information that is displayed as words.

- **Kinesthetic learners** prefer to learn through experience and practice, whether simulated or real.

To determine your learning style according to the VARK Inventory, respond to the following questionnaire (You can also take the VARK online at http://vark-learn.com/the-vark-questionnaire/).

The VARK Questionnaire

How Do I Learn Best?

This questionnaire is designed to tell you about your preferences in working with information. Choose answers that explain your preference(s). Check the box next to those items. For each question, select *as many boxes as applies to you.* If none of the response options apply to you, leave the item blank.

1. You are helping someone who wants to go to the airport, town center, or railway station. You would:
- ☐ A. go with her.
- ☐ B. tell her the directions.
- ☐ C. write down the directions.
- ☐ D. draw, or show her a map, or give her a map.

2. You are planning a vacation for a group. You want some feedback from them about the plan. You would:
- ☐ A. describe some of the highlights they will experience.
- ☐ B. use a map to show them the places.
- ☐ C. give them a copy of the printed itinerary.
- ☐ D. phone, text or e-mail them.

3. A website has a video showing how to make a special graph. There is a person speaking, some lists and words describing what to do and some diagrams. You would learn most from:
- ☐ A. reading the words.
- ☐ B. listening.
- ☐ C. watching the actions.
- ☐ D. seeing the diagrams.

4. You are going to cook something as a special treat for your family. You would:
- ☐ A. cook something you know without the need for instructions.
- ☐ B. ask friends for suggestions.
- ☐ C. look on the Internet or in some cookbooks for ideas from the pictures.
- ☐ D. use a cookbook where you know there is a good recipe.

(continued)

5. A group of tourists want to learn about the parks or wildlife reserves in your area. You would:
   - ☐ A. talk about, or arrange a talk for them, about parks or wildlife reserves.
   - ☐ B. show them maps and Internet pictures.
   - ☐ C. take them to a park or wildlife reserve and walk with them.
   - ☐ D. give them a book or pamphlets about the parks or wildlife reserves.

6. You are about to purchase a digital camera or mobile phone. Other than price, what would most influence your decision?
   - ☐ A. Trying or testing it
   - ☐ B. Reading the details or checking its features online
   - ☐ C. It is a modern design and looks good.
   - ☐ D. The salesperson telling me about its features.

7. Remember a time when you learned how to do something new. Avoid choosing a physical skill (e.g., riding a bike). You learned best by:
   - ☐ A. watching a demonstration.
   - ☐ B. listening to somebody explaining it and asking questions.
   - ☐ C. diagrams, maps, and charts—visual clues.
   - ☐ D. written instructions—e.g., a manual or book.

8. You have a problem with your heart. You would prefer that the doctor:
   - ☐ A. gave you something to read to explain what was wrong
   - ☐ B. used a plastic model to show what was wrong.
   - ☐ C. described what was wrong.
   - ☐ D. showed you a diagram of what was wrong.

9. You want to learn a new program, skill or game on a computer. You would:
   - ☐ A. read the written instructions that came with the program.
   - ☐ B. talk with people who know about the program.
   - ☐ C. use the controls or keyboard.
   - ☐ D. follow the diagrams in the book that came with it.

10. I like websites that have:
    - ☐ A. things I can click on, shift or try.
    - ☐ B. interesting design and visual features.
    - ☐ C. interesting written descriptions, lists and explanations.
    - ☐ D. audio channels where I can hear music, radio programs, or interviews.

11. Other than price, what would most influence your decision to buy a new non-fiction book?
    - ☐ A. The way it looks is appealing.
    - ☐ B. Quickly reading parts of it.
    - ☐ C. A friend talks about it and recommends it.
    - ☐ D. It has real-life stories, experiences and examples.

12. You are using a book, CD, or website to learn how to take photos with your new digital camera. You would like to have:
    - ☐ A. a chance to ask questions and talk about the camera and its features.
    - ☐ B. clear written instructions with lists and bullet points about what to do.
    - ☐ C. diagrams showing the camera and what each part does.
    - ☐ D. many examples of good and poor photos and how to improve them.

13. Do you prefer a teacher or a presenter who uses:
    - ☐ A. demonstrations, models or practical sessions.
    - ☐ B. question and answer, talk, group discussion, or guest speakers.
    - ☐ C. handouts, books, or readings.
    - ☐ D. diagrams, charts or graphs.

14. You have finished a competition or test and would like some feedback. You would like to have feedback:
    - ☐ A. using examples from what you have done.
    - ☐ B. using a written description of your results.
    - ☐ C. from somebody who talks it through with you.
    - ☐ D. using graphs showing what you had achieved.

15. You are going to choose food at a restaurant or café. You would:
    - ☐ A. choose something that you have had there before.
    - ☐ B. listen to the waiter or ask friends to recommend choices.
    - ☐ C. choose from the descriptions in the menu.
    - ☐ D. look at what others are eating or look at pictures of each dish.

16. You have to make an important speech at a conference or special occasion. You would:
    - ☐ A. make diagrams or get graphs to help explain things.
    - ☐ B. write a few key words and practice saying your speech over and over.
    - ☐ C. write out your speech and learn from reading it over several times.
    - ☐ D. gather many examples and stories to make the talk real and practical.

Scoring the VARK

If you took the VARK online, the scoring was done for you. If not, now you need to match up each of the boxes you selected with a category from the VARK using the scoring chart in Table 4.1. Circle the letter (V, A, R, or K) that corresponds to each of your responses (A, B, C, or D). For example, if you marked both B and C for question 3, circle both the V and the R in the third row of the scoring chart.

Count the number of each VARK letter you have circled to get your score for each VARK category.

Because you can choose more than one answer for each question, scoring is not just a simple matter of counting. It is like four stepping stones across a stream. Enter your scores from highest to lowest on the stones in the following figure, with their V, A, R, and K labels.

Responses to Question 3			
A	**B**	**C**	**D**
K	(V)	(R)	A

Table 4.1 ▽ **Scoring Chart**

Question	A category	B category	C category	D category
1	K	A	R	V
2	V	A	R	K
3	K	V	R	A
4	K	A	V	R
5	A	V	K	R
6	K	R	V	A
7	K	A	V	R
8	R	K	A	V
9	R	A	K	V
10	K	V	R	A
11	V	R	A	K
12	A	R	V	K
13	K	A	R	V
14	K	R	A	V
15	K	A	R	V
16	V	A	R	K

Total number of **V**s circled = _____

Total number of **A**s circled = _____

Total number of **R**s circled = _____

Total number of **K**s circled = _____

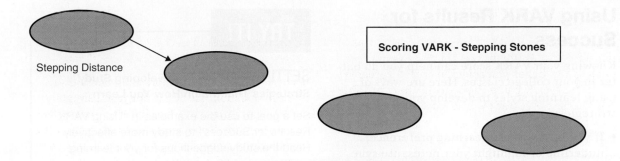

Stepping Distance

Your stepping distance comes from Table 4.2:

Table 4.2 ▽ **Stepping Distance**

The total of my four VARK scores is:	My stepping distance is:
16–21	1
22–27	2
28–32	3
More than 32	4

Follow these steps to establish your preferences:

1. Your first preference is always your highest score. Check the first stone as one of your preferences.

2. Now subtract your second-highest score from your highest score. If that figure is larger than your stepping distance (see Table 4.2), you have a single preference. Otherwise, check this stone as another preference and continue with step 3 below.

3. Subtract your third-highest score from your second-highest one. If that figure is larger than your stepping distance, you have a bimodal preference. If not, check your third stone as a preference and continue with step 4 below.

4. Subtract your fourth or lowest score from your third one. If that figure is larger than your stepping distance, you have a strong preference for three learning styles (trimodal). Otherwise, check your fourth stone as a preference, and you have all four modes as your preferences.

Note: If you are bimodal or trimodal or have checked all four modes as your preferences, you can be described as *multimodal* in your VARK preferences.

TRY IT!

FEELING CONNECTED ▷ **Connect with VARK "Buddies"**

Your first-year seminar class will allow you to connect with other students who have the same VARK profile as you. Once you've gotten your VARK score and determined your preferences, find a few other students who share your learning style and agree to practice some of the study strategies on the next page. Challenge each other to come up with one new idea for studying that relates to your learning preference.

Using VARK Results for Success

Knowing your VARK score can help you do better in your college classes. Here are ways of using learning styles to develop your own study strategies:

- If you have a visual learning preference, underline or highlight your notes; use symbols, charts, or graphs to display your notes; use different arrangements of words on the page; and redraw your pages from memory.

- If you are an aural learner, talk with others to verify the accuracy of your lecture notes. Record your notes and listen to them, or record class lectures. Read your notes out loud; ask yourself questions and speak your answers.

- If you have a read/write learning preference, write and rewrite your notes, and read your notes silently. Organize diagrams or flowcharts into statements, and write imaginary exam questions and respond in writing.

- If you are a kinesthetic learner, you'll need to use all your senses in learning—sight, touch, taste, smell, and hearing. Supplement your notes with real-world examples; move and gesture while you are reading or speaking your notes. ∎

TRY IT!

SETTING GOALS ▷ **Developing Study Strategies That Match How You Learn**

Set a goal to use the examples in "Using VARK Results for Success" to study more effectively. Read the study suggestions for your learning preference, and practice each one during the next week. You might also experiment with study strategies for another learning style to tap into other strengths that you might have. For instance, even if you're an aural or read/write learner, you may find that tapping into kinesthetic strategies such as walking or gesturing helps you learn and remember. Even if you're not a visual learner as determined by the VARK, you might benefit from using a graph or mind map in understanding concepts and details. As your learning improves, you will be motivated to find other study methods and to share them with others.

> " Knowing your VARK score can help you do better in your college classes. "

When Learning Styles Clash with Teaching Styles

This may not be surprising, but instructors tend to teach in ways that fit their *own* particular styles of learning. So an instructor who learns best in a read/write mode or aural mode will probably just lecture and give the class little opportunity for either interaction or visual and kinesthetic learning. But an instructor who prefers a more interactive, hands-on environment will likely involve students in discussion and learning through experience.

Which learning situations work best for you? Think about the following questions:

- Do you enjoy listening to lectures, or do you find yourself bored?
- When your instructor assigns a group discussion, what is your immediate reaction?
- Do you dislike talking with other students, or is that the way you learn best?
- How do you react to lab sessions when you have to conduct an actual experiment? Is this an activity you look forward to or one that you do not like?

Each of these learning situations is more interesting for some students than for others, but each is certainly going to be part of your college experience. Your college has intentionally designed courses that give you opportunities to listen to instructors who are well educated and trained in their fields, to interact with other students in structured groups, and to learn by doing. Because these are all

"As we start a new school year, Mr. Smith, I just want you to know that I'm an Abstract-Sequential learner and trust that you'll conduct yourself accordingly!"

△ **Learn to Adapt**

In college you will find that some instructors may have teaching styles that are challenging for you. Seek out the kinds of classes that conform to the way you like to learn, but also develop your adaptive strategies to make the most of any classroom setting. William G. Browning, Minneapolis, MN.

essential components of your college education, it's important for you to make the most of each situation, learn the content of each course, and in general learn how to learn better.

Don't depend on the instructor or the classroom environment to give you everything you need to make the most of your learning. Use your own preferences, talents, and abilities to develop many different ways to study and retain information. Look back through this chapter to remind yourself of the ways that you can use your own learning style to be more successful in any class you take. If you are interested in reading more about learning styles, the library and your college learning center will have many resources.

Learning with a Learning Disability

While everyone has a learning style, not all—but many—people have a learning disability, a general term that covers a wide variety of specific learning problems resulting from neurological disorders that can make it difficult to acquire certain academic and social skills. A learning disability is a very common challenge to learning for students of any age. Learning disabilities are usually recognized and diagnosed in grade school, but some students can enter college without having been properly diagnosed or assisted.

Learning disabilities can show up as specific difficulties with spoken and written language, coordination, self-control, or attention. Such difficulties can impede learning to read, write, or do math. The term *learning disability* covers a broad range of symptoms and outcomes. Because of this, it is sometimes difficult to diagnose a learning disability or pinpoint the causes. The types of learning disabilities that most commonly affect college students are *attention disorders,* which affect the ability to focus and concentrate, and *cognitive disorders,* which affect the development of academic skills, including reading, writing, and mathematics.

You might know someone who has been diagnosed with a learning disability, such as dyslexia, a reading disability that occurs when the brain does not properly recognize and process certain symbols, or an attention deficit disorder that affects concentration and focus. It is also possible that you have a special learning need and are not aware of it. This section seeks to increase your self-awareness and your knowledge about such challenges to learning. The earlier in life, and college, you address any learning challenges you might have, the better you will perform.

Attention Disorders

Attention disorders are common in children, adolescents, and adults. Some students who have attention disorders appear to daydream a lot; even if you do get their attention, they can be easily distracted. Individuals with attention deficit disorder (ADD) or attention deficit hyperactivity disorder (ADHD) often have trouble organizing tasks or completing their work. They don't seem to listen to or follow directions, and their work might be messy or appear careless. Although ADD and ADHD are not strictly classified as learning disabilities, they can seriously interfere with academic performance, leading some educators to group them with other learning disabilities.[4]

If you have trouble paying attention or getting organized, you won't really know whether you have ADD or ADHD until you are evaluated. Check out resources on campus or in the community. Your campus learning center or counseling center would be a natural place to start. After you have been evaluated, follow the professional advice you get, which may mean taking medication. If you receive a prescription for medication, be sure to take it according to the physician's directions. In the meantime, if you're having trouble getting and staying organized, whether or not you have an attention disorder you can improve your focus through your own behavioral choices.

The world-famous Mayo Clinic offers the following suggestions for adults with ADD or ADHD:[5]

- Make a list of tasks to be accomplished each day. Make sure you're not trying to do too much.

- Break down tasks into smaller, more manageable steps.

- Use sticky pads to write notes to yourself. Put them on the fridge, on the bathroom mirror,

[4]Adapted and reprinted from the public domain source by Sharyn Neuwirth, *Learning Disabilities* (Darby, PA: National Institute of Mental Health, 1993), 9–10.

[5] "Adult ADHD: Lifestyle and Home Remedies," Mayo Clinic, March 7, 2013, www.mayoclinic.org/diseases-conditions/adult-adhd/basics/lifestyle-home-remedies/con-20034552.

in the car or in other places where you'll benefit from having a reminder.

- Keep an electronic calendar to track appointments and deadlines.

- Carry a notebook or electronic device with you so that you can note ideas or things you'll need to remember.

- Take time to set up systems to file and organize information, both on your electronic devices and for paper documents. Get in the habit of using these systems consistently.

- Follow a routine that's consistent from day to day and keep items, like keys and your wallet, in the same place.

- Ask for help from family members or friends.

Cognitive Learning Disabilities

Cognitive learning disabilities are related to mental tasks and processing. Dyslexia, for example, is a developmental reading disorder classified as a cognitive learning disability. A person can have problems with any of the tasks involved in reading. However, scientists have found that a significant number of people with dyslexia are not able to distinguish or separate the sounds in spoken words. For instance, dyslexic individuals sometimes have difficulty assigning the right sounds to letters, either individually or when letters combine to form words. There is, of course, more to reading than recognizing words. If the brain is unable to form images or relate new ideas to those stored in memory, the reader can't understand or remember the new concepts. So other types of reading disabilities can appear when the focus of reading shifts from identifying words to comprehending a written passage.[6]

Writing, too, involves several brain areas and functions. The networks of the brain that control vocabulary, grammar, hand movement, and memory must all be in good working order. So a developmental writing disorder might result from problems in any of these areas. Someone who can't distinguish the sequence of sounds in

[6] "Dyslexia," Learning Disabilities Association of America, 2001, http://ldaamerica.org/types-of-learning-disabilities/dyslexia/.

△ **Speaking Out**
Actor Orlando Bloom attended the Child Mind Institute lecture series in New York City, where he spoke about living with dyslexia. Here Bloom is embraced by a young fan who also deals with dyslexia. Stories of how people overcome challenges can inspire all of us. The key is learning about and using the tools that are available. © Richie Buxo/Splash News/Corbis.

a word will often have problems with spelling. People with writing disabilities, particularly an expressive language disorders (the inability to express oneself using accurate language or sentence structure), are often unable to write complete, grammatical sentences.[7] A student with a developmental arithmetic disorder will have difficulty recognizing numbers and symbols, memorizing facts such as the multiplication table, and understanding abstract concepts such as place value and fractions.[8]

Exploring Resources

If you have a documented learning disability, make sure to notify the office for students with disabilities at your college or university to receive reasonable accommodations as required by law. Reasonable accommodations might include use of a computer during some exams, readers for tests, in-class note takers, extra time for assignments and tests, and use of audio textbooks, depending on need and the type of disability.

If you think you might have a learning disability but it has not yet been "documented," the office for students with disabilities would be a good place to start. You could also discuss this issue with your academic adviser, a learning center professional, or a counselor in your college counseling center. All of them can get you to the right source for evaluation and assistance.

The following questions may help you determine whether you or someone you know should be screened for a possible learning disability:

- Do you perform poorly on tests even when you feel that you have studied and are capable of performing better?

- Do you have trouble spelling words?

- Do you work harder than your classmates at basic reading and writing?

[7] Ibid.

[8] "Dyscalculia," Learning Disabilities Association of America, 2001, http://ldaamerica.org/types-of-learning-disabilities/dyscalculia/.

- Do your instructors point out inconsistencies in your classroom performance, such as answering questions correctly in class but incorrectly on a written test?

- Do you have a really short attention span, or do your family members or instructors say that you do things without thinking?

Although responding yes to any of these questions does not mean that you have a disability, the resources of your campus learning center or the office for student disability services can help you address any potential problems and devise ways to learn more effectively.

Anyone who is diagnosed with a learning disability is in good company. According to national data, between 15 and 20 percent of Americans have a learning disability. In fact, some of the most intelligent individuals in human history have had a learning disability—Benjamin Franklin, George Washington, Alexander Graham Bell, and Woodrow Wilson. Actors Keanu Reeves, Keira Knightley, and Daniel Radcliffe; filmmaker Steven Spielberg; celebrity chef Jamie Oliver; and college football star Tim Tebow are just a few of the famous and successful people who have diagnosed learning disabilities.

> "Between 15 and 20 percent of Americans have a learning disability."

Here is a final important message: A learning disability is a learning difference but is in no way related to intelligence. Having a learning disability is not a sign that you are stupid. Remember, some of the most intelligent individuals in human history have had a learning disability. ∎

Chapter Review

Steps to Success:
Understanding How You Learn

○ **Pick one of the learning theories mentioned in this chapter, and do some additional research on it.** You may also want to expand your knowledge of other learning theories to see if they apply to you.

○ **Take a learning styles inventory, either in this chapter or at your campus learning center or counseling center.** See whether the results might at least partly explain your level of performance in each class you are taking this term.

○ **Learn about and accept your unique learning preferences.** Especially make note of your strengths in terms of those things you learn well and easily. See whether those skills could be applied to other learning situations.

○ **Use your learning style to develop study strategies that work best for you.** You can walk, talk, read, listen, or even dance while you are learning.

○ **If you need help with making the best use of your learning style, visit your campus learning center.** Consider taking some courses in the social and behavioral sciences that would help you better understand how humans learn.

○ **If you think you might have a learning disability, go to your campus learning center and ask for a diagnostic assessment so that you can develop successful coping strategies.** Make sure to ask for a personal interpretation and follow-up counseling or tutoring.

Applying what you've learned . . .

Now that you have read and discussed this chapter, consider how you can apply what you have learned to your academic and personal lives. The following prompts will help you reflect on the chapter material and its relevance to you both now and in the future.

1. It is important to understand various learning styles and how your own style(s) of learning can affect your experience in the classroom. Considering your learning style(s), what kinds of teaching and learning methods do you think will work best for you? What teaching and learning methods will be especially challenging?

2. It is important to understand various learning styles for education purposes, but it is also important to understand how learning preferences affect career choices. Considering your preferred learning style, what might be the best careers for you? Why?

Use Your Resources

GO TO ▷ The library or the Internet: If you want to conduct research on theories of learning.

GO TO ▷ The learning center: If you want to take another learning inventory.

GO TO ▷ The career center: If you need guidance on how the information you discovered about how you learn can be used in career planning.

GO TO ▷ A counselor in the office for students with disabilities: If you need advice on learning disability testing, diagnosis, and accommodations.

GO TO ▷ Your first-year seminar instructor: If you want to find out more about learning styles and learning disabilities.

GO ONLINE TO ▷ LD Pride (www.ldpride.net/learningstyles.MI.htm): If you want general information about learning styles and learning disabilities and an interactive diagnostic tool to determine your learning style.

GO ONLINE TO ▷ The National Center for Learning Disabilities (www.ncld.org): If you want to access a variety of resources for diagnosing and understanding learning disabilities.

NOW... How do you measure up?

1. I would describe myself as an engaged learner.
   - ○ Agree
   - ○ Don't Know
   - ○ Disagree

2. I understand how I learn.
   - ○ Agree
   - ○ Don't Know
   - ○ Disagree

3. I know where to get help with a learning problem I might have.
   - ○ Agree
   - ○ Don't Know
   - ○ Disagree

4. I know where to get help with a learning problem I might have.
   - ○ Agree
   - ○ Don't Know
   - ○ Disagree

How do your answers here compare to your responses to the quiz you took at the start of the chapter? Which sections of this chapter left a strong impression on you? What topics left you wanting to learn more? Remember that your campus has resources for finding answers to every question you might have. Take advantage of all your college or university has to offer.

LaunchPad
macmillan learning

LaunchPad Solo for College Success is a great resource. Go online to master concepts using the LearningCurve study tool and much more. **macmillanhighered.com/collegesuccessmedia**

05

73
Preparing for Class

74
Pay Attention! Listening, Participating, and Note Taking

77
Approaches to Note Taking

84
Keep It Fresh by Reviewing Your Notes

Getting the Most Out of Class

PureSolution/Shutterstock.

LaunchPad
macmillan learning

To access the LearningCurve study tool, Video Tools, and more, go to *LaunchPad Solo for College Success*. **macmillan highered.com/ collegesuccessmedia**

In every college class you take, you will need to master two skills to earn high grades: listening and note taking. It all begins with listening. If you are thinking about what happened the night before or your plans later in the day, you won't be able to listen effectively. If you are sleepy or distracted by people around you, your attention to what's going on in class will suffer. Successful listening in college classes is about "being in the moment" and focusing on the lecture or discussion related to the topic of the day. By taking an active role in your classes—genuinely participating by asking questions, contributing to discussions, and providing answers—you will listen better and take more meaningful notes. Your experience with note taking before coming to college may be limited. High schools and other educational or work settings sometimes require note taking, but more often they do not. Some students even find it difficult to listen and take notes at the same time. If this is a problem for you, don't give up. With practice and

experience, you'll be able to both listen and write down what's most important. The reward for your efforts will be greater understanding of course material, a feeling of empowerment that comes from offering your perspectives in class discussions, and improvement in your ability to find new possibilities, understand abstract ideas, organize those ideas, and recall the material once the class is over.

You can then connect your understanding of what went on in class with your understanding of the reading assignments. This increased capacity to analyze and understand complex material will result in better academic performance while you are in college and will also be valued by a wide range of employers.

This chapter provides valuable suggestions for becoming a skilled listener, note taker, and class participant. Decide which techniques work best for you. Practice them regularly until they become part of your study routine.

How do you measure up?

1. I do a good job of identifying key points of lectures and discussions and writing them down in my notes.

   ○ Agree
   ○ Don't Know
   ○ Disagree

2. When I don't understand something, I know how important it is to ask questions in class—even in large classes.

   ○ Agree
   ○ Don't Know
   ○ Disagree

3. In math or science courses students should write down everything the instructor puts on the board or screen.

   ○ Agree
   ○ Don't Know
   ○ Disagree

4. I know that one of the most effective ways to learn is to join study groups for each of my classes.

   ○ Agree
   ○ Don't Know
   ○ Disagree

Review the items you marked "Don't Know" or "Disagree." Pay special attention to these topics in this chapter—you will find motivating strategies to develop in these areas. A follow-up quiz at the end of the chapter will prompt you to consider what you have learned.

△ **Amy Gailliard**

© Matelly/cultura/Corbis.

Tongue-Tied

"So, Amy, why do you think Harper Lee chose to give *To Kill a Mockingbird* a child narrator?" my professor asked me at our second literature class. Minutes earlier I'd been tapping my pencil on my notebook, feeling happy as we discussed my favorite book. Suddenly I was grasping for something to say.

"Er," I managed. Thirty-two twenty-something-year-old faces were looking at me. I felt my face go beet red. They didn't want to hear from the "old lady" in the class, twice their age.

"Anyone else?" he asked, looking around. "Speak up."

"Scout has an innocent perspective," said the girl sitting next to me.

"Exactly," said Professor Kelso. "And why is that such an effective device here?"

Because the difference between what the reader sees happening in the book and what Scout perceives generates a lot of irony, I thought to myself. Because we see her learn something important. Because her childlike tone disguises the serious purpose of the plot.

"Because we see her start to understand how her world works—in good and bad ways," said a student across the room.

The professor crossed his arms and nodded. "Good job, Aziz. That's a point toward your class participation grade." Then he caught a glance at my stricken face. "Amy, did you have something to add?"

"Uh, well . . . I, um," I said. Yep, it looked like being back in college was going to be rough.

How is Amy's reticence about speaking in front of her younger classmates affecting her performance in college? What kind of preparation before class would have helped Amy? Flip through the chapter. What other suggestions can you find that would have helped her speak up?

Preparing for Class

Imagine you're a track star. Would you come to a meet without having trained—a lot? Of course not. Think of each class as an important event, like a track meet. To do your best, you'll need to prepare ahead of time, just like any athlete would. A great way to prepare is to follow the active learning steps listed below. Doing so before you hit the classroom will get you in shape and help make the time you spend in class much more valuable.

1. **Pay attention to your course syllabus.** A syllabus is not something you ignore or discard. It is an important, formal statement of course expectations, requirements, and procedures.

2. **Do the assigned reading.** Unless you do the assigned reading before class, you may not be able to follow the lecture. When you have done the reading, you will find that the lecture means more to you and class participation is a lot easier.

3. **Use additional materials provided by the instructor.** Many professors post lecture outlines or notes online. If you download and print these materials, they can create an organizational structure for note taking.

4. **Warm up for class.** Before class begins, preview by reviewing chapter introductions and summaries as well as your notes.

5. **Get organized.** Decide whether a three-ring binder, a spiral notebook, a digital device, or some combination of the three will work best for you. You might also want to create a folder for each course. If you use a laptop or tablet, create a Documents folder for each class, and carefully label the notes for each class meeting. ∎

TRY IT!

SETTING GOALS ▷ **Do All Your Assigned Reading before Class**

It's easy to think that doing the assigned reading is something you could skip or postpone until after class or just before the exam. However, that's putting the cart before the horse. Instructors assign reading prior to class for a reason: They want you to have a good understanding of the material *before* they expand on it during the lecture. They also want you to participate knowledgeably in class discussions—something you can't do unless you have done the reading. Material presented in textbooks or other sources will often give you the basics—a foundation that instructors will assume you've been exposed to before they give you their views and interpretations. Set a goal to do all assigned reading before you go to class; if you don't quite finish, complete your reading assignment as soon as possible after class.

◁ **Prepare Better by Working Together**
A great way to prepare for class is to discuss readings, lectures, and other course materials with your classmates. Some of them are sure to know the material, and they may understand concepts that you find challenging. At the same time, explaining concepts to your classmates will help you solidify your own understanding. © Peter Muller/Corbis.

Pay Attention! Listening, Participating, and Note Taking

Think about your conversations with friends and family members. When you listen carefully to what the other person says, you can communicate effectively. But if you "tune out," you won't have much to contribute, and you might get caught off guard if asked a direct question. The same is true in class—there is a give-and-take between students and the instructor, especially in classes where the

instructor emphasizes interactive discussion, calls on students by name, shows students signs of approval and interest, and avoids criticizing anyone for an incorrect answer.

Listening carefully in class—really paying attention—is one of the most important skills you can develop. If you don't listen, you won't know what your instructor identifies as the most important concepts—concepts that are likely to show up on tests. And of course, paying attention will help you remember and understand what you have heard, and it naturally will make you more likely to participate in a class, especially when you are prepared.

> " Listening carefully in class—really paying attention—is one of the most important skills you can develop. "

Listening Critically

Have you taken a learning inventory and discovered that aural (auditory) learning, which is learning by listening, is one of your learning

△ **Listen Up**

Develop your listening skills by practicing the eight steps to becoming a critical listener. Making use of these suggestions and reviewing your notes after class will help the information stick. © Hero Images/Corbis.

  05 Getting the Most Out of Class

preferences? About one-third of us prefer to learn by listening. The other two-thirds do not. If you are taking classes in which instructors lecture all or part of the time, then aural learning is a skill you will need to develop to be academically successful, whether or not learning by listening is your preference. Critical listening involves examining how we listen and evaluating what is said so that we can form our own ideas and opinions.

Here are some suggestions for being a critical listener:

1. **Be ready for the message.** Prepare yourself to hear, listen, and receive the message. If you have done the assigned reading, you will know the details in the text, so you can focus your notes on key concepts during the lecture.

2. **Listen for the main concepts and central ideas, not just facts and figures.** Facts will be easier to remember when you can place them in the context of a broader theme.

3. **Listen for new ideas.** Even if you know a lot about a topic, you can still learn something new.

4. **Repeat mentally.** Think about what you hear and restate it silently in your own words. If you don't understand a concept, ask for clarification.

5. **Decide whether what you have heard is not important, somewhat important, or very important.** If a point in the lecture is not important, let it go. If it is very important, highlight or underline the point in your notes. If it is somewhat important, relate it to a very important topic.

6. **Keep an open mind.** Your classes will expose you to new ideas and different perspectives. But instructors want you to think for yourself, and they do not expect you to agree with everything they or your classmates say.

7. **Listen to the entire message.** Concentrate on the big picture, but also pay attention to specific details and examples that can assist you in understanding and retaining the information.

8. **Sort, organize, and categorize.** When you listen, try to match what you are hearing with what you already know. Take an active role in deciding how best to recall what you are learning.

Becoming an Active Class Participant

In all your classes, try using the following techniques to ramp up your participation:

1. **Sit as close to the front as possible.** If students are seated by name and your name begins with a letter that comes toward the end of the alphabet, request to be moved up front.

2. **Keep your eyes on the instructor.** Sitting close to the front of the classroom will make this easier for you to do.

3. **Focus on the lecture.** Do not let yourself be distracted by other students.

4. **Raise your hand when you don't understand something.** But don't overdo it—the instructor and your peers will tire of too many questions that disrupt the class.

5. **Speak up in class.** It becomes easier every time you do so.

6. **Never feel that you're asking a "stupid" question.** You have a right to ask for an explanation.

7. **When the instructor calls on you to answer a question, don't bluff.** If you know the answer, give it. If not, just say so.

8. **If you've recently read a book or an article that is relevant to the class, bring it in.** You can provide additional information that was not covered in class.

TRY IT!

FEELING CONNECTED ▷ **Work Up the Nerve**

Participating in class not only helps you learn but also shows your instructor that you're interested and engaged, and it will help you connect to what is happening in each class and become an active participant in the learning experience. Like anything else, raising your hand for the first time might make you anxious. After that first time, though, you'll likely find that contributing to class raises your interest and enjoyment. Think about the number of times during the past week you have raised your hand in class to ask a question. Do you ask questions frequently, or is it something you avoid? Make a list of the reasons you either do or don't ask questions in class. Would asking more questions help you earn better grades? How does participating in class make you feel about being there?

Taking Notes

Listening and note taking go hand in hand. Some students find it difficult to take notes while they are listening. As you gain experience, you will improve your ability to do these things simultaneously. If you find your notes are missing lots of important details, you may want to record the lecture (with the instructor's permission), using one of the many apps available such as QuickVoice Recorder, Smart Voice Recorder, or Audio Class Notes. Continue to take notes regardless. Listening to the recording will actually improve your auditory learning abilities.

Listening and note-taking skills are especially important in college because your instructors are likely to introduce material in class that your texts don't cover. This is one way that college is very different from most high schools. College and university professors have spent entire careers developing their own ideas that might add to—or even differ from—what you read in your textbooks. Be aware that an instructor often thinks that what is discussed in class is more important than what is in the text. Chances are very good that your instructors will include much of the material they introduce in class on weekly quizzes and major exams.

While you are listening and taking notes, also be sure to participate in class discussion when you have something important to say or a

> " Listening and note-taking skills are especially important in college because your instructors are likely to introduce material in class that your texts don't cover. "

question to ask. The instructor is always the best place to start for answers. You will tend to remember what you have said or answers to questions you have asked more easily than what you have only heard. If you have questions about your notes, you might choose to approach the instructor after class or go over your notes with a classmate.

Learning how to balance these three aspects of being in class—listening, participating, and taking notes—will help you get the most out of each class meeting. ■

Learning Online

Today many students in high school and college take courses online. You might already have lots of experience with this mode of learning, or you might be taking your first online course. Some students take online courses because they find it difficult to come to campus. They may live many miles away or have family responsibilities that keep them at home. Other students find that their college or university offers certain courses only online, even to students who live on or commute to campus.

The many advantages to online learning include being able to stay at home or in your residence hall room and work on your own schedule instead of at a time and place determined by the college. You can read and study when you are your freshest, and your course materials will always be available without a special trip to the library. If you tend to be distracted by other students in a classroom, online learning may make it easy for you to

concentrate more effectively. Also, online classes provide anonymity that can increase the honesty and quality of the class discussion. You won't always know who is making what comment, so you'll set aside any preconceived notions you have about whose comments matter most.

There are also challenges in online learning, and one of them may be finding a meaningful way to participate in the course. If you are an online learner, be sure to take advantage of all the opportunities you have to become involved in the class—chat groups, discussion boards, and getting to know other students and the instructor through the Internet. And remember this: If you are not a self-starter, if you tend to procrastinate, and if you need the motivation of a face-to-face lecture to make you listen and pay attention, online courses may not be the best way for you to learn in the first year of college.

Approaches to Note Taking

Taking notes in college classes isn't optional. You must do it in order to make the best use of your class time, but first you have to decide on a note-taking system that works best for you.

Cornell Format

In the Cornell format, you create a "recall" column on each page by drawing a vertical line a few inches from the left border (see Figure 5.1).

As you take notes during the lecture—whether writing down ideas, making lists, or using an outline or paragraph format—write only in the wider column on the right; leave the recall column blank. Then, as soon after class as feasible, sift through your notes and write down the main ideas and important details in the recall column. Many students have found the recall column to be an important study device for tests and exams.

Figure 5.1 ▽ Note Taking in the Cornell Format

Psychology 101
1/29/15
Theories of Personality

Personality trait: define	Personality trait = "durable disposition to behave in a particular way in a variety of situations"
Big 5: Name + describe them	Big 5—McCrae + Costa–(1) extroversion, (or positive emotionality)=outgoing, sociable, friendly, upbeat, assertive; (2) neuroticism=anxious, hostile, self-conscious, insecure, vulnerable; (3) openness to experience=curiosity, flexibility, imaginative; (4) agreeableness=sympathetic, trusting, cooperative, modest; (5) conscientiousness=diligent, disciplined, well organized, punctual, dependable
Psychodynamic Theories: Who?	Psychodynamic Theories–focus on unconscious forces
3 components of personality: name and describe	Freud—psychoanalysis—3 components of personality–(1)id=primitive, instinctive, operates according to pleasure principle (immediate gratification); (2) ego=decision-making component, operates according to reality principle (delay gratification until appropriate); (3) superego=moral component, social standards, right + wrong
3 levels of awareness: name and describe	3 levels of awareness—(1) conscious=what one is aware of at a particular moment; (2) preconscious=material just below surface, easily retrieved; (3) unconscious=thoughts, memories, + desires well below surface, but have great influence on behavior

Outline Format

You probably already know what a formal outline looks like, with key ideas represented by Roman numerals and other ideas relating to each key idea represented, in order, by uppercase letters and Arabic numbers (see Figure 5.2). If you use this approach, try to determine how the instructor is outlining the lecture or presentation, and re-create that outline in your notes.

Figure 5.2 ▽ Note Taking in the Outline Format

Psychology 101
1/29/15
Theories of Personality

I. Personality trait = "durable disposition to behave in a particular way in a variety of situations"

II. Big 5—McCrae + Costa

 A. Extroversion (or positive emotionality)=outgoing, sociable, friendly, upbeat, assertive

 B. Neuroticism=anxious, hostile, self-conscious, insecure, vulnerable

 C. Openness to experience=curiosity, flexibility, imaginative

 D. Agreeableness=sympathetic, trusting, cooperative, modest

 E. Conscientiousness=diligent, disciplined, well organized, punctual, dependable

III. Psychodynamic Theories—focus on unconscious forces—Freud —psychoanalysis

 A. 3 components of personality

  1. Id=primitive, instinctive, operates according to pleasure principle (immediate gratification)

  2. Ego=decision-making component, operates according to reality principle (delay gratification until appropriate)

  3. Superego=moral component, social standards, right + wrong

 B. 3 levels of awareness

  1. Conscious=what one is aware of at a particular moment

  2. Preconscious=material just below surface, easily retrieved

  3. Unconscious=thoughts, memories, + desires well below surface, but have great influence on behavior

Paragraph Format

The paragraph format involves writing detailed paragraphs, with each paragraph containing a summary of a particular topic (see Figure 5.3). You might decide to write summary paragraphs when you are taking notes on what you are reading. This method might not work as well for class notes, however, because it's difficult to summarize a topic until your instructor has covered it completely.

Figure 5.3 ▽ **Note Taking in the Paragraph Format**

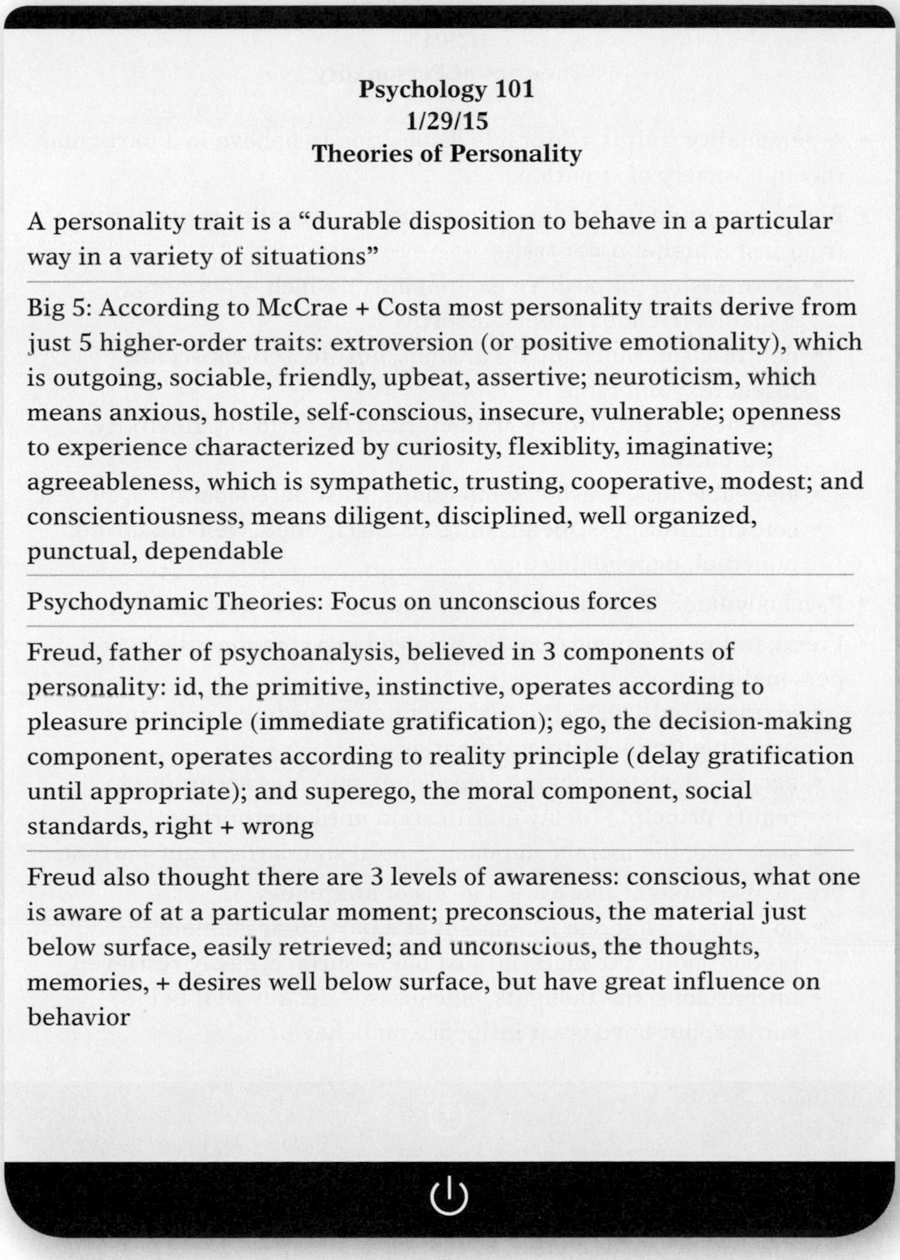

Psychology 101
1/29/15
Theories of Personality

A personality trait is a "durable disposition to behave in a particular way in a variety of situations"

Big 5: According to McCrae + Costa most personality traits derive from just 5 higher-order traits: extroversion (or positive emotionality), which is outgoing, sociable, friendly, upbeat, assertive; neuroticism, which means anxious, hostile, self-conscious, insecure, vulnerable; openness to experience characterized by curiosity, flexiblity, imaginative; agreeableness, which is sympathetic, trusting, cooperative, modest; and conscientiousness, means diligent, disciplined, well organized, punctual, dependable

Psychodynamic Theories: Focus on unconscious forces

Freud, father of psychoanalysis, believed in 3 components of personality: id, the primitive, instinctive, operates according to pleasure principle (immediate gratification); ego, the decision-making component, operates according to reality principle (delay gratification until appropriate); and superego, the moral component, social standards, right + wrong

Freud also thought there are 3 levels of awareness: conscious, what one is aware of at a particular moment; preconscious, the material just below surface, easily retrieved; and unconscious, the thoughts, memories, + desires well below surface, but have great influence on behavior

List Format

The list format can be effective when taking notes on terms and definitions, sequences, or facts (see Figure 5.4). It's easy to use lists in combination with the Cornell format.

Figure 5.4 ▽ Note Taking in the List Format

Psychology 101
1/29/15
Theories of Personality

- A personality trait is a "durable disposition to behave in a particular way in a variety of situations"
- Big 5: According to McCrae + Costa most personality traits derive from just 5 higher-order traits
    - extroversion (or positive emotionality), which is outgoing, sociable, friendly, upbeat, assertive
    - neuroticism, which means anxious, hostile, self-conscious, insecure, vulnerable
    - openness to experience characterized by curiosity, flexiblity, imaginative
    - agreeableness, which is sympathetic, trusting, cooperative, modest
    - conscientiousness, means diligent, disciplined, well organized, punctual, dependable
- Psychodynamic Theories: Focus on unconscious forces
- Freud, father of psychoanalysis, believed in 3 components of personality
    - id, the primitive, instinctive, operates according to pleasure principle (immediate gratification)
    - ego, the decision-making component, operates according to reality principle (delay gratification until appropriate)
    - superego, the moral component, social standards, right + wrong
- Freud also thought there are 3 levels of awareness
    - conscious, what one is aware of at a particular moment
    - preconscious, the material just below surface, easily retrieved
    - unconscious, the thoughts, memories, + desires well below surface, but have great influence on behavior

Taking Notes in Class

Once you've decided on an approach to note taking, you'll need to actually use it in class. To do so effectively, try these techniques:

1. **Identify the main ideas.** Well-organized lectures always contain key points. The first principle of effective note taking is to write down the main ideas around which the lecture is built. Some instructors announce the purpose of a lecture or offer an outline, thus providing the class with the skeleton of main ideas, followed by the details. Others develop overhead transparencies or PowerPoint presentations and may make these materials available on a class Web site before the lecture.

2. **Don't try to write down everything.** Attempting to record every word from a class lecture or discussion will distract you from an essential activity: thinking. If you're an active listener, you will ultimately have shorter but more useful notes.

3. **Don't be thrown by a disorganized lecturer.** When a lecturer is disorganized, it's your job to organize what he or she says into general and specific frameworks. When the order is not apparent, indicate the gaps in your notes. After the lecture, consult your reading material, your study team, or a classmate to fill in these gaps, or visit the instructor during office hours with your questions.

4. **Prepare to use your notes as a study tool.** As soon after class as feasible, preferably within an hour or two, sift through your notes and create a recall column to identify the main ideas and important details for tests and examinations. In anticipation of using your notes later, treat your notes as part of an exam-preparation system.

Make Adjustments for Different Classes

As you become comfortable with the different systems for note taking, you will learn to adjust your approach depending on the kind of class. Nonlecture courses pose special challenges because they tend to be less organized and more free-flowing. Be ready to adapt your note-taking methods to match the situation. Group discussion has become a popular way to teach in college because it involves active learning. On your campus you may also have Supplemental Instruction (SI) classes that provide further opportunity to discuss the information presented in lectures. Take advantage of this option if it's available, and keep a record of what's happening in such classes.

Students who participate in Supplemental Instruction predictably earn higher grade point averages than students who do not. But it doesn't work to attend only a few SI sessions. You have to attend regularly in order to reap the benefits. At some colleges, Supplemental Instruction isn't optional—it's required for certain courses, especially those in which students tend to struggle. Generally these courses are a "gateway" to pre-med, science, engineering, and math majors. Even if SI isn't required, be sure to take advantage of this valuable option, and keep a written record of what is happening in SI classes.

Imagine you are taking notes in a problem-solving group assignment. You would begin your notes by asking yourself, "What is the problem?" and writing the problem down. As the discussion progresses, you would list the solutions offered. These solutions would be your main ideas. The important details might include the positive and negative aspects of each view or solution. The important thing to remember when taking notes in nonlecture courses is that you need to record the information presented by your classmates as well as by the instructor and to consider all reasonable ideas, even though they may differ from your own.

How to organize the notes you take in a class discussion depends on the purpose or form of the discussion. It usually makes good sense to begin with the list of issues or topics that the discussion leader announces. Another approach is to list the questions that the participants raise for discussion. If the discussion is an exploration of the reasons for and against a particular argument, it's reasonable to divide your notes into columns or sections for pros and cons. When conflicting views arise in the discussion, record the different perspectives and the rationales behind them.

Use Specific Strategies for Note Taking in Quantitative Courses

Taking notes in math and science courses can be different from taking notes in other types of classes, where it may not be a good idea to try to write down every word the instructor says. In a quantitative course, quote the instructor's words as precisely as possible. Technical terms often have exact meanings and cannot be paraphrased.

Quantitative courses such as mathematics, chemistry, and physics often build on each other from term to term and from year to year. When you take notes in these courses, you are likely to need to refer to them in future terms. For example, when taking organic chemistry, you may need to go back to notes taken in earlier chemistry courses. This review process can be particularly important when time has passed since your last course, such as after a summer break. Here are some ideas for getting organized:

1. **Create separate binders for each course.** Keep your notes and supplementary materials (such as instructors' handouts) for each course in a separate three-ring binder labeled with the course number and name.

2. **Download materials from your instructor *before* class.** Your instructor may post a broad range of materials on a class Web site, such as notes, outlines, diagrams, charts, graphs, and other visual explanations. Be sure to download these materials before class and bring them with you. You can save yourself considerable time and distraction during the lecture if you do not have to copy complicated graphs and diagrams while the instructor is talking.

3. **Take notes only on the front of each piece of loose-leaf paper.** Later, you can use the back of each sheet to add further details, annotations, corrections, comments, questions, and a summary of each lecture. Alternatively, once you've placed what have now become the left-hand pages in the binder, you can use them the same way that you would use the recall column in the Cornell format, noting key ideas to be used for testing yourself when preparing for exams.

4. **Listen carefully to other students' questions and the instructor's answers.** Take notes on the discussion and during question-and-answer periods.

5. **Use asterisks, exclamation points, question marks, or symbols of your own** to highlight important points or questions in your notes.

6. **Consider taking your notes in pencil or erasable pen.** In science and math classes it can be hard to create diagrams on a screen even if you would otherwise prefer to type your notes.

7. **Refer to the textbook after class.** The text may contain diagrams and other visual representations that are more accurate than those you are able to draw while taking notes in class.

8. **Write down any equations, formulas, diagrams, charts, graphs, and definitions that the instructor puts on the board or screen,** and expect that you'll need to erase and make changes. You want to keep your notes as neat as possible.

9. **Use standard symbols, abbreviations, and scientific notation.**

10. **Write down all worked problems and examples, step by step.** These often provide the format for exam questions. Actively try to solve each problem yourself as it is solved at the front of the class. Be sure that you can follow the logic and understand the sequence of steps.

11. **Organize your notes in your binder chronologically.** Then create separate tabbed sections for homework, lab assignments, returned tests, and other materials.

12. **Label and store handouts immediately.** If the instructor distributes handouts in class, label them and place them in your binder either immediately before or immediately after the notes for that day.

13. **Keep your binders for math and science courses until you graduate** (or even longer if there is any chance that you will attend graduate school in the future). They will serve as beneficial review materials for later classes in math and science sequences and for preparing for standardized tests such as the Graduate Record Exam (GRE) or the Medical College Admission Test (MCAT). ■

Take Better Notes in Better Ways

Studies have shown that people remember only half of what they hear, which is a major reason to take notes during lectures. Solid note taking will help you distill key concepts and make it easier to study for tests. Note taking also engages the brain in a process known as rehearsal. Writing things down is important for you to start the process of creating your own way of understanding the materials. Along with making use of the note-taking formats that will be presented in this section, use your smartphone, tablet, or laptop to save information and create tools that will help you study.

1. Microsoft Word is great for most classes. To highlight main ideas, you can bold or underline text, change the size and color, highlight whole sections, and insert text boxes or charts. You can make bullet points or outlines and insert comments. As you review your notes, you can cut and paste to make things more coherent.

2. Microsoft Excel works well for any class that involves calculations or financial statements. You can embed messages in the cells of a spreadsheet to explain calculations. (The notes will appear whenever you hover your cursor over that cell.)

3. Microsoft PowerPoint can be invaluable for visual learners. Instead of creating one giant, potentially confusing Word file, you can make a slide show with a new slide for each key point. Some instructors also post the slides that they plan to use in class before each session. You can write notes on printouts of the slides, or download them and add your notes in PowerPoint.

Some Cool Apps for Note Taking and Reviewing

- Pocket (iOS and Android) allows you to store and review written content from your phone.
- Evernote (iOS and Android) lets you take a picture of handwritten or printed notes—or anything else you want to recall—and then you can file content and search it by key word later.
- CamScanner (iOS and Android) allows you to scan and store notes and convert and share documents in PDF or JPEG formats.
- TinyTap (iOS) lets you create multiple-choice quizzes that you can take as practice and share with other students.
- StudyBlue (iOS, Android, and Web apps) allows you to make amazing-looking flash cards.

No matter what program or app you use, some rules always apply:

- Write down main points using phrases or key terms instead of long sentences.
- Date your notes; keep them in order and in one place; save files using file names with the course number, name, and date of the class; and back up everything.
- Create a folder for each class so you can find everything you need easily.
- Keep a pen and paper handy for sketching graphs and diagrams.

If you find it hard to keep up, practice your listening and typing skills. Consider a typing class, program, or app to learn how to type properly. If you prefer a spiral notebook and a ballpoint pen, that's OK; these formats are tried and true. Practice teaching others what you learned in class. You can also learn note-taking strategies from your peers.

Keep It Fresh by Reviewing Your Notes

Most forgetting of information takes place within the first twenty-four hours of encountering it, a phenomenon known as "the forgetting curve." If you do not review your notes almost immediately after class, it can be difficult to retrieve the material later. In two weeks, you will have forgotten up to 70 percent of the material or information! Don't let the forgetting curve take its toll on you. As soon after class as possible, review your notes and fill in the details you still remember but missed writing down. If you are an aural learner, you might want to repeat your notes out loud.

> " Most forgetting of information takes place within the first twenty-four hours of encountering it. "

For interactive learners, the best way to learn something might be to teach it to someone else. You will understand something better and remember it longer if you try to explain it. Explaining material to someone else helps you discover your own reactions and uncover gaps in your comprehension. (Asking and answering questions in class can also provide you with the feedback you need to make certain your understanding is accurate.) Now you're ready to embed the major points from your notes in your memory. Use the following three important steps for remembering the key points from the lecture.

1. **Write down the main ideas.** For five or ten minutes, quickly review your notes and select key words or phrases that will act as labels or tags for main ideas and key information in your notes.

2. **Recite your ideas out loud.** Recite a brief version of what you understand from the

class. If you don't have a few minutes after class when you can concentrate on reviewing your notes, find some other time during that same day to review what you have written. You might also want to ask your instructor to glance at your notes to determine whether you have identified the major ideas.

3. **Review your notes from the previous class just before the next class session.** As you sit in the classroom waiting for the lecture to begin, use the time to quickly review your notes from the previous class session. As discussed above, this is an effective way to prepare for class. This review will put you in tune with the lecture that is about to begin and prompt you to ask questions about material from the previous lecture that might not have been clear to you.

Compare Notes

Comparing notes with other students in a study group, SI session, or test review session has a number of benefits: You will probably take better notes when you know that someone else will see them, you can tell whether your notes are as clear and organized as those of other students, and you can use your comparisons to see whether you agree on what the most important points are.

Take turns testing each other on what you have learned. This will help you predict exam questions and find out if you can answer them. In addition to sharing specific information from the class, you can also share tips on how you take and organize your notes. You might get new ideas that will help your overall learning.

Be aware, however, that merely copying another student's notes, no matter how good those notes are, does not benefit you as much as comparing notes. If you had to be absent from a class because of illness or a family emergency, it's fine to look at another student's notes to see what you missed, but just rewriting those notes

might not help you learn the material. Instead, summarize the other student's notes in your own words to enhance your understanding of the important points.

Class Notes and Homework

Good class notes can help you complete homework assignments, too. Follow these steps.

1. **Take ten minutes to review your class notes.** Skim the notes and put a question mark next to anything you do not understand at first reading. Draw stars next to topics that are especially important. The "Try It!" exercise is devoted to this helpful tip.

2. **Do a warm-up for your homework.** Before starting the assignment, look through your notes again. Use a separate sheet of paper to rework examples, problems, or exercises. If there is related assigned material in the textbook, review it. Go back to the text examples. Cover the solutions and attempt to answer each question or complete each problem.

3. **Do assigned problems and answer assigned questions.** When you start your homework, read each question or problem and ask: What am I supposed to find or find out? What is essential and what is extraneous? Read each problem several times and restate it in your own words. Work the problem without referring to your notes or the text.

4. **Don't give up.** When you encounter a problem or question that you cannot readily handle, move on only after a reasonable effort. After you have reached the end of the assignment, return to the items that stumped you. Try once more, and then take a break. You may need to mull over a particularly difficult problem for several days.

5. **Complete your work.** When you finish an assignment, consider what you learned from the exercise. Think about how the problems and questions were different from one another, which strategies you used to solve them, and what form the answers took. Review any material you have not mastered. Ask the professor, a classmate, your study group, someone in the campus learning center, or a tutor to help you with difficult problems and questions. ■

MANAGING TIME ▷ Review Your Notes before Class

Depending on the amount of time between class sessions—two days, a weekend, or longer—you might find that it's hard to remember exactly what happened in the previous class. That's why good class notes are so important. Before class, take ten or fifteen minutes to read over your notes from the previous class, and draw stars next to topics that you remember were especially important. Put a question mark next to anything you wrote down but don't completely understand. This review will get you ready for the lecture that is about to begin and remind you to ask questions about material from the previous lecture that isn't clear to you. If you find yourself confused about something the instructor said, you can be sure that other classmates are confused as well. Speaking up to clarify any confusing points or misunderstandings you might have is a great way for you to participate in class.

What if you have three classes in a row and no time for studying between them? Recall and recite as soon after class as possible. Review the most recent class first. Never delay recall and recitation longer than one day; if you do, it will take you longer to review, select main ideas, and recite. With practice, you can quickly complete the review of your main ideas from your notes, perhaps between classes, during lunch, or while riding the bus.

Chapter Review

Steps to Success:
Getting the Most Out of Class

○ **Prepare for class before class; it is one of the simplest and most important things you can do.** Read your notes from the previous class and do the assigned readings.

○ **Practice the behaviors of effective learning during class.** These behaviors include listening attentively, taking notes, and contributing to class discussion.

○ **As you review your notes before each class, make a list of any questions you have and ask both your instructor and fellow students for help.** Other students will appreciate your asking these questions. Don't wait until just before the exam to try to find answers to your questions.

○ **Identify the different types of note taking covered in this chapter, and decide which one(s) might work best for you.** We recommend the Cornell method; however, any method can work as long as you use it consistently. Compare your notes with those of another good student to make sure that you are covering the most important points.

Applying what you've learned . . .

Now that you have read and discussed this chapter, consider how you can apply what you have learned to your academic and personal lives. The following prompts will help you reflect on the chapter material and its relevance to you both now and in the future.

1. How would you rate your current level of participation in the classes you are taking this term? Do you speak up, contribute to discussion, and ask questions, or do you daydream or sit silently? Do your instructors encourage you to participate, or do they seem to intentionally discourage your involvement? Research finds that students learn more when they contribute to class discussions and feel comfortable asking and responding to questions. Think about how your own level of participation—whether it's high or low—relates to learning and enjoyment in the classes you're currently taking.

2. Review the content on note-taking systems in this chapter. How would you describe your current method of taking notes? Are you organized or disorganized? What software programs or apps do you use? How is your current method of taking notes similar to or different from the methods suggested in "Approaches to Note Taking"? Do your notes help you study for exams? If not, what suggestions from this chapter might help you become a better note-taker?

Use Your Resources

GO TO ▷ The learning center: If you need help with developing strategies for learning and good study skills. Students at all levels use campus learning centers to improve in the skills discussed in this chapter.

GO TO ▷ Fellow students: If you need help finding a tutor or joining a study group. Often the best help you can get is from your fellow students—look for the most serious, purposeful, and directed students.

GO ONLINE TO ▷ Articles on overcoming the fear of public speaking: If you become more comfortable speaking in public, you will be able to participate more in class. Look online for helpful articles such as this one: www.themuse.com/advice/how-i-finally-got-over-my-fear-of-public-speaking.

NOW... How do you measure up?

1. I do a good job of identifying key points of lectures and discussions and writing them down in my notes.

○ Agree
○ Don't Know
○ Disagree

2. When I don't understand something, I know how important it is to ask questions in class—even in large classes.

○ Agree
○ Don't Know
○ Disagree

3. In math or science courses students should write down everything the instructor puts on the board or screen.

○ Agree
○ Don't Know
○ Disagree

4. I know that one of the most effective ways to learn is to join study groups for each of my classes.

○ Agree
○ Don't Know
○ Disagree

How do your answers here compare to your responses to the quiz you took at the start of the chapter? Which sections of this chapter left a strong impression on you? What listening and note-taking strategies have you begun to use, and are they working? What other strategies will you commit to trying?

LaunchPad
macmillan learning

LaunchPad Solo for College Success is a great resource. Go online to master concepts using the LearningCurve study tool and much more. **macmillanhighered.com/collegesuccessmedia**

06

91
Four-Step Plan for Active Reading

97
Different Courses—Different Kinds of Textbooks

101
Improving Your Reading

Reading for Success

WunderfulPixel/Shutterstock

To access the LearningCurve study tool, Video Tools, and more, go to *LaunchPad Solo for College Success.* **macmillan highered.com/ collegesuccessmedia**

Why is reading a college textbook more challenging than reading a high school text or reading for pleasure? The answer is that college textbooks are loaded with terms, concepts, and complex information that you are expected to learn on your own in a short time. The amount of material you will be expected to read, especially for courses like English literature, history, psychology, and sociology, may come as a surprise. To accomplish this, you will find it helpful and worthwhile to learn and use the active reading strategies in this chapter, which together form a textbook reading plan that will help you get the most out of your college reading.

How much reading did you do in high school? Many college students tell us that they did very little reading—only what they were required to do. Today, many readers opt for online sources, which tend to be shorter and often use more informal language. But whatever your previous reading habits might have been, college will require a higher level of focus and attention. Some students may be able to read quickly but find that their comprehension level is low. While you're in college, you will find that occasionally you need to reread a particularly difficult set of pages more than once so that you really understand the concepts. Depending on how much reading you did before coming to college—reading for pleasure, reading for classes, reading for work—you might find that reading is your favorite way to learn, or it may be your least favorite. Even if it *isn't* your favorite thing to do, however, reading is absolutely essential to doing well in college and in life. Any professional career that you might choose—such as medicine, engineering, law, accounting, or teaching—will require you to do lots of reading.

How do you measure up?

1. It's important to skim or "preview" a textbook chapter before beginning to read.
   - ○ Agree
   - ○ Don't Know
   - ○ Disagree

2. It's not a good idea to underline, highlight, or annotate the text when reading a page or section for the very first time.
   - ○ Agree
   - ○ Don't Know
   - ○ Disagree

3. Taking notes on textbook readings helps you keep up with key ideas without having to read the material over and over.
   - ○ Agree
   - ○ Don't Know
   - ○ Disagree

4. When reading a textbook with lots of new words, it's a good idea to have a dictionary close by to check word meanings.
   - ○ Agree
   - ○ Don't Know
   - ○ Disagree

Review the items you marked "Don't Know" or "Disagree." Pay special attention to these topics in this chapter—you will find motivating strategies to develop in these areas. A follow-up quiz at the end of the chapter will prompt you to consider what you have learned.

You Can't Put a Price on Knowledge

△ **Titus Indra**

Santhosh Kumar/Shutterstock.

The day after I registered for classes and got my list of assigned textbooks, I looked up the books on the campus online bookstore. My biology textbook alone was $200. I figured borrowing the textbook from a classmate or from the library would be OK. I could even photocopy a few sections if necessary, or I could order an old edition online. We'd probably cover most chapters in class anyway.

That was the plan, but because we had a ton of assigned reading, nobody wanted to share a book. Most of my classmates were pre-med and studied nonstop. My lab partner said that I could borrow his book on *Saturday nights* if I returned it by 8:00 a.m. each Sunday. The 400-page beast was as thick as a toaster, and photocopying was a pain.

I realized three things: (1) the lone library copy would never be available; (2) old editions were marked up and lacked important updates; and (3) a huge part of learning in college involves teaching yourself. I went to see my instructor during her office hours. She suggested I buy an e-book version from the publisher's Web site, which saved me some money. It felt good to have the book on my iPad so I could stay on pace with the syllabus.

Titus demonstrated poor judgment at the start, but he showed initiative in meeting with his biology instructor to figure out a solution that worked for him before he fell too far behind. Why is it so important to keep up with your outside reading assignments in college?

Four-Step Plan for Active Reading

A textbook reading plan can pay off by increasing your focus and concentration, promoting greater understanding of what you read, and preparing you to study for tests and exams. The plan you'll learn in this section is based on four main steps: previewing, reading and marking, reading with concentration, and reviewing.

Step 1: Previewing

When you read actively, you use strategies that help you stay focused. The first strategy, previewing, will give you an idea or overview of what is to come in the chapter. By previewing, you get the big picture—you see what you are about to read, and you can begin to consider how it's connected to what you already know and to the material the instructor is covering in class. Begin your preview by reading the title of the chapter. Next, skim the learning objectives (if they appear at the beginning of the chapter) and the introductory paragraphs, and then scan the list of key terms and read the summary at the end of the chapter (if the chapter includes either of these features). Skim the chapter headings and subheadings. Finally, look for any study exercises at the end of the chapter.

As part of your preview, check the number of pages in the chapter. Estimate how many pages you can reasonably expect to cover in your first fifty-minute study period. You may require more or less time to read different types of textbooks. For example, depending on your interests and previous knowledge, you may be able to read a psychology text more quickly than a foreign language text that presents a whole new system of words and meanings.

As you preview the text, look for connections between the text material and the related lecture material. Call to mind the terms and concepts that you remember from the lecture. Use these strategies to warm up. Ask yourself: Why am I reading this? What do I need to learn? You'll find that if you have previewed a chapter, you will be able to read it more quickly and with greater comprehension.

△ **Be Prepared**
Go through the textbook before class and see what you think the main points might be. Later you'll be able to compare your thoughts on the main points with what your instructor emphasized. Was there any overlap, and if so, where? What did you miss?

TRY IT!

SETTING GOALS ▷ **Be Motivated to Do All Your Required Reading**

Some first-year students, especially those who have trouble managing their time, think they can skip some required reading and still get good grades on tests and exams. The best students, however, will tell you that this isn't a smart strategy. Instructors assign readings that are important to your understanding, and they include concepts and details from readings on tests. Maintain your motivation to do well by completing all assigned reading, and you'll see the payoff in better grades.

Map It!

Mapping a chapter as you preview it provides a visual guide for how different chapter ideas fit together. Because about 75 percent of students identify themselves as visual learners, mapping is an excellent learning tool.

To map a chapter while you are previewing, draw either a wheel structure or a branching structure (see Figure 6.1). In the wheel structure, place the central idea in the chapter in the circle. You should find the central idea in the chapter introduction; it may also be apparent in the chapter title. For example, the central idea of this chapter is "reading successfully." Place secondary ideas on the spokes radiating from the circle, and draw offshoots of those ideas on the lines attached to the spokes. In the branching structure, put the main idea (most likely the chapter title) at the top, followed by supporting ideas on the second tier, and so forth. If you prefer a more step-by-step visual image, make an outline of the headings and subheadings of the chapter (see Figure 6.2).

Figure 6.1 ▽ Wheel and Branching Maps
Practice using one of these maps by taking the content of the sample outline in Figure 6.2 and writing it where it belongs on the map.

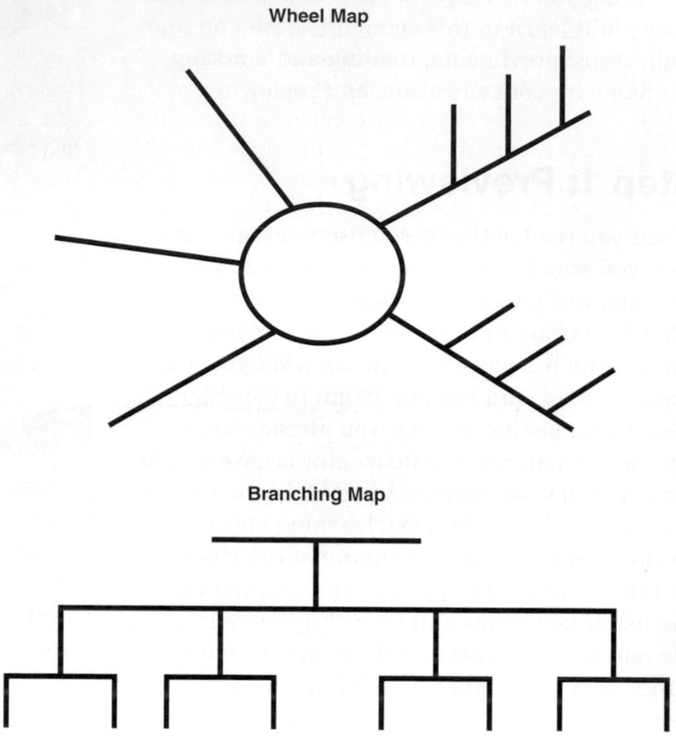

Wheel Map

Branching Map

Figure 6.2 ◁ Sample Outline
Figure 6.2 shows how a student might have outlined the first section of this chapter.

I. Four Steps in Active Reading

  A. Step 1, Preview: Get lay of the land, skim
    1. Mapping
    2. Outlining or listing
  B. Step 2, Read and mark textbooks
    1. Marking is highlighting, outlining, writing annotations in margin
    2. Read and think BEFORE marking
    3. Take notes while marking
    4. Avoid bad habits (like highlighting everything!)
  C. Step 3, Read with concentration
    1. Focus! Find proper location, turn off phone, set aside blocks of time with breaks, set study goals
    2. Monitor comprehension
  D. Step 4, Review: Do it regularly (use notes, flash cards, marked-up reading)

Step 2: Reading and Marking

Marking your textbooks is another active reading strategy that will help you concentrate on the material as you read. Marking means underlining, highlighting, or using margin notes or annotations. Figure 6.3 provides an example of many of these methods. No matter

which method you prefer, remember these important guidelines:

1. **Read and think before you mark.** Finish reading a section before you decide which are the most important ideas and concepts. When you read a text for the first time, everything can seem important. After you

---

Figure 6.3 ▽ Examples of Reading and Marking

Using a combination of highlighting and margin notes, the reader has made the content of this page easy to review. Without reading the text, note the highlighted words and phrases and the margin notes, and see how much information you can gather from them. Then read the text itself. Does the markup serve as a study aid? Does it cover the essential points? Would you have marked this page any differently? Why or why not?

Source: "The Stress of Adapting to a New Culture." Adapted from *Psychology*, 6th ed., p. 534, by D. H. Hockenbury and S. E. Hockenbury. © 2013 by Worth Publishers. Used with permission.

CULTURE AND HUMAN BEHAVIOR

The Stress of Adapting to a New Culture

(margin note) differences affecting cultural stress

Refugees, immigrants, and even international students are often unprepared for the dramatically different values, language, food, customs, and climate that await them in their new land. The process of changing one's values and customs as a result of contact with another culture is referred to as *acculturation*. **Acculturative stress** is the stress that results from the pressure of adapting to a new culture (Sam & Berry, 2010).

(margin note) acceptance of new culture reduces stress

Many factors can influence the degree of acculturative stress that a person experiences. For example, when the new society accepts ethnic and cultural diversity, acculturative stress is reduced (Mana & others, 2009). The transition is also eased when the person has some familiarity with the new language and customs, advanced education, and social support from friends, family members, and cultural associations (Schwartz & others, 2010). Acculturative stress is also lower if the new culture is similar to the culture of origin.

(margin note) also speaking new language, education, & social support

Cross-cultural psychologist John Berry (2003, 2006) has found that a person's attitudes are important in determining how much acculturative stress is experienced (Sam & Berry, 2010). When people encounter a new cultural environment, they are faced with two questions: (1) Should I seek positive relations with the dominant society? (2) Is my original cultural identity of value to me, and should I try to maintain it?

(margin note) how attitudes affect stress

(margin note) 4 patterns of acculturation

The answers produce one of four possible patterns of acculturation: integration, assimilation, separation, or marginalization (see the diagram). Each pattern represents a different way of coping with the stress of adapting to a new culture (Berry, 1994, 2003).

1 *Integrated* individuals continue to value their original cultural customs but also seek to become part of the dominant society. They embrace a *bicultural* identity (Hunyh & others, 2011). Biculturalism is associated with higher self-esteem and lower levels of depression, anxiety, and stress, suggesting that the bicultural identity may be the most adaptive acculturation pattern (Schwartz & others, 2010). The successfully integrated individual's level of acculturative stress will be low (Lee, 2010).

2 *Assimilated* individuals give up their old cultural identity and try to become part of the new society. They adopt the customs and social values of the new environment, and abandon their original cultural traditions.

Assimilation usually involves a moderate level of stress, partly because it involves a psychological loss—one's previous cultural identity. People who follow this pattern also face the possibility of being rejected either by members of the majority culture or by members of their original culture (Schwartz & others, 2010). The

(margin note) possible rejection by both cultures

Acculturative Stress Acculturative stress can be reduced when immigrants learn the language and customs of their newly adopted home. Here, two friends, one from China, one from Cuba, help each other in an English class in Miami, Florida.

process of learning new behaviors and suppressing old behaviors can also be moderately stressful.

3 Individuals who follow the pattern of *separation* maintain their cultural identity and avoid contact with the new culture. They may refuse to learn the new language, live in a neighborhood that is primarily populated by others of the same ethnic background, and socialize only with members of their own ethnic group.

In some cases, separation is not voluntary, but is due to the dominant society's unwillingness to accept the new immigrants. Thus, it can be the result of discrimination. Whether voluntary or involuntary, the level of acculturative stress associated with separation tends to be high.

(margin note) *separation may be self-imposed or discriminating

(margin note) higher stress with separation

4 *Finally, the *marginalized* person lacks cultural and psychological contact with *both* his traditional cultural group and the culture of his new society. By taking the path of marginalization, he lost the important features of his traditional culture but has not replaced them with a new cultural identity.

Although rare, the path of marginalization is associated with the greatest degree of acculturative stress. Marginalized individuals are stuck in an unresolved conflict between their traditional culture and the new society, and may feel as if they don't really belong anywhere. Fortunately, only a small percentage of immigrants fall into this category (Schwartz & others, 2010).

(margin note) *marginalized = higher level of stress

		Question 1: Should I seek positive relations with the dominant society?	
		Yes	**No**
Question 2: Is my original cultural identity of value to me, and should I try to maintain it?	**Yes**	Integration	Separation
	No	Assimilation	Marginalization

Patterns of Adapting to a New Culture According to cross-cultural psychologist John Berry, there are four basic patterns of adapting to a new culture (Sam & Berry, 2010). Which pattern is followed depends on how the person responds to the two key questions shown.

complete a section, reflect on it to identify the key ideas. Ask yourself: What are the most important ideas? What will I see on the test? This step can help you avoid marking too much material. On a practical note, if you find that you have made mistakes in how you have highlighted, or if another student has already highlighted your textbook, select a different color highlighter to use.

2. **Take notes while you read and mark.** Think about it: If you rely on marking alone, you will have to read all the pages again. But if you take notes while you preview in addition to making a map, an outline, a list, or flash cards (see Figure 6.4 on page 96), you are actively learning and also creating tools you can use to review, whether on your own or with a friend or study group.

3. **Avoid developing bad habits with marking.** Highlights and underlines are intended to pull your eye only to important terms and facts. For some, highlighting or underlining is actually a form of procrastination. If you are reading through the material but aren't planning to learn it until sometime later, you might be giving yourself a false sense of security and thus doing yourself more harm than good. And don't highlight or underline nearly everything you read; you won't be able to identify important concepts quickly if they're lost in a sea of color or underlines. Ask yourself whether your highlighting or underlining is helping you be more active in your learning process. If not, you might want to try a different technique, such as making margin notes or annotations. When you force yourself to put something in your own words while taking notes, you not only are predicting exam questions but also are evaluating whether you can answer them.

66 Ask yourself: What are the most important ideas? What will I see on the test? 99

TRY IT!

SETTING GOALS ▷ Practice Marking a Chapter

You probably have reading assignments for every class. Have you been marking your assigned chapters to identify the most important points? If so, have you been following the suggestions in the preceding list? If marking chapters is not something you do when you study, set a goal for this week to mark every chapter you are assigned to read. You can underline, use margin notes, or use a light-colored highlighter—one that you can see through to read the text. Try using a different method in each chapter to see which approach works best for you. As your understanding of the material grows and your performance on tests improves, you will be motivated to maintain your new good habits.

Step 3: Reading with Concentration

Instructors cannot provide all you need to know about an academic topic only by lecturing. Learning in any class will also depend on your doing the assigned textbook reading. Reading a college textbook, especially if the material is completely unfamiliar or highly technical, is a challenge for most new college students, but using tested strategies such as those outlined here will make you a more effective reader.

Focus, focus, focus. Like many students, you may have trouble concentrating or understanding the content when reading textbooks. Many factors may affect your ability to concentrate and to understand texts: the time of day, your energy level, your interest in the material, and your study location.

Consider the following suggestions, and decide which would be most helpful in improving your reading ability.

- **Find a quiet study location.** If you are on campus, the library is your best option. Set your mobile phone to mute with vibrate off, and store it where you can't see it. If you are reading an electronic document, download the information and disconnect from the network to reduce online distractions.

- **Read in blocks of time, with short breaks in between.** Reading in small blocks throughout the day instead of cramming in all your reading at the end of the day should help you understand and retain the material more easily.

- **Set goals for your study period,** such as "I will read twenty pages of my psychology text in the next fifty minutes." Reward yourself with a ten-minute break after each fifty-minute study period.

- **If you're having trouble concentrating or staying awake, do something about it!** Take a quick walk around the library or down the hall. Stretch and take some deep breaths and think positively about your study goals. Then resume studying.

- **Jot study questions in the margins, take notes, or recite key ideas.** Reread confusing parts of the text, and make a note to ask your instructor for clarification.

- **Focus on the important portions of the text.** Pay particular attention to the first and last sentences of paragraphs and to words in italics or in bold print.

- **Define unfamiliar terms** by using the glossary in the text or a dictionary.

Monitor your comprehension. An important aspect of textbook reading is monitoring your comprehension. As you read, ask yourself whether you understand the material, and check your understanding with a study partner. If you don't understand it, stop and reread the material. Look up words that you don't know. Try to clarify the main points and their relationship to one another.

After you have read the first section of the chapter and marked or taken notes on the key ideas, proceed to each subsequent section until you have finished the chapter. After you have completed each section—and before you move on to the next section—ask yourself again: What are the key ideas? What will I see on the test? At the end of each section, try to guess what information the author will present in the following section. Effective reading should lead you from one section to the next, with each new section adding to your understanding.

> " Ask yourself again: What are the key ideas? What will I see on the test? "

Make the Most of Your Textbook

It's important to know how to get the most out of your textbook, whether it's printed or digital. As you begin reading, you can learn more about the textbook and its author(s) by reading the first pages of the book, where you will find a preface, an introduction, and an "About the Author" section. The preface explains why the book was written, how it is organized, what material is covered, and how to use the features in each chapter to their fullest extent. Make the time to read these pages.

At the end of each chapter of a textbook, you will often find lists of key terms as well as questions that you can use as a study guide or as a

quick check of your understanding of the chapter's main points. Take time to read and respond to these questions, whether or not your instructor requires you to do so. If you are using a digital textbook, tools for review are integrated throughout each chapter.

Because some textbooks offer "test banks" to aid instructors in creating quizzes and tests, your instructors may draw their exams directly from the textbook. On the other hand, they may consider the textbook to be supplementary to their lectures. When in doubt, ask for a clarification of what will be covered on tests and what types of questions will be used.

Step 4: Reviewing

The final step in effective textbook reading is reviewing. Reviewing involves looking through your assigned reading again. Many students expect the improbable—that they will read through the text material once and be able to remember the ideas at exam time, which may be four, six, or even twelve weeks later. Realistically, you will need to include regular reviews in your study process. Here is where your notes, study questions, annotations, flash cards, visual maps, or outlines will be most useful. See Figure 6.4 for an example of how to prepare flash cards. Aim to review the material from each chapter every week.

Consider ways to use your many senses to review. Recite aloud. Tick off each item in a list on each of your fingertips. Post diagrams, maps, or outlines around your living space so that you will see them often and will likely be able to visualize them while taking the test. ■

Figure 6.4 ▽ Examples of Flash Cards

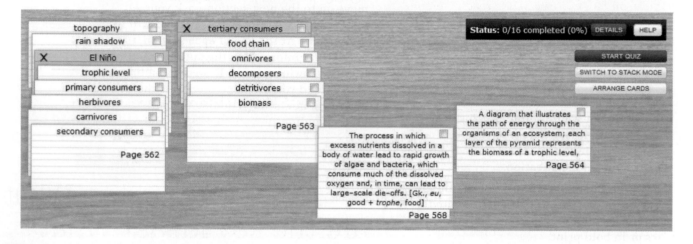

Reading Online

Are you taking an online class, reading in a learning management system (LMS) environment, reading an e-book version of a class text, or interacting with course material in a publisher's digital learning environment on a mobile device? If so, how is your reading experience different from reading a print book?

In the article "Being a Better Online Reader, which appeared in the *New Yorker* on July 16, 2014, Maria Konnikova reports that educational researchers are just beginning to study how reading online changes the way people read and comprehend material. While some students comprehend more from reading a print book or article, just the opposite is true for other students. In general, however, people tend to read more quickly online, performing an action that Ziming Kiu, a professor at San Jose State University, calls "skimming." Many of us skim or browse the Internet when we are looking for a particular key word or moving from source to source by clicking on different URLs. Skimming, however, is very different from reading deeply, the type of reading that you'll need to do when reading college texts.

May Dyson, a psychologist at the University of Reading in England, has found that when we read online, we experience more distractions—not only distractions from e-mails or pop-up Web sites, but also distractions from differences in layout and even in color of the online material. She adds that these distractions can be exhausting. College publishers are intentionally developing digital learning environments to reduce distractions and to keep students grounded in the content; for instance, many digital textbooks do not have any live links, which keeps students within the learning environment, and note-taking and highlighting tools are available, which facilitates deep reading. So if you are reading textbooks online or on a device, set yourself up to stay focused. Keep tempting messaging apps and Web browsers closed so that you aren't lured away from your assignments, and discipline yourself to use the four-step active reading plan: (1) previewing your reading by noting subheads and study exercises; (2) highlighting or annotating using the devices available in the online platform; (3) reading with concentration; and finally (4) reviewing to make sure that you understand what you have read and can apply it to what you're learning through other classroom activities whether online or face-to-face.

Different Courses—Different Kinds of Textbooks

Because of the variation in college textbooks, you will need to learn and use different reading strategies depending on the material in the text. But no matter how differently books are organized or written—some are better organized and better written than others—you can depend on the four-step active reading plan to help you navigate all of them. Some textbooks may be easier to understand than others, but don't give up if the reading level is challenging.

Different instructors use textbooks in different ways. Some instructors expect you to read the textbook carefully, while others are much more concerned that you understand broad concepts that come primarily from their lectures. Ask your instructors what the tests will cover and what types of questions will be used.

If your textbook seems disorganized or hard to understand, let your instructor know your opinion; other students likely feel the same way. Your instructor might spend some class time explaining the text. He or she can also meet with you during office hours to help you with the material, and you might visit the learning center for help as well.

Reading Math Textbooks

Textbooks in different major disciplines, or areas of academic study, tend to be quite different from each other. Let's start with math textbooks, which are filled with sample problems, graphs, and figures that you will need to understand to grasp the content and the classroom presentations. Math textbooks are also likely to have fewer long blocks of text and more practice exercises than other textbooks. As you read, also pay special attention to the definitions—learning the meaning of each term in a new topic is the first step toward complete understanding.

Math texts usually have symbols, derivations of formulas, and proofs of theorems. You must understand and be able to apply the formulas

and theorems, but unless your course has an especially theoretical emphasis, you are less likely to be responsible for all the proofs. So if you get lost in the proof of a theorem, go on to the next item in the section.

When you come to a sample problem, pick up pencil and paper and work through it. Then look at the solution and think through the problem on your own. You'll spend the most time completing the exercises that follow each text section of the math book.

To be successful in any math or science course, you must keep up with all assignments. Always do your homework on time, whether or not your instructor collects it. After you complete an assignment, skim through the other exercises even if they weren't assigned. Just reading the unassigned problems will deepen your understanding of the topic and its scope. Finally, talk yourself through the assignment. As you do, focus on understanding the problem and its solution, not just on memorization.

Reading Science Textbooks

Science textbooks have many similarities to math textbooks. Your approach to a particular science textbook will depend somewhat on whether you are studying a math-based science such as physics or a text-based science such as biology or zoology. First, you need to familiarize yourself with the overall format of the book. Review the table of contents, the glossary of terms, and the appendices. The appendices will include lists of physical constants, unit conversions, and various charts and tables.

As you begin an assigned section in a science text, skim the material quickly to get a general idea of the topic. Begin to absorb the new vocabulary and technical symbols. Then skim the end-of-chapter problems so you'll know what to look for as you do a second and more detailed reading of the chapter. State a specific goal—for example, if you are taking a biology

△ **Getting the Most Out of Your Textbooks**
Math and science texts are filled with graphs and figures that you will need to understand to grasp the content and the classroom presentations. If you have trouble reading and understanding any of your textbooks, get help from your instructor or your learning center.

class: "I'm going to distinguish between mitosis and meiosis," or "Tonight I'll focus on the topics in this chapter that were stressed in class."

You may decide to underline or highlight words in a subject such as anatomy, which involves a lot of memorization of terms. Be restrained in your use of a highlighter; highlighting should pull your eye only to important terms and facts.

In most sciences, outlining the text chapters is the best strategy. You can usually identify main topics, subtopics, and specific terms under each subtopic by the size of the type. Headings printed in larger type will introduce major sections; smaller type is used for subtopics within these sections. Refer to Figure 6.2 for an example of a chapter outline. To save time when you are outlining, don't write full sentences, but include clear explanations of new technical terms and symbols. Pay special attention to

topics that were covered in the lecture class or in the lab. If you aren't sure whether your outlines contain too much or too little detail, compare them with those of a classmate or the members of your study group.

Reading Social Science and Humanities Textbooks

Many of the suggestions that apply to reading science textbooks also apply to reading in the social sciences (sociology, psychology, anthropology, economics, political science, and history). Social science texts are filled with terms that are unique to a particular field of study. They also describe research and theory building and have references to many primary sources. In addition, your social science texts may describe differences in opinions or perspectives.

Your reading can become more interesting if you seek out different opinions about a common issue by looking at a variety of resources in your campus library or on the Internet.

Textbooks in the humanities (philosophy, religion, literature, music, and art) provide facts, examples, opinions, and original material such as stories and essays. You will often be asked to react to your reading by identifying central themes or characters.

Some professors believe that the way courses and majors are structured artificially divides human knowledge and experience. Those with this view may argue that subjects such as history, political science, and philosophy are closely linked and that studying each subject separately results in only partial understanding. These instructors will stress the connections between courses and encourage you to think in an interdisciplinary manner. You might be asked to consider how the book you're reading, the music you're studying, or a particular painting reflects the political atmosphere or prevailing culture of the period. ■

The Value of Primary Source Material

While textbooks cover a lot of material in a fairly limited space, they can't tell you everything you want to know about a topic, and they may omit things that would make your reading more interesting. If you find yourself fascinated by a particular topic, go to the primary sources—the original research or documents used in writing the text. You'll usually find these sources cited in footnotes or in endnotes at the end of each chapter or at the end of the book. If you are using an e-book or digital textbook, you might find more extensive primary source material or links that will take you directly to it.

These primary sources may be journal articles from a literary or scientific journal such as the *Journal of the American Medical Association*; research papers or dissertations (the major research papers that students write to earn a doctoral degree); recent laws enacted by the U.S. Congress or the Supreme Court; personal letters from soldiers on the front line of major wars; diaries belonging to U.S. presidents such as George Washington, John Quincy Adams, Thomas Jefferson, or Harry Truman; or the inaugural addresses of presidents or governors. Reading primary source material gives you the real scoop that you won't always find in your textbooks.

Many primary sources were originally written for other instructors or researchers. Therefore they often use language and refer to concepts you may never have heard before. If you are reading a journal article that describes a theory or research study, one technique for easier understanding is to read the article from the end to the beginning. Read the conclusion or "discussion" section, and then go back to see how the experiment was done. In almost all scholarly journals, each article is introduced by an abstract, a paragraph-length summary of the methods and major findings described in the article. Reading an abstract is sort of like reading a CliffsNotes study guide—you'll get the gist of a research article before you dive in. As you're reading research articles, always ask yourself: So what? Was the research important to what we know about the topic, or was it a waste of time and money, in your opinion?

MANAGING TIME ▷ Plan Your Reading Assignments

Create a simple table with four columns and with horizontal lines for all your reading assignments for this week. Following the example provided, use the first column to list each reading assignment. In the second column, rate each assignment on a scale of 1 to 5 according to how easy (1) or difficult (5) you think the reading will be. Estimate how many hours each assignment will take and enter that estimate in the third column. (Remember that a difficult reading will take longer.) Use the fourth column to keep track of how much time you actually spend reading.

Estimated reading time this week:

Assignment	Difficulty (1–5)	Estimated time	Actual time
History (Ch. 1)	4	1.5 hr.	2.0 hr.
Psychology (Chs. 2 & 3)	4	1.5 hr.	4.0 hr.
Math (Ch. 3)	5	2.0 hr.	2.5 hr.
Speech (Ch. 2)	2	1.0 hr.	1.25 hr.
College Success (Ch. 5)	2	1.0 hr.	1.0 hr.

Total actual reading time: 10.75 hours

Thoughts: *I used all four steps of active reading. My reading took me a bit longer, but I can tell that I learned much more. I also feel like I knew how to use my textbooks better after reading this chapter from my college success textbook.*

Estimated reading time this week:

Assignment	Difficulty (1–5)	Estimated time	Actual time

Total actual reading time:

Thoughts:

At the end of the week, go back and analyze the table. Did you spend more time or less time reading than you predicted? How accurate were your predictions about the difficulty levels of the readings?

Improving Your Reading

With effort, you can improve your reading dramatically. Remember to be flexible. How you read should depend on the material. Evaluate the relative importance and difficulty of the assigned reading, and then adjust your reading style and the time you allot. Connect one important idea to another by asking yourself: Why am I reading this? Where does this fit in? Reading textbooks and other assignments with good understanding and recall takes planning.

Developing Your Vocabulary

When reading books and articles for your college classes, you will inevitably encounter lots of unfamiliar words. Some terminology will be specific to a particular academic field, but other terms can be used in a variety of settings and contexts. Increasing your ability to use language is something you'll do throughout your life, not only while you're in college but also after you begin your career.

If words are such a basic and essential component of knowledge, what is the best way to learn them? As you do your assigned reading, follow the basic vocabulary-building strategies outlined here:

- **Pay attention to key terms in bold type.** Often these key terms are defined in the text margin, repeated at the end of the chapter, and then compiled in a glossary at the back of the book. These features are there to help students master the content.

- **Notice and write down unfamiliar words.** Consider making flash cards or lists of new words you want to remember. Practice by using the flash cards that are often available for each chapter in digital books.

- **Consider the context.** When you encounter a challenging or unfamiliar term, see if you can predict its meaning by using the surrounding words.

- **Analyze terms to uncover meaning.** If context by itself is not enough, try analyzing the term to discover its root, or base part, or other meaningful parts of the word. For example,

△ **Word Power**
The popular app Words with Friends by Zynga includes a dictionary powered by Dictionary.com, which allows players to check the definition and pronunciation of 170,000 words, and a Word of the Day which helps expand players' vocabularies.

emissary has a root that means "to emit" or "to send forth," so we can guess that an emissary is someone sent forth with a message. Similarly, note prefixes and suffixes. For example, *anti-* means "against" and *pro-* means "for." Use the glossary in the text, a print dictionary, or the Merriam-Webster Online Dictionary (www.merriam-webster.com) to locate the definition. If a word has more than one definition, search for the meaning that fits the usage you are looking for.

- **Take every opportunity to use new terms in your writing and speaking.** If you use a new word a few times, you'll soon know it. In addition, studying new terms on flash cards or study sheets can be handy at exam time.

- **Consult a thesaurus.** A thesaurus is like a dictionary except that it groups words that mean more or less the same thing. If you think there may be a better word to convey your meaning, a thesaurus will help you discover the right word to express what you want to say. Online dictionaries often have access to a hyperlinked thesaurus, and word processing programs generally include a limited thesaurus to help you check out similar words.

- **Play word games.** Doing so will increase the words you know. If you never played Scrabble when you were growing up, you'll find that it's fun, even for adults. Try playing the popular app Words with Friends. Or you might download a crossword puzzle app or pick up some puzzle books. By working crossword puzzles, you'll become familiar with lots of new words.

- **Review word lists.** You may want to start building your vocabulary, especially if you're planning to go to graduate or professional school; an expansive vocabulary will help you perform well in interviews and on high-stakes exams like the Scholastic Aptitude Test (SAT)

or the Graduate Record Exam (GRE). The word lists at Majortests.com (www.majortests .com/word-lists) can be very helpful; see how many of the words on the lists you already know, and identify words you need to add to your working vocabulary.

What to Do When You Fall Behind in Your Reading

Occasionally, life might get in the way of doing your assigned readings on time. You may get sick or have to take care of a sick family member for a few days, you may have to work extra hours, or you may have a personal problem that prevents you from concentrating on your courses for a short time. While there are valid reasons for getting behind, some students simply procrastinate and think that they can catch up. This is a myth. The less you read the harder you'll have to work to make up for lost time. Try to follow the

▽ **A Marathon, Not a Sprint**
If you fall behind in your reading, you won't be alone—eventually almost every student does. Remember that your studies are more like a marathon than a sprint, so you should plan to make up lost ground slowly but steadily: Do your assigned readings, study with others, get help, and *do not give up!* Jerome Prevost/TempSport/Corbis.

schedule of readings for each course, but if you fall behind, don't panic. Here are some suggestions for getting back on track:

- **Plan to do the assigned readings as scheduled.** Add one or two hours a day to your study time so you can go back and read the parts that you missed. In particular, take advantage of every spare moment to read; for example, read during your lunch hour at work, or while you are waiting for public transportation or at the doctor's office.

- **Join a study group.** If each member of your study group reads a section of the assigned chapter and shares and discusses his or her notes, summary, or outline with the group, you can all cover the content more quickly.

- **Ask for help.** Visit your campus learning center to work with a tutor who can help you with difficult concepts in the textbook.

66 If you fall behind, don't panic. 99

TRY IT!

FEELING CONNECTED ▷ **Two (or More) Are Better Than One**

One way to get immediate feedback on your reading comprehension is to work with a study partner or study group. The give-and-take that you will experience will improve your learning and your motivation. Another way that study group members can work together is to divide up a chapter for previewing and studying and then get together later to teach the material to one another.

- **Talk to your instructor.** If you have a valid reason for falling behind, such as sickness or a personal problem, ask for extra time to make up your assignments. Most instructors are willing to make a one-time exception to help students catch up.

- **Do not give up.** You may have to work harder for a short period of time, but you will soon get caught up. ■

If English Is Not Your First Language

Learning English is difficult when it is not your first language. You'll notice that words are often spelled differently from the way they sound and that the language is full of idioms—phrases that are peculiar and cannot be understood from the meanings of the individual words. If you are learning English and are having trouble reading your texts, don't give up. Reading the material slowly and more than once can help you improve your comprehension. Make sure that you have two good dictionaries—one in English and one that links English with your primary language—and look up every word that you don't know. Be sure to practice thinking, writing, and speaking in English, and take advantage of your campus's helping services. Your campus may have ESL (English as a second language) tutoring and workshops. Ask your adviser or your college success instructor to help you locate these services.

Chapter Review

Steps to Success: Reading for Success

○ **Practice the four steps of active reading: previewing, reading and marking, reading with concentration, and reviewing.** If you practice these steps, you will understand and retain more of what you read.

○ **Take your course textbooks seriously.** They contain essential information that you'll be expected to learn and understand. Never try to "get by" without the text.

○ **Remember that not all textbooks are the same.** They vary by subject area and style of writing. Some may be easier to comprehend than others, but don't give up if the reading level is challenging.

○ **Learn and practice the techniques suggested in this chapter for reading and understanding texts on different subjects.** Which texts are easiest for you to read? Which are the hardest? Why?

○ **In addition to the textbook, read all assigned supplemental materials.** You should also try to find additional materials to take your reading beyond just what is required. The more you read, the more you will understand, and the better your performance will be.

○ **As you read, take notes on the material.** Indicate in your notes the specific ideas you need help in understanding.

○ **Get help with difficult material before much time goes by.** College courses use sequential material that builds on previous material. You will need to master the material as you go along.

○ **Discuss difficult readings in study groups.** Explain to one another what you do and don't understand.

○ **Find out what kind of assistance your campus offers to increase reading comprehension and speed.** Check out your learning and counseling centers for free workshops. Even faculty and staff sometimes take advantage of these services. Most everyone wants to improve his or her reading speed and comprehension.

○ **Use reading as a means to build your vocabulary.** Learning new words is a critical learning skill and outcome of college. The more words you know, the more you'll understand.

Applying what you've learned . . .

Now that you have read and discussed this chapter, consider how you can apply what you have learned to your academic and personal lives. The following prompts will help you reflect on the chapter material and its relevance to you both now and in the future.

1. Choose a reading assignment for one of your upcoming classes. After previewing the material, begin reading until you reach a major heading or until you have read at least a page or two. Now stop and write down what you remember from the material, and then go back and review what you just read. Were you able to remember all the main ideas?

2. It's easy to say that there is not enough time in the day to get everything done, especially a long reading assignment. However, your future depends on how well you do in college. Challenge yourself not to use that excuse. How can you modify your daily activities to make time for reading?

Use Your Resources

GO TO ▷ **The learning center:** If you need help with your reading. Most campuses have a learning center, and reading assistance is among its specialties. The best students, good students who want to be the best students, and students with academic difficulties all use learning centers. Services are offered by both full-time professionals and highly skilled student tutors.

GO TO ▷ **Fellow college students:** If you need help understanding your reading assignments. Often the best help is closest to you. Keep an eye out in your classes, residence hall, and campus groups for the best students—those who appear to be the most serious, purposeful, and directed. Hire a tutor. Join a study group. If you do these things, you are much more likely to be successful.

GO ONLINE TO ▷ **Niagara University's Office for Academic Support (www.niagara .edu/general-study-skills):** If you want to read helpful articles about reading and marking textbooks and other general study skills.

NOW... How do you measure up?

1. It's important to skim or "preview" a textbook chapter before beginning to read.
   - ○ Agree
   - ○ Don't Know
   - ○ Disagree

2. It's not a good idea to underline, highlight, or annotate the text when reading a page or section for the very first time.
   - ○ Agree
   - ○ Don't Know
   - ○ Disagree

3. Taking notes on textbook readings helps you keep up with key ideas without having to read the material over and over.
   - ○ Agree
   - ○ Don't Know
   - ○ Disagree

4. When reading a textbook with lots of new words, it's a good idea to have a dictionary close by to check word meanings.
   - ○ Agree
   - ○ Don't Know
   - ○ Disagree

How do your answers here compare to your responses to the quiz you took at the start of the chapter? Which sections of this chapter left a strong impression on you? What strategies for reading college textbooks have you started to use? Are they working? What other strategies will you commit to trying?

LaunchPad
macmillan learning

07

109
Preparing for Tests

114
Studying to Make It Stick

117
Taking Tests and Exams

121
Academic Honesty and Misconduct

Taking Exams & Tests

© Redberry/Shutterstock.

To access the LearningCurve study tool, Video Tools, and more, go to *LaunchPad Solo for College Success.* **macmillan highered.com/ collegesuccessmedia**

In this chapter you will find advice for preparing academically for tests and exams, as well as advice for preparing physically and emotionally. This chapter also discusses what kind of collaboration is acceptable and reminds you why the guidelines for academic honesty and integrity are so important in college and beyond.

Does the thought of your first college test or exam make you anxious? Many students who have had particular problems with certain subjects such as math or science or with certain kinds of tests will feel that they are doomed to repeat old problems in college. Nothing could be further from the truth. You were admitted to this college because of your potential to do well, but good grades on tests and exams don't happen by magic. It is your responsibility to attend all classes, take good notes, do all assigned readings, and seek help when you need it. Helping services available on campus will include tutoring, Supplemental Instruction, the learning center, and special help from your instructor with test-preparation sessions or one-on-one assistance. If you prepare and seek help when you have trouble, you should do well.

Most college instructors will expect you to be responsible for your own learning. They'll provide good information but won't give you specific instructions about how to study and prepare for tests and major projects. Although some study strategies, such as not waiting until the last minute to prepare for an exam or a project, will apply to all courses, the usefulness of other strategies will vary according to the subject matter. This chapter will help you determine the most effective study strategies for different courses.

How do you measure up?

1. To do well on exams, students should maintain good eating, sleeping, and exercise habits, especially before the exam date.
   ○ Agree
   ○ Don't Know
   ○ Disagree

2. In order to prevent last-minute cramming, it's important to begin studying for an exam at least a week in advance.
   ○ Agree
   ○ Don't Know
   ○ Disagree

3. Doing well on essay exam questions requires reading each question carefully and responding with complete and precise answers.
   ○ Agree
   ○ Don't Know
   ○ Disagree

4. I understand clearly how cheating is defined in each of my classes.
   ○ Agree
   ○ Don't Know
   ○ Disagree

Review the items you marked "Don't Know" or "Disagree." Pay special attention to these topics in this chapter—you will find motivating strategies to develop in these areas. A follow-up quiz at the end of the chapter will prompt you to consider what you have learned.

Just Say No

racron/Shutterstock.

I took a college success course in my first year of college and learned how to prepare well for tests and how to manage my time so that I can get my projects and papers finished before they are due. Classmates sometimes ask to copy my notes, and a few have wanted to copy a term paper I wrote in the past for a course they're taking now. I'm glad to compare notes with other students—our instructors encourage us to share our notes to learn from each other—but

△ **Emily Vonn**

I'm uncomfortable just handing out my notes to be copied. And agreeing to let another student copy a major paper that I wrote would definitely be over the line. I actually think the instructors would remember my papers because I routinely run my topics by them and ask them to suggest sources of information. Even if the instructor didn't recognize the paper as mine, I don't think that giving someone my work is fair to me, nor is it doing that person any favors. The first couple of times a student asked to copy one of my papers, I felt slightly flattered but also a little guilty for refusing. I guess I was afraid of being thought of as a goody two-shoes. But our campus honor code is clear that this is plagiarism; I decided it was worth it to just say no.

Emily has made the most of the test-taking and time-management strategies that she learned in her college success course, and she has also applied what she learned about maintaining academic integrity. Can you relate to Emily's experience of being asked for her papers and notes? Or can you relate more to the students who asked Emily for favors?

Preparing for Tests

In your first months of college, you will notice that students have different ways of preparing for tests. Some keep up with their assignments so that when test day comes, they need only to review what they have already studied. Others wait until the last minute and try to cram their test preparation into one night. Needless to say, cramming rarely results in good test grades.

You actually began preparing for tests and examinations on the first day of the term. Your note taking, assigned reading, and homework are all part of your preparation; keeping up with all this work during each term will contribute to good test performance. Review assigned readings before class and again after class, and note any material covered in both the reading assignments and class. You will likely see this material again—on your test.

Work with Instructors, Peers, and Tutors

Preparing for tests does not have to be a lonely pursuit. In fact, it shouldn't be. Enlisting the help of *human* resources—people—will help you succeed.

Start with your instructor. Pay close attention to what your instructors emphasize in class. Take good notes, and learn the material before each exam. Unless they tell you otherwise, instructors are quite likely to stress in-class material on exams. Well in advance of test day, you need to get information. Before each exam, talk to your instructor to find out the types of questions you'll have to answer, the time you will have to complete them, and the content to be covered. Ask how the exam will be graded and whether all questions will have the same point value. Keep in mind, though, that most instructors dislike being asked, "Is this going to be on the test?" They believe that everything that goes on in class is important enough for you to learn, whether or not you'll actually be tested on it.

Use the information that you get from your instructor to design an exam plan. It is very

Figure 7.1 ▽ **Exam Schedule from Sample Course Syllabus**

History 111, US History to 1865
Fall 2016

Examinations
Note: In this course, most of your exams will be on Fridays, except for the Wednesday before Thanksgiving. This is to give you a full week to study for the exam and permit me to grade them over the weekend and return the exams to you on Monday. I believe in using a variety of types of measurements. In addition to those scheduled below, I reserve the right to give you unannounced quizzes on daily reading assignments. Also, current events are fair game on any exam! Midterm and final exams will be cumulative (on all material since beginning of the course). Other exams cover all classroom material and all readings covered since the prior exam. The schedule is as follows:

Friday, 9/9: Objective type

Friday, 9/23: Essay type

Friday, 10/7: Midterm: essay and objective

Friday, 11/4: Objective

Wednesday, 11/23: Essay

Friday, 12/16: Final exam: essay and objective

important to check the exam dates on your syllabus, as in Figure 7.1. Then you can create a schedule that will give you time to review effectively for the exam instead of waiting until the night before to review. Develop a to-do list of the major steps you need to take to be ready. Be sure you have read and learned all the material by one week before the exam. Try to attend all test or exam review sessions offered by your instructor.

Join a study group. Your instructor may allow class time for the formation of study groups. If not, ask your instructor, adviser, or campus tutoring or learning center to help you identify other interested students, and then decide on guidelines for the group. Study groups can meet throughout the term, or they can just review for midterms or final exams. Group members should complete their assignments before the group meets and should prepare study questions or points of discussion ahead of time.

Numerous research studies have shown that joining a study group is one of the most effective strategies to use when preparing for exams. You can hear other group members' views of your instructor's goals, objectives, and emphasis; have partners quiz you on facts and concepts; and gain the enthusiasm and friendship of others, which will help build and sustain your motivation.

Get a tutor. Tutoring is not just for students who are struggling. Often the best students seek tutorial assistance. Most campus tutoring centers offer their services for free. Ask your academic adviser or counselor or the campus learning center about arranging for tutoring. Learning centers often employ student tutors who have done well in the same courses you are taking. Many learning centers also have computer tutorials that can help you refresh basic skills. And think about eventually becoming a tutor yourself; tutoring other students will greatly deepen your own learning.

TRY IT!

FEELING CONNECTED ▷ Tutoring and Study Groups

Believe it or not, one of the best ways to feel connected with other students is by participating in tutoring or in a study group. You can probably locate options for tutoring on your institution's Web site, or you can visit the campus learning center to find out about tutoring for a course that is difficult for you. Remember also that you can seek tutoring help for classes in which you are doing well in order to stretch your mental muscles, so to speak.

Whether or not you need one-on-one help, you'll benefit from joining a study group. Research proves that students learn more studying in a group than they do studying alone, and so we reinforce this idea often in this book. Study groups can also be about more than academic work. As a plus, you might find that you and some of your "study buddies" develop strong friendships that last throughout your college experience.

Prepare Properly for Math and Science Exams

More than in other academic areas, your grades in math and science courses will be determined by your scores on major exams. To pass a math or science course, you must perform well on timed tests. Here are some strategies you can use to prepare properly:

Ask about test rules and procedures. Are calculators allowed? Are formula sheets permitted? If not, will any formulas be provided? Will you be required to give definitions? Derive formulas? State and/or prove theorems?

Work as many problems as you can before the test. Practicing with sample problems is the best way to prepare for a problem-solving test (see Figure 7.2).

Practice understanding the precise meaning and requirements of problems. Failure to read problems carefully and to interpret and answer what is asked is the most common mistake made by students taking science and math exams.

Prepare in advance to avoid other common mistakes. Errors with parentheses (failing to use them when they are needed, failing to distribute a multiplier) and mistakes with negative signs are common in math-based courses. Pay attention to these details in class so that you don't fall into the typical traps when you are taking an exam.

Study from your outline. In a subject such as anatomy, which requires memorizing technical terms and understanding the relationships among systems, focus your preparation on your study outline.

Prepare Physically and Emotionally

Academic preparation—the studying you do to get ready for a test—is important, but physical and emotional preparation will also play a role in your success. Here are some tips for physical preparation:

> " Your grades in math and science courses will be determined by your scores on major exams. "

Maintain a regular sleep routine. To do well on exams, you need to be alert so that you can think clearly, and you are more likely to be alert when you are well rested. Last-minute, late-night cramming is not an effective study strategy.

Follow a regular exercise program. Walking, running, swimming, and other aerobic activities are effective stress reducers. They provide positive and much-needed breaks from intense studying and may help you think more clearly.

Eat right. Avoid drinking too many caffeinated drinks and eating too much junk food. Be sure to eat breakfast before a morning exam. Ask the instructor if you can bring a bottle of water with you to exams.

Know the material. Study by testing yourself or by quizzing others in a study group so that you will be sure you really know the material. If you allow adequate time to review, on exam day you will enter the classroom confident that you are prepared.

Practice relaxing. If you experience an upset stomach, sweaty palms, a racing heart, or other unpleasant physical symptoms of test anxiety before an exam, see your counseling center about relaxation techniques. Practice them regularly.

Use positive self-talk. Instead of telling yourself, "I never do well on math tests," or "I'll never be able to learn all the information for my history essay exam," make positive statements such as "I have attended all the lectures, done my homework, and passed the quizzes. Now I'm ready to pass the test." ■

(c) What is the probability that 5 cards drawn at random from a 52-card deck will yield a royal flush?

■ **30.** Biblical permutations: The King James Version of the Old Testament has its 39 books canonized in a different order than the Hebrew Bible does. What mathematical expression would yield the number of possible orders of these 39 books? Is this number larger than you expected?

8.4 Continuous Probability Models

31. Generate two random real numbers between 0 and 1 and take their sum. The sum can take any value between 0 and 2. The density curve is the shaded triangle shown in Figure 8.13.

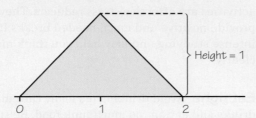

Figure 8.13 The density curve for the sum of two random numbers, for Exercise 31.

(a) Verify by geometry that the area under this curve is 1.
(b) What is the probability that the sum is less than 1? (Sketch the density curve, shade the area that represents the probability, and then find that area. Do this for part (c) as well.)
(c) What is the probability that the sum is less than 0.5?

32. Suppose two data values are each rounded to the nearest whole number. Make a density curve for the sum of the two roundoff errors (assuming each error has a continuous uniform distribution).

33. On the TV show *The Price Is Right,* the "Range Game" involves a contestant being told that the suggested retail price of a prize lies between two numbers that are $600 apart. The contestant has one chance to position a red window with a span of $150 that will contain the price. On one episode, the price of a piano is between $8900 and $9500. If we assume a uniform continuous distribution (i.e., that all prices within the $600 interval are equally likely), what is the probability that the contestant will be successful?

8.5 The Mean and Standard Deviation of a Probability Model

34. You have a campus errand that will take only 15 minutes. The only parking space anywhere nearby is a faculty-only space, which is checked by campus police about once every hour. If you're caught, the fine is $25.

(a) Give the probability model for the money that you may or may not have to pay.
(b) What's the expected value of the money that you will pay for your unauthorized parking?

35. Exercise 15 gives a probability model for the grade of a randomly chosen student in Statistics 101 at North Carolina State University, using the 4-point scale. What is the mean grade in this course? What is the standard deviation of the grades?

36. In Exercise 14, you gave a probability model for the intelligence of a character in a role-playing game. What is the mean intelligence for these characters?

37. Exercise 16 gives probability models for the number of rooms in owner-occupied and rented housing units. Find the mean number of rooms for each type of housing. Make probability histograms for the two models and mark the mean on each histogram. You see that the means describe an important difference between the two models: Owner-occupied units tend to have more rooms.

38. Typographical and spelling errors can be either "nonword errors" or "word errors." A nonword error is not a real word, as when "the" is typed as "teh." A word error is a real word, but not the right word, as when "lose" is typed as "loose." When undergraduates write a 250-word essay (without spell-checking), the number of nonword errors has this probability model:

Errors	0	1	2	3	4
Probability	0.1	0.2	0.3	0.3	0.1

The number of word errors has this model:

Errors	0	1	2	3
Probability	0.4	0.3	0.2	0.1

(a) What is the mean number of nonword errors in an essay?
(b) What is the mean number of word errors in an essay?
(c) How does the difference between the means describe the difference between the two models?

39. Find (and explain how you found) the mean for:

(a) the continuous probability model in Exercise 31.
(b) the probability model in Exercise 32.

■ **40.** The idea of insurance is that we all face risks that are unlikely but carry a high cost. Think of a fire destroying your home. Insurance spreads the risk: We all pay a small amount, and the insurance policy pays a large amount to those few of us whose homes burn down. An insurance

SETTING GOALS ▷ Be at Your Best for the Next Test

Doing your best on tests and exams takes more than hours of study. You must be physically and emotionally ready. Visualize the good grades you will earn, and imagine the pride you will feel in your accomplishments to motivate yourself to prepare thoroughly. Set a goal to stay in good physical shape during this term and

especially before midterms and final exams. That means paying attention to the suggestions in this chapter in addition to making sure that you get regular exercise and enough rest and that you have a nutritious diet. If you take care of yourself, you'll find that all the hard work you've put into studying really pays off.

Studying to Make It Stick

The benefits of having a good memory are obvious. In college, your memory will help you retain information and ace tests. After college, the ability to recall names, procedures, presentations, and appointments will save you energy and time and will prevent a lot of embarrassment. Learning how to exercise the "memory muscle" is just as important as using the tools and activities that can enhance memory.

Help Your Memory Help You

For many college courses, remembering concepts and ideas can be much more important than recalling details and facts. One of your primary tasks as a student is to figure out whether the instructor wants you to concentrate on the big-picture concepts and ideas, the smaller individual facts and details, or both types of information. Having these answers will help you focus properly when you study. To embed important ideas in your mind as you review your notes and books, ask yourself these questions:

1. What is the essence of the idea?

2. Why does the idea make sense? What is the logic behind it?

3. How does this idea connect to other ideas in the material?

4. What are some possible arguments against the idea?

The human mind has discovered ingenious ways to remember information. Here are some tips that you may find useful as you're trying to sort out the causes of World War I or remember the steps in a chemistry problem.

- **Pay attention.** This is perhaps the most basic and the most important suggestion. If you are sitting in class thinking about everything except what the instructor is saying, your memory doesn't have a chance. If you are reading and you find that your mind is wandering, you're wasting your study time. Force yourself to focus, and pay attention to what you are hearing and reading.

- **"Overlearn" the material.** Once you think you understand the material you're studying, go over it again to make sure that you'll retain it for a long time. Test yourself or ask someone else to test you. Recite what you're trying to remember aloud and in your own words.

- **Use the Internet.** If you're having trouble remembering what you have learned, Google a key word and try to find interesting details that will engage you in learning more about the subject. Many first-year courses cover such a large amount of material that you'll overlook the more interesting information unless you seek it out and explore it for yourself. As your interest increases, so will your memory.

- **Get the big picture.** Whenever you begin a course, review the syllabus, talk with someone who has already taken the course, and look briefly at all the reading assignments. Having the big picture in mind will help you understand and remember the details of what you're learning. For example, the big picture for a first-year college success class is to give students the knowledge and strategies to be successful in college.

- **Look for connections between your life and the content of your courses.** Finding connections between course material and your daily life can help you remember what you're learning. For example, if you're taking a sociology class and studying marriage and the family, think about how your own family experiences relate to those described in your readings or in the lectures.

- **Look for repeated ideas, themes, and facts as you reread your notes.** These are likely to appear on tests.

- **Think through and say aloud the key concepts and terminology of the course.** The more your brain uses these ideas and words, the more likely you are to remember them.

- **Get organized.** If your desk and computer are organized, you won't waste time trying to remember where you put a particular document or what name you gave a file. And as you rewrite your notes, ordering them in a way that makes sense to you (for example, by topic or by date) will help you learn and remember them.

- **Manage stress.** We don't know how much worry or stress causes us to forget, but most people agree that stress can be a distraction. Healthful, stress-reducing activities such as meditating, exercising, and getting enough sleep are especially important.

Use Review Sheets, Mind Maps, and Flash Cards

To prepare for an exam covering large amounts of material, you need to condense the volume of notes and text pages into manageable study units. Review your materials with these questions in mind: Is this one of the key ideas in the chapter or unit? Will it be on the test? You may prefer to highlight, underline, or annotate the most important ideas, or you may create outlines, lists, or visual maps containing the key ideas.

Use your notes to develop review sheets. Make lists of key terms and ideas that you need to remember. Also, do not underestimate the value of using a recall column from your lecture notes to test yourself or others on information presented in class. A recall column is a narrow space on the left side of your notebook paper that you can use to rewrite the ideas from the lecture that you most want to remember. A mind map is essentially a review sheet with a visual element (see Figure 7.3). Its word and visual

Figure 7.3 ▽ **Sample Mind Map on Listening and Learning in the Classroom**

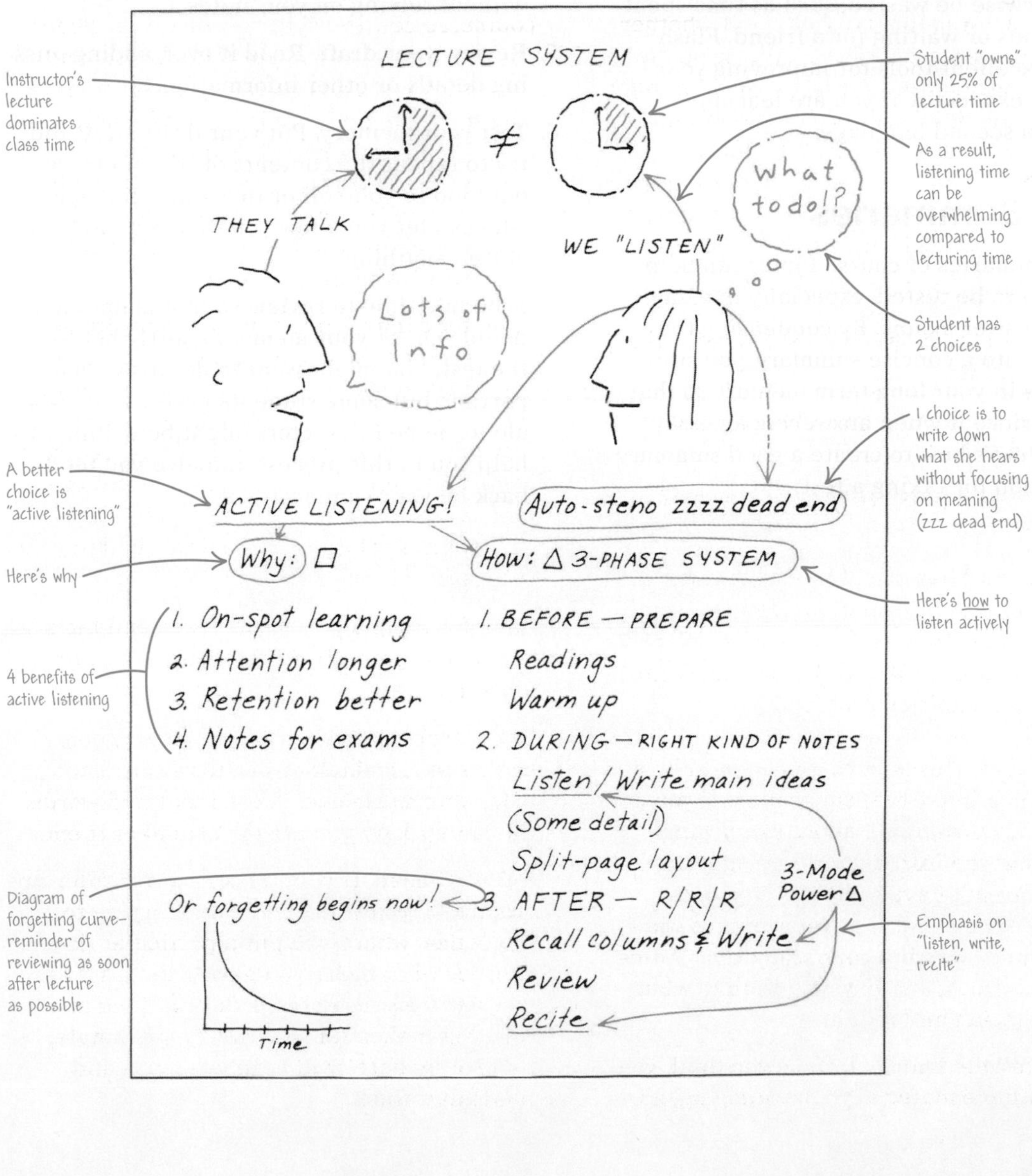

patterns provide you with graphic clues to jog your memory. If you have already used a wheel or branching map to organize your reading, you'll find the mind map offers you even more opportunity to be creative—to use art, color, and graphics to map your learning. You can also use these maps when you're studying several chapters for a test. The maps can help you make connections between the concepts in each chapter. Because the mind map approach is visual, it helps many students recall information easily.

In addition to using review sheets and mind maps, you may want to create flash cards. An advantage of flash cards is that you can keep them in a pocket or backpack and pull them out anywhere to study. Apps such as Chegg Flashcards and StudyBlue enable you to create flash cards on your electronic devices. Flash cards can help you make good use of time that might otherwise be wasted, such as time spent riding the bus or waiting for a friend. Flash cards are excellent tools for improving your vocabulary, especially if you are learning English as a second language.

Create Summaries

Writing summaries of course topics can help you prepare to be tested, especially in essay and short-answer exams. By condensing the main ideas into a concise summary, you store information in your long-term memory so that you can retrieve it when answering an essay question. Here's how to create a good summary in preparation for taking a test:

1. **Read the assigned material, your class notes, and your instructor's PowerPoint slides.** Underline or mark main ideas as you go, make explanatory notes or comments about the material, or make an outline on a separate sheet of paper. Predict test questions based on your active reading.

2. **Make connections between main points and key supporting details.** Reread to identify each main point and the supporting evidence. Create an outline in the process.

3. **Review underlined material.** Put those ideas into your own words and in a logical order.

4. **Write your ideas in a draft.** In the first sentence, state the purpose of your summary. Follow this statement with each main point and its supporting ideas. See how much of the draft you can develop from memory without relying on your notes.

5. **Review your draft.** Read it over, adding missing details or other information.

6. **Test your memory.** Put your draft away and try to repeat the contents of the summary out loud to yourself or to a study partner who can let you know whether you have forgotten anything.

7. **Schedule time to review your summary and double-check your memory shortly before the test.** You might want to do this with a partner, but some students prefer to review alone. Some instructors might be willing to help you in this process and give you feedback on your summaries. ■

Taking Tests and Exams

Throughout your college career, you will take tests in many different formats, in many subject areas, and with many different types of questions. Some test-taking tips, however, apply to nearly all test situations.

- **Write your name on the test.** Unless you're directed not to, write your name on the test and on the answer sheet.

- **Analyze, ask, and stay calm.** Read all the directions so that you understand what to do. Ask the instructor or exam monitor for clarification if anything confuses you. Be confident. Don't panic.

- **Use your time wisely.** Quickly survey the entire test, and decide how much time you will spend on each section. Be aware of the point values of different sections of the test.

- **Answer the easy questions first.** Expect that you'll be puzzled by some questions. Make a note to come back to them later. If different sections consist of different types of questions (such as multiple-choice, short-answer, and essay), complete the types you are most comfortable with first. Be sure to leave enough time for any essays.

- **If you feel yourself starting to panic or go blank, stop whatever you are doing.** Take a long, deep breath and slowly exhale. Remind yourself that you know the material and can do well on this test. Then take another deep breath. If necessary, go to another section of the test and come back later to the item that triggered your anxiety.

- **If you finish early, don't leave.** Stay and check your work for errors. Reread the directions one last time. If you are using a Scantron answer sheet, make sure that the question number on the answer sheet corresponds to the number of the question on the test and that all your answer bubbles are filled in accurately and completely.

Be Ready for Every Kind of Pitch

Just like a batter in baseball has to be ready for any pitch—fastball, curve, slider, changeup—on test day you have to be ready for whatever may be coming your way. Some test-taking tips depend on the type of exam you are taking or the type of test questions that you have to answer within the exam. Different types of exam questions call for different strategies.

Essay questions. Essay exams include questions that require students to write a few paragraphs in response. Some college instructors have a strong preference for essay exams, for a simple reason: They promote critical thinking, whereas other types of exams tend to be exercises in memorization. To succeed on essay exams, follow these guidelines:

1. **Budget your exam time.** Quickly survey the entire exam, and note the questions that are easiest for you to answer, along with their point values. Take a moment to weigh their values, estimate the approximate time you should allot to each question, and write the time beside each item number. Be sure you understand whether you must answer every question or choose among the questions provided.

2. **Actively read the whole question.** Many well-prepared students write a good answer to a question that was not asked—when that happens, they may lose points or even fail the exam. Many other students write a good answer to only part of the question—they also may lose points or even fail the exam.

3. **Develop a brief outline of your answer before you begin to write.** First make sure that your outline responds to all parts of the question. Then use your first paragraph to introduce the main points, and use subsequent paragraphs to describe each point in more depth.

If you begin to lose your concentration, you will be glad to have the outline to help you regain your focus. If you find that you are running out of time and cannot complete an essay question, at least provide an outline of key ideas. Instructors usually assign points based on your coverage of the main topics from the material. Thus you will usually earn more points by responding to all parts of the question briefly than by addressing just one aspect of the question in detail.

4. **Write concise, organized answers.** Some students answer essay questions by quickly writing down everything they know on the topic. Long answers are not necessarily good answers. Answers that are too general, unfocused, or disorganized may not earn high scores.

5. **Know the key task words in essay questions.** The following key task words appear frequently on essay tests: *analyze, compare, contrast, criticize/critique, define, describe, discuss, evaluate, explain, interpret, justify, narrate, outline, prove, review, summarize,* and *trace.* Take time to learn them so that you can answer essay questions accurately and precisely.

TRY IT!

MANAGING TIME ▷ Time Flies—Even during an Essay Test

Have you ever taken an essay test or exam and the instructor called "time" before you had finished all your answers? Don't let this happen to you. Remember that writing long responses to the first few questions can be a costly error, because doing so takes up precious time that you may need to answer the questions at the end of the exam. Divide the total time by the number of questions, wear a watch to monitor your time as you move through the exam, and remember to give yourself enough time at the end for a quick review.

Multiple-choice questions. Multiple-choice questions provide any number of possible answers, often between three and five; the answer choices are usually numbered (1, 2, 3, 4, . . .) or lettered (a, b, c, d, . . .), and the test taker is supposed to select the correct or best answer for each question. Preparing for multiple-choice tests requires you to actively review all the course material. Reciting from flash cards,

summary sheets, mind maps, or the recall column in your lecture notes is a good way to review.

Take advantage of the many cues that multiple-choice questions include. Note terms in the question such as *not, except,* and *but* so that the answer you choose fits the question. Also, read each answer choice carefully; be suspicious of choices that use words such as *always, never,* and *only.* These choices are often (but not always) incorrect. Often the correct answer is the option that is the most comprehensive.

In some multiple-choice questions, the first part of the question is an incomplete sentence (called the stem), and each answer choice completes the sentence. In these questions, any answer choices that do not use correct grammar are usually incorrect. For example, in Figure 7.4, "Margaret Mead was an" is the stem. Which of the four options is grammatically wrong and can be ruled out?

To avoid becoming confused by answer choices that sound alike, predict the answer to each question before reading the options. Then choose the answer that best matches your prediction. If a question totally confuses you, place a check mark in the margin and come back to it later. Sometimes a question later in the exam will provide a clue for the one you are unsure about. If you have absolutely no idea, look for an answer that at least has some pieces of information. If there is no penalty for guessing, fill in an answer for every question, even if it is sometimes just a guess. If there is a penalty for guessing, don't just choose an answer at random; leaving an answer blank might be a wiser choice. Finally, if you have time at the end, always go back and double-check that you chose the right answer for the right question, especially if you are using a Scantron form.

Fill-in-the-blank questions. Fill-in-the-blank questions consist of a phrase, sentence, or paragraph with a blank space indicating where the student should provide the missing word or words. In many ways, preparing for fill-in-the-blank questions is similar to getting ready for multiple-choice items, but fill-in-the-blank questions can be harder because you do not have a choice of possible answers right in front of you. Not all fill-in-the-blank questions are constructed the same way. Sometimes the answer consists of a single word, while at other times the instructor is

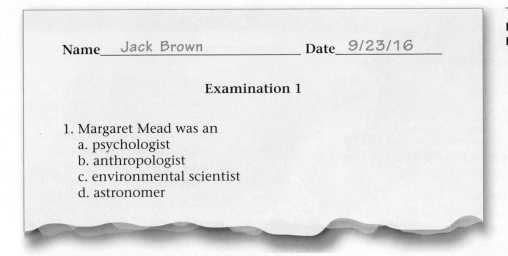

Figure 7.4 ◁ **Example of a Multiple-Choice Question**

Name ___Jack Brown_____ Date __9/23/16____

Examination 1

1. Margaret Mead was an
   a. psychologist
   b. anthropologist
   c. environmental scientist
   d. astronomer

looking for a phrase. In the latter case, there may be a series of blanks to give you a clue about the number of words in the answer, or there may be just one long blank. If you are unsure, ask the instructor whether the answer is supposed to be one word or more than one word.

True/false questions. True/false questions ask students to determine whether a statement is accurate or not. For the statement to be true, every detail in the statement must be true. As in multiple-choice tests, statements containing words such as *always, never,* and *only* tend to be false, whereas less definite terms such as *often* or *frequently* suggest that the statement may be

true. Read through the entire exam to see if information in one question will help you answer another. Do not second-guess what you know or doubt your answers just because a sequence of questions appears to be all true or all false.

Matching questions. Matching questions are set up with terms in one column and descriptions in the other, and you must make the proper pairings. Before matching any items, review all the terms and descriptions. Match those terms you are sure of first. As you do so, cross out both the term and its description, and then use the process of elimination to assist you in matching the remaining items.

You Bombed a Test—Now What?

Has your college experience already included bombing a test—maybe even a test that you studied hard for? You're not alone. Almost all first-year students are occasionally stunned by a bad test grade that they didn't expect. What can you do now? First and foremost, be sure to review the test to understand what questions you missed and why. If you throw the test in the trash without figuring out what went wrong, you lose a golden opportunity to learn from your mistakes (and it's always possible that your instructor made an error in grading or that there was a glitch if the test was machine-scored). Be sure to make an appointment with your instructor to discuss the test and get his or her advice on how you could do better next time. You might be embarrassed and tempted to avoid your instructor, but that's not a smart move. When you take the initiative to talk over your test, find out what

you misunderstood, and get the clarification you need, your instructor will know that you're a serious student.

Did the test you bombed cover in-class lecture or discussion material more than what you read in your text, or vice versa? Think about how you are studying now. Are you spending too much time studying the wrong material? And did you honestly put in enough study time, or did you think you could do well by only skimming the material? Does your personal study regimen include working alone with no distractions and working with other students? Both techniques have value, and over time you'll figure out what works best for you.

Finally, once you have analyzed why you earned a poor test grade, be resilient—bounce back! Don't let a bad grade get you down. Make some changes in what and how you study, and find the motivation to succeed on your next test.

△ **Online and On Target**
What strategies can this student use to succeed on this online test? His instructor allows students to reference their notes and the textbook as needed during tests. OJO_Images/istock.

Online Tests

Many students take online tests in traditional, hybrid, and online courses. Online tests might include any of the question types described above. Don't let these tests trip you up. Avoid rookie mistakes by using these strategies:

1. **Don't wait until the last minute to study.** Whether the online test is part of a self-paced online course or a face-to-face course, start a study group (either in person or online) as far in advance as possible.

2. **Resist the temptation to look online for answers.** The answer you pick might not be what your instructor is looking for. It's much better to check your notes to see what you were taught in class.

3. **Collaborate if it is allowed.** If your instructor doesn't forbid collaboration on tests, open up an instant message window with a fellow student. Take the test together, and take it early.

4. **Don't get distracted.** When you're taking an online exam, it's easy to fall prey to real-life diversions like Twitter, Netflix, or a sudden urge to rearrange your closet. Whatever you do, take the test seriously. Go somewhere quiet where you can concentrate—not Starbucks. A quiet, remote spot in the library is ideal. You might try wearing noise-canceling headphones!

5. **Be aware that you might lose your Internet connection in the middle of the test, and plan accordingly.** To be on the safe side, type all your answers and essays into a Word document. Then leave time at the end to cut and paste them into the test itself.

6. **Use any extra time wisely.** Take a few minutes to obsessively check your answers and spelling. Your online test platform may not have spellcheck. (Of course, double-checking your answers is good advice for traditional tests, too.) ■

Academic Honesty and Misconduct

Imagine what our world would be like if researchers reported fraudulent results that were then used to develop new machines or medical treatments or to build bridges, airplanes, or subway systems. Integrity is a cornerstone of higher education, and activities that compromise that integrity damage everyone: your country, your community, your college or university, your classmates, and yourself.

Cheating

Institutions vary widely in how they define broad terms such as *lying* or *cheating*.

One university defines cheating as "intentionally using or attempting to use unauthorized materials, information, notes, study aids, or other devices . . . [including] unauthorized communication of information during an academic exercise." This would apply to looking over a classmate's shoulder for an answer, using a calculator when it is not authorized, obtaining or discussing an exam (or individual questions from an exam) without permission, copying someone else's lab notes, purchasing a term paper over the Internet, watching the movie version of a book instead of reading it, and duplicating computer files.

△ **Exam Day—Give It Your Best**

Whether or not your exams are monitored by the instructor, be sure to do your own work and protect it from the wandering eyes of others. Put away all materials, including your mobile devices, which will likely arouse the suspicion of instructors. Chris Ryan/Getty Images.

Plagiarism

Plagiarism, or taking another person's ideas or work and presenting them as your own, is especially intolerable in an academic culture. Just as taking someone else's property constitutes physical theft, taking credit for someone else's ideas constitutes intellectual theft. On most tests, you don't have to credit specific sources. In written reports and papers, however, you must give credit any time you use (1) another person's actual words; (2) another person's ideas or theories, even if you don't quote the person directly; or (3) information that is not considered common knowledge.

Many schools prohibit certain activities in addition to lying, cheating, unauthorized assistance, and plagiarism. Some examples of prohibited behaviors are intentionally inventing information or results, earning credit more than once for the same piece of academic work without permission, giving your work or exam answers to another student to copy during the actual exam or before that exam is given to another section, giving or selling a paper you have written to another student, and bribing someone in exchange for any kind of academic advantage. Most schools also prohibit helping or attempting to help another student commit a dishonest act.

TRY IT!

MAKING DECISIONS ▷ Ignorance Is No Excuse

Make a decision to learn about the rules of academic honesty for each of your classes by asking questions in class or by setting up appointments with your instructors during their office hours. Some rules will be the same for all classes; others will depend on how the course is taught or how students are expected to study. Pleading ignorance of the rules is not a good strategy. Having all the information at hand each term will allow you to make good decisions with regard to maintaining your academic integrity.

Consequences of Cheating and Plagiarism

Although some students may seem to be getting away with cheating or plagiarizing, such behaviors can have severe and life-changing consequences. In recent years college students have been suspended or expelled for cheating on examinations or plagiarizing major papers, and some college graduates have even had their degrees revoked. Writers and journalists such as Jayson Blair, formerly of *The New York Times,* and Stephen Glass, formerly of the *New Republic,* have lost their jobs and their journalistic careers after their plagiarism was discovered. Even college presidents have occasionally been guilty of using the words of others in writing and speaking. Such discoveries can result not only in embarrassment and shame but also in lawsuits and criminal actions.

Because plagiarism can be a problem on college campuses, faculty members are now using electronic systems such as www.turnitin.com to identify passages in student papers that have been plagiarized. Many instructors routinely check their students' papers to make sure that the writing is original. So even though the temptation to cheat or plagiarize might be strong, the chance of possibly getting a better grade isn't worth misrepresenting yourself or your knowledge and suffering the potential consequences.

Reducing the Likelihood of Academic Dishonesty

To avoid becoming intentionally or unintentionally involved in academic misconduct, consider the reasons why it could happen:

- **Ignorance.** Some students are unaware of the rules for academic honesty in each class. In a survey at the University of South Carolina, 20 percent of students incorrectly thought that buying a term paper wasn't cheating. Forty percent thought that using a test file (a collection of actual tests from previous terms) was fair behavior. Sixty percent thought that it was acceptable to get answers from someone who had taken the exam earlier in the same or a prior term.

- **Cultural and campus differences.** In other countries and on some U.S. campuses, students are encouraged to review past exams as practice exercises. Some student government associations maintain test files for student use. Make sure you know the policy on your campus.

- **A belief that grades are all that matter.** This might reflect our society's competitive atmosphere. It also might be the result of pressure from parents, peers, or teachers. In truth, grades mean nothing if you have cheated to earn them. Even if your grades help you get a job, what you have actually learned is what will help you keep the job and be promoted. If you haven't learned what you need to know, you won't be ready to work in your chosen field.

- **Unclear boundaries and concern that you'll seem rude.** If another student asks you to help him or her cheat, clearly state your boundaries. Tell the student that you both would risk failing the assignment, failing the course, or worse. Protect your paper during an exam. During class or outside class, resist showing another student your homework or a major paper you have written, unless your judgment says that doing so presents a good opportunity for student collaboration and you can ensure that your work doesn't leave your sight. Turning someone down can be hard because so many of us are instinctively

polite and helpful, but assure yourself that saying no is the right thing to do.

- **Lack of preparation or inability to manage your time and activities.** If your lack of preparation is a time-management problem, be honest with yourself and unlearn old habits of procrastination. If you've done your best and still need extra time, ask an instructor to extend a deadline so that a project can be done well.

- **Feeling overwhelmed and alone.** Find out where you can obtain assistance with study skills, time management, and test taking. If your methods are in good shape but the content of the course is too difficult, consult your instructor, join a study group, or visit your campus learning center or tutorial service. As a last resort, consider withdrawing from the course. Your college will have a deadline for dropping a course without penalty. But before withdrawing, be sure to talk with your academic adviser or instructor.

- **Impossibly high standards of family and friends.** Rather than giving in to unfair pressure from others to achieve impossibly high standards, stick to your own goals. If you are being pressured to enter a career that does not interest you, sit down with a counselor or career services professional to explore alternatives. ■

Chapter Review

Steps to Success:
Taking Exams & Tests

○ **Start preparing for test taking the very first day of the course.** Classes early in the term are the most important ones *not* to miss.

○ **Learn as much as you can about the type of tests you will be taking.** You will study differently for an essay exam than you will for a multiple-choice test.

○ **Prepare physically through proper sleep, diet, and exercise.** These behaviors are as important as studying the actual material. You may not control what is on the exams, but you can control your physical readiness to do your best.

○ **Prepare emotionally by being relaxed and confident.** Confidence comes from the knowledge that you are well prepared and know the material.

○ **Seek help from your counseling center if you experience severe test anxiety.** Professionals can help you deal with this problem.

○ **Develop a systematic plan of preparation for every test.** Be specific about when you are going to study, how long you'll study, and what material you will cover.

○ **Join a study group and participate conscientiously and regularly.** Students who join study groups perform better on tests. Studying with a group is a habit you should practice.

○ **Never cheat or plagiarize.** Experience the satisfaction that comes from learning and doing your own work and from knowing that you don't have to worry about getting caught or using material that may be incorrect.

○ **Learn what constitutes cheating and plagiarism on your campus so that you don't inadvertently do either.** If you are not clear about your institution's policies, ask your instructors or the professionals in your campus learning center or writing center.

Applying what you've learned . . .

Now that you have read and discussed this chapter, consider how you can apply what you have learned to your academic and personal lives. The following prompts will help you reflect on the chapter material and its relevance to you both now and in the future.

1. Identify your next test or exam. What class is it for? When is it scheduled (morning, afternoon, or evening)? What type of test will it be (problem-solving, multiple-choice, open-book, etc.)? List the specific strategies described in this chapter that will help you prepare for and take this test.

2. Do you know how your institution or your different instructors define cheating or plagiarism? Look up the definitions of these terms in your institution's student handbook, and read about the penalties for students who are dishonest. Then check your syllabi for class-specific guidelines. If you still have questions about what behaviors are or are not acceptable in a particular class, check with your instructor.

Use Your Resources

GO TO ▷ The learning center: If you need help solving your academic problems. The best students, good students who want to be the best students, and students with academic difficulties all use learning centers and tutoring services. These services are offered by both full-time professionals and highly skilled student tutors.

GO TO ▷ Your college's counseling services center: If you need help dealing with test anxiety. College and university counseling centers offer a wide array of services, often including workshops and individual or group counseling.

GO TO ▷ Fellow college students: If you need help staying on track academically. Seek the help of classmates who are serious, purposeful, and directed. Or you can secure a tutor or join a study group.

GO ONLINE TO ▷ The Academic Center for Excellence, University of Illinois at Chicago (www.uic.edu/depts/ace/strategies.shtml): If you need help studying and preparing for exams. This Web site provides a list of tips to help you prepare for exams. Do your own search using terms like "test preparation and academic support" to locate other online resources.

NOW... How do you measure up?

1. To do well on exams, students should maintain good eating, sleeping, and exercise habits, especially before the exam date.
   - ○ Agree
   - ○ Don't Know
   - ○ Disagree

2. In order to prevent last-minute cramming, it's important to begin studying for an exam at least a week in advance.
   - ○ Agree
   - ○ Don't Know
   - ○ Disagree

3. Doing well on essay exam questions requires reading each question carefully and responding with complete and precise answers.
   - ○ Agree
   - ○ Don't Know
   - ○ Disagree

4. I understand clearly how cheating is defined in each of my classes.
   - ○ Agree
   - ○ Don't Know
   - ○ Disagree

How do your answers here compare to your responses to the quiz you took at the start of the chapter? Which sections of this chapter left a strong impression on you? What strategies for taking exams and tests have you started to use? Are they working? What other strategies will you commit to trying?

LaunchPad
macmillan learning

LaunchPad Solo for College Success is a great resource. Go online to master concepts using the LearningCurve study tool and much more. **macmillanhighered.com/collegesuccessmedia**

129
College-Level Thinking

130
Developing Strong Thinking Skills

134
Applying Your Critical-Thinking Skills

138
Bloom's Taxonomy and Your First Year of College

Thinking in College

WunderfulPixel/Shutterstock

LaunchPad
macmillan learning

To access the LearningCurve study tool, Video Tools, and more, go to *LaunchPad Solo for College Success*. **macmillan highered.com/ collegesuccessmedia**

The most important skill you'll acquire in college is the ability to think for yourself. Learning to think—using the mind to produce ideas, opinions, decisions, and memories—is part of normal human development. Just as our bodies grow, so does our ability to think logically and rationally about abstract concepts. Courses in every discipline will encourage you to ask questions, to sort through different information and ideas, and to form and defend your own opinions.

You may have heard the term *critical thinking* before. The term refers to thoughtful consideration of the information, ideas, and arguments that you encounter in order to guide belief and action—this is the kind of

thinking you will do in college, and it's what this chapter is all about. We will provide you with valuable strategies to develop strong thinking skills, and we will explain how developing and applying your critical-thinking skills can make the search for answers an exciting and rewarding adventure. Finally, we will help you understand why the ability to think is one of the most important and desirable skills for succeeding in college and the workplace and for living in a democracy. When employers say they want workers who can locate and analyze information, draw conclusions, and present the information convincingly to others, they are seeking employees who are good thinkers.

How do you measure up?

1. Even when people are irritating, it's important to try to listen to what they have to say.
   - ○ Agree
   - ○ Don't Know
   - ○ Disagree

2. There can be more than one right answer to almost any question.
   - ○ Agree
   - ○ Don't Know
   - ○ Disagree

3. It's important not to allow emotions to get in the way of making the right decision.
   - ○ Agree
   - ○ Don't Know
   - ○ Disagree

4. Good thinkers listen to all sides of an argument before taking a position.
   - ○ Agree
   - ○ Don't Know
   - ○ Disagree

Review the items you marked "Don't Know" or "Disagree." Pay special attention to these topics in this chapter—you will find motivating strategies to develop in these areas. A follow-up quiz at the end of the chapter will prompt you to consider what you have learned.

Seeing Things in New Ways

△ **Tamara Jacobs**

bikeriderlondon/Shutterstock.

For a week before our first college debate team meeting, I had nightmares about being thrown in the deep end with some horrendous topic, like whether terrorism can be justified. When the day arrived, our team adviser, Mr. Randall, gave us a subject I could really work with: capital punishment. Even better, he put me in the "pro" camp. I mean, how can you argue against executing violent murderers?

"Be sure to set aside your opinions on the subject and use your critical-thinking skills," Mr. Randall said. "Remember: You'll be arguing only one side of the issue. But you'll need to understand both sides if you want to outthink your opponent."

Fast-forward to the next debate meeting: "So I've been studying both sides of the issue," I told Mr. Randall. "It turns out that it's more expensive to put people to death in the United States than it is to keep them locked up. Also, many studies show that the death penalty doesn't prevent murders from happening. What's worse, a lot of people who've been put to death turned out to be innocent . . . So now I don't know what to think."

"Don't worry, Tamara," said Mr. Randall. "That just means that your mind is working—and that's a good thing. It sounds like it's going to be a great debate."

Can you think of a time when learning more about an issue caused you to question your prior opinions? Did you, like Tamara, feel confused about "what to think"?

College-Level Thinking

In college the level of thinking that your instructors expect from you exceeds the kind of thinking you probably did in high school, both in terms of the questions that are asked and the answers that are expected. If a high school teacher asked, "What are the three branches of the U.S. government?" there was only one acceptable answer: "legislative, executive, and judicial." A college instructor, on the other hand, might ask, "Under what circumstances might conflicts arise among the three branches of government, and what does this tell you about the democratic process?" There is no single or simple answer, and that's the point of higher education. Questions with complicated answers will require you to think deeply. The shift to this higher or deeper level of thinking can be an adjustment—it might even catch you off guard and cause you some stress.

> ❝Questions with complicated answers will require you to think deeply.❞

Important questions usually do not have simple answers, and to answer them well, you will have to discover many ways of thinking and to become comfortable with uncertainty. You also must be willing to challenge assumptions and conclusions, even when they are presented by experts. Rather than just taking in information, studying it, and then recalling it for a test, in college you'll go far beyond these skills and gain the confidence to arrive at your own conclusions—to think for yourself. Educational researchers describe this process as "constructing" knowledge for yourself rather than merely "receiving" knowledge from others.

> ❝We can also define critical thinking as the search for truth.❞

The Nobel Prize–winning economist Daniel Kahneman describes two types of thinking: "fast thinking" and "slow thinking." He characterizes fast thinking as automatic, emotional, stereotypic, and subconscious. Slow thinking takes more effort and attention and is more logical, rational, and deep.[1] By improving your slower-thinking abilities, you will become a better learner and problem solver.

At the start of the chapter, we described critical thinking as thoughtful consideration of the information, ideas, and arguments that you encounter in order to guide belief and action. We can also define critical thinking as the search for truth. It is similar to slow thinking as described by Kahneman, but it also emphasizes the importance of evaluating information to guide belief and action—this is the kind of thinking you will do in college. ∎

TRY IT!

FEELING CONNECTED ▷ **Reflecting on How You Think**

Come up with examples from this term of instances when you were asked to do deep or slow thinking in one or more of your courses and to arrive at your own conclusions. Has it caught you off guard to be asked questions with complicated answers? Discuss your experiences with your classmates.

[1] Daniel Kahneman, *Thinking, Fast and Slow* (New York: Farrar, Straus and Giroux, 2013).

Developing Strong Thinking Skills

A high-priority goal for all colleges is to develop students' thinking and decision-making skills. As you become more competent and confident as a thinker, you will contribute to the larger society by helping solve community and national problems.

Challenge Assumptions and Beliefs

We develop an understanding of information and issues we encounter based on our values, worldviews, and family backgrounds; then we form opinions and perspectives. Many of our beliefs are based on gut feelings or blind acceptance of things we have heard, read, or been told—to some extent, this is unavoidable. Some assumptions, or beliefs we accept as true, should be examined more thoughtfully, especially if they will influence an important decision. College is a time to challenge and to think critically about ideas we have always had.

Ask Questions

An important step in learning to think critically is to be curious. This involves asking questions. You can begin by asking yourself questions about beliefs and assumptions that you hold in order to dig deeper into why you hold them. Instead of accepting statements and claims made by others at face value, question them. Here are a few suggestions:

- What approach should you take when you come across an idea or a statement that you consider interesting, confusing, or suspicious?

- Do you fully understand what is being said, or do you need to pause and think what it means?

- Do you agree with the statement? Why or why not?

- Can the statement or idea be interpreted in more than one way?

Don't stop there.

- Ask whether you can trust the person or group supporting the idea or making a particular claim and whether there is enough evidence to back up that claim.

- Ask who might agree or disagree and why.

- Ask how the new idea relates to what you already know.

- Think about where you might find more information about the subject, and what you could do with what you learn.

- Ask yourself about the effects of accepting a new idea as truth.
  - Will you have to change or give up what you have believed in for a long time?
  - Will accepting the new idea require you to do something differently?
  - Should you try to bring other people around to a new way of thinking?

Consider Multiple Points of View and Draw Conclusions

Before you draw any conclusions about the validity of information or opinions, it's important to consider more than one point of view. You might encounter differences of opinion in college reading assignments or as you do research for a project. Your own belief system will influence how you interpret information. For example, consider your own ideas about the cost of college in the United States. American citizens, politicians, and others often voice opinions on private versus public schools. What kind of higher education do *you* think is best, and *why* do you hold this viewpoint?

The more ideas you consider, the better your thinking will become. Ultimately, you will discover not only that it is OK to change your mind but also that a willingness to do so is the mark of a reasonable, educated person. After considering multiple viewpoints and drawing conclusions, the next step is to maintain or revise your own viewpoints based on evidence and facts. Drawing conclusions based on your consideration of opinions and evidence involves looking at the outcome of your inquiry in a more demanding, critical way. If you have found new evidence, what does that new evidence show? Do your original beliefs hold up, or do they need to be modified or abandoned? Most important, consider what you would need to do or say to persuade someone else that your ideas are valid.

Make Arguments

What does the word *argument* mean to you? If you're like most people, the first image it brings up might be an ugly fight you had with a friend, a yelling match you witnessed on the street, or a heated disagreement between family members. While these unpleasant confrontations are arguments, the word also refers to a

TRY IT!

SETTING GOALS ▷ **Make Up Your Own Mind**

What would motivate you to draw your own conclusions based on evidence rather than to blindly follow others? What if you were faced with a decision that could affect your health? For instance, if you were out with friends who were trying e-cigarettes, and they were attempting to persuade you that e-cigarettes aren't dangerous like conventional cigarettes are, would you risk believing them without checking further? Be motivated to develop an attitude of healthy skepticism. That doesn't mean you have to be rude or combative. Instead, you can request more time to ask questions, do research, or think carefully about a decision before following the crowd. It never works to blame others when you blindly follow them over a cliff.

calm, reasoned effort to persuade someone of the value of an idea.

Arguments are central to academic study, work, and life in general. Scholarly articles, business memos, and requests for spending money all have something in common: The effective ones make a general claim, provide reasons to support it, and back up those reasons with evidence. That's what argument is.

It's important to consider multiple arguments in tackling new ideas and complex questions, but remember that all arguments are not equally valid. Whether examining an argument or making one, a good critical thinker is careful to ensure that ideas are presented in an understandable, logical way and to assess whether those making the arguments have presented enough information to justify their positions.

Examine Evidence

Another important part of thinking critically is checking that the evidence supporting an argument—whether someone else's or your own—is of the highest possible quality. To do that, simply ask a few questions about the argument:

- What idea am I being asked to accept?

- Are good and sufficient reasons given to support the overall claim?

- Are those reasons backed up with evidence in the form of facts, statistics, and quotations?

- Does the evidence support the conclusions?

- Is the argument based on logical reasoning, or does it appeal mainly to emotions?

- Can I think of any counterarguments, and if so, what facts can I use as proof?

- What do I know about the person or organization making the argument?

If you have evaluated the evidence used in support of a claim and are still uncertain, it's best to keep looking for more evidence. Drawing on questionable evidence for an argument has a tendency to backfire. A little persistence will help you find better sources.

PENGUINS ARE BLACK AND WHITE. SOME OLD TV SHOWS ARE BLACK AND WHITE. THEREFORE, SOME PENGUINS ARE OLD TV SHOWS.

GLASBERGEN

Logic: another thing that penguins aren't very good at.

△ **Logic That Just Doesn't Fly**
This cartoon is an obvious example of faulty reasoning. Some conversations or arguments tend to include reasoning like this. Can you think of an illogical leap like this one that someone used in an argument with you? How did you use critical thinking to counter it? Or did your emotions get the best of you? © Randy Glasbergen.

Recognize and Avoid Faulty Reasoning

Although logical reasoning is essential to solving any problem, you need to go one step further to make sure that an argument hasn't been compromised by faulty reasoning. Here are some of the most common missteps—logical fallacies or flaws in reasoning—that people make in their use of logic:

- **Attacking the person.** Arguing against other people's positions or attacking their arguments is perfectly acceptable. Going after their personalities, however, is not OK.

- **Begging.** "Please, officer, don't give me a ticket! If you do, I'll lose my license, and I have five little children to feed, and I won't be able to feed them if I can't drive my truck." None of the driver's statements offer any evidence, in any legal sense, as to why this person shouldn't be given a ticket. An appeal to facts and reason would be more effective: "I fed the meter, but it didn't register the coins. Since the machine is broken, I'm sure you'll agree that I don't deserve a ticket."

- **Appealing to false authority.** Citing true authorities can offer valuable support for an argument. However, we see examples of false authority all the time in advertising: Sports stars who are not doctors, dieticians, or nutritionists urge us to eat a certain brand of food; famous actors and singers who are not dermatologists extol the medical benefits of a costly remedy for acne.

- **Jumping on a bandwagon.** Sometimes we are more likely to believe something that many others also believe. Even accepted truths can turn out to be wrong, however. At one time nearly everyone believed that the earth was flat, until someone came up with evidence that it was round.

- **Assuming that something is true because it hasn't been proven false.** If you go to a library or look online, you'll find dozens of books detailing close encounters with flying saucers or ghosts. These books describe the people who had such encounters as honest and trustworthy. Because no one could disprove the claims of the witnesses, the events are said to have actually occurred. Even in science, few things are ever proved completely false, but evidence can be discredited.

- **Falling victim to false cause.** A basis for many superstitions is that just because one event followed another, the first event must have caused the second. The ancient Chinese once believed that they could make the sun reappear after an eclipse by striking a large gong, because it had happened once before. Most effects, however, are usually the result of several causes. Don't be satisfied with easy cause-and-effect claims; they are rarely correct.

- **Making hasty generalizations.** If someone selected a green marble from a barrel containing a hundred marbles, you wouldn't assume that the next marble drawn from the barrel would also be green. However, if you were given fifty draws from the barrel and you drew only green marbles, you would be more willing to conclude that the next marble drawn would be green, too. Reaching a conclusion based on the opinion of one source is like assuming that all the marbles in the barrel are green after pulling out only one marble.

- **Accepting a slippery slope argument.** "If we allow tuition to increase, the next thing we know, it will be $20,000 per term." Such an argument is an example of "slippery slope" thinking.

Fallacies like these can slip into even the most careful reasoning. One false claim can derail an entire argument, so be on the lookout for weak logic in what you read and write. Never forget that accurate reasoning is a key factor in succeeding in college and in life. ■

© Randy Glasbergen.
www.glasbergen.com

◁ **Comparison Shopping**
Use shopping to practice your critical-thinking abilities. You need to ask the right questions to find out if a deal is really a deal. © Randy Glasbergen.

Applying Your Critical-Thinking Skills

As is true for any skill that you want to develop, you need to practice thinking critically in order to get good at it. Now that you are aware of what good thinking is, and isn't, you can look for opportunities to improve.

Collaborate

One way to become a better critical thinker is to practice with other people. By getting feedback from others, you can see the possible flaws in your own position or approach. Whether debating an issue in a political science class or making a dress in a fashion design class, learn to appreciate how fellow students and instructors bring their own life experiences, personal taste, knowledge, and expertise to the table. There are often several ways of approaching any task. Getting input from others can help make your finished product a masterpiece.

Researchers who investigate student thinking across grade levels find that critical thinking and collaboration go hand in hand. Students are more likely to exercise their critical-thinking abilities when they are confronted by the experiences and opinions of others; that is why study groups are so important in college. Having more than one student involved in the learning process generates a greater number of ideas and discussions that can challenge your thinking and assumptions, thereby improving your critical-thinking skills. Creative brainstorming and group discussion encourage original thought. These habits also teach participants to consider alternative points of view carefully and to express and defend their own ideas clearly.

As you leave college and enter the working world, you will find that collaboration—not only with people in your work setting but also with others around the globe—is essential to almost any career you may pursue. Whether in person or through electronic communication, teamwork improves your ability to think critically.

Be Creative

Another way to develop strong thinking skills is to take advantage of opportunities to be creative. Our society is full of creative individuals who think outside the box or simply ask questions that others are not asking. Many have achieved fame by using their thinking skills and actions to change the world. As you move through your other first-year courses such as sociology, psychology, history, or math, you will encounter assignments that will encourage you to be creative. You will also learn about people who have used their creative-thinking abilities to find a sense of purpose and to become world changers in academic and nonacademic areas.

Learn to Problem-Solve

Your success both in college and in your future life will depend on how well you make decisions and solve problems. Making decisions and solving problems involve thinking logically, weighing evidence, and formulating conclusions. Here are some examples of situations that you might experience in college that will require these skills:

- Deciding what sources are most important to include in your research paper

- Finding a way to negotiate a problem situation with your roommate

- Determining the kinds of exercise you need to maintain a healthy fitness level and avoid weight gain

- Understanding the advantages and disadvantages of accessing information sources, including Facebook, Twitter feeds, CNN, *USA Today, The New York Times*, the satirical newspaper, the *Onion,* and your school newspaper.

In addition to these situations, the college years also represent a time in your life when you get to know yourself and what you believe. You will begin to develop your own positions on societal and political issues, learn more about what is important to you, and develop into a contributing citizen of your country and also the world.

In college you'll be exposed to ideas and often-conflicting opinions about contemporary issues such as same-sex marriage, military operations, immigration, global human rights, public education in the United States, and student loan debt and loan forgiveness. Before accepting any opinion on any issue as "the truth," look for evidence that supports different positions on these debates. In fact, look for opportunities to participate in such debates. ∎

◁ **Get a Second Opinion and a Third**
Each person brings his or her own perspective and life experience to a project—whether answering an essay question in an English class, doing a chemistry lab, framing a roof in a carpentry class, or making a dress in a fashion design class. Getting feedback on your project can help inform the decisions that you make and usually results in a better finished product. Getting comfortable giving and getting input helps prepare you for working in your chosen career field.
© Zero Creatives/Corbis.

Figure 8.1 ▽ Rate Your Critical-Thinking Skills

Now that you have been reading about what is involved with developing strong thinking skills, it's a good time to rate yourself as a critical thinker. Use Figure 8.1 to rate your critical-thinking skills. What have you learned in this chapter that can help you improve?

Circle the number that best fits you in each of the situations described below.

Situations	Never				Sometimes					Always
In class, I ask lots of questions when I don't understand.	1	2	3	4	5	6	7	8	9	10
If I don't agree with what the group decides is the correct answer, I challenge the group opinion.	1	2	3	4	5	6	7	8	9	10
I believe there are many solutions to a problem.	1	2	3	4	5	6	7	8	9	10
I admire those people in history who challenged what was believed at the time, such as "the earth is flat."	1	2	3	4	5	6	7	8	9	10
I make an effort to listen to both sides of an argument before deciding which way I will go.	1	2	3	4	5	6	7	8	9	10
I ask lots of people's opinions about a political candidate before making up my mind.	1	2	3	4	5	6	7	8	9	10
I am not afraid to change my belief if I learn something new.	1	2	3	4	5	6	7	8	9	10
Authority figures do not intimidate me.	1	2	3	4	5	6	7	8	9	10

The more 7–10 scores you have circled, the more you use your critical-thinking skills. The lower scores indicate that you may not be using critical-thinking skills very often or use them only during certain activities.

Role Models in Creativity

The following are some critical thinkers of our past and present who made contributions that continue to affect our lives.

- **Abraham Lincoln.** When we think of great leaders, Lincoln often comes to mind. Lincoln was able to think about the relationship between national policy and human rights in new and different ways. By working slowly and deliberately, Lincoln changed American laws and began a long process toward guaranteeing equal rights for all U.S. citizens.
- **Martin Luther King Jr.** King could be considered one of the greatest activists of all time. When racial segregation ruled in the South, he contributed to the civil rights movement by voicing his concerns and presenting his dream of a different world. He created opportunities for change in many unfair policies and practices.
- **Twitter creators Jack Dorsey, Evan Williams, Biz Stone, and Noah Glass.** Twitter was created in 2006 as a social networking and microblogging site to enhance communication around the world through hashtag statements that are limited to 140 characters each. In spite of early public resistance, the site quickly gained popularity and changed our way of communicating in times of national and international crisis due to its quick information-sharing ability.
- **Steve Jobs.** As an innovative thinker, Jobs shaped the way our society views technology and digital capabilities. He was resilient and did not give up even when faced with challenges such as losing his position as the head of Apple at one time.
- **Lady Gaga.** Pushing her artistic expression through fashion and activism, Lady Gaga projects an identity that challenges gender expectations and voices her belief in equality for all individuals.

Think—and Find What You're Looking For

You have probably heard that colleges and universities expect their students to be able to conduct research when they write papers or create projects. In high school or a casual setting, doing research usually means going to a search engine like Google, Yahoo, or Ask.com. Many of us do this so automatically that we say, "Let me Google that." And when you do, you're likely to find people basically doing three things: yelling, selling, or telling.

Yelling: Someone has a viewpoint and puts it forward on Blogger or YouTube, but how do you know if this person is biased or a member of a fringe or hate group when you use his or her video in your project?

Selling: Often, people promote products or services in a way that makes them sound like credible sources of information when they are really simply trying to get you to buy something.

Telling: These places and people actually have credible information that you find informative and useful, but how can you verify their credibility?

A Google search, however, isn't exactly what your instructors have in mind when they ask you to conduct research. If you need to conduct research for a paper and you're not sure how else to do it, remain calm. You can apply the critical-thinking skills you've learned in this chapter. Here's how:

- **Start with good questions.** If you are researching a topic, such as "marijuana legalization," generate some questions you have about that subject rather than just going to Google and typing "marijuana" into the search box. Generating questions will save you time by clarifying what you need to know, so you will recognize useful results and ignore the ones that won't help you. Here are some possible questions:
  - What is the history of marijuana use in the United States?
  - Why was it made illegal in the first place?
  - Where has it been legalized, and why?
  - What have been some of the positive and negative outcomes of making it legal?

- **Ask a librarian.** Show the reference librarians your list of questions. They can help you fine-tune them and will recommend good places to find certain kinds of answers.
- **Use databases.** Your school pays for research databases, which collect a variety of credible, scholarly research. When you use research databases, you can be sure that the information is reliable, and you can refine your search terms to produce 20 or 30 returns, as opposed to 20 or 30 million. Most databases are available online with login information that your college can provide, so you can use them anytime from home or on your laptop.
- **Use a variety of locations to confirm information.** When you see the same information in a variety of credible sources, you can start to trust its accuracy. *Remember that there are good sources of information available only in print form.*
- **Consider the quality of the information and evaluate the sources.** Where did it come from? Who said it, and why? How current is it? Has anything major happened in this area since information was published?

As you Google this or that, use the steps to develop strong thinking skills to scrutinize the yellers, sellers, and tellers, and apply these skills when you need to conduct solid research.

Bloom's Taxonomy and Your First Year of College

Benjamin Bloom, a professor of education at the University of Chicago, worked with a group of other researchers to design a system of classifying goals for the learning process. This system is known as Bloom's Taxonomy, and it is now used at all levels of education to define and describe the process that students use to understand and think critically about what they are learning.

Bloom identified six levels of learning, as you can see in Figure 8.2. The higher the level, the more critical thinking it requires.

You have been using the levels of Bloom's Taxonomy throughout your education, perhaps without being aware of it. As you work through the courses in your first year of college, you will recognize material you've learned before,

and you will practice your skills of defining and remembering. You'll become aware that the skills on Bloom's first level aren't going to get you very far. To retain new information, you'll need to move to level 2, understanding the information clearly enough so that you can describe the concepts to someone else. Many of your classes will require you to apply what you learn to your experience and to new situations (level 3)—as you engage with material in this way, your comprehension grows, as does your ability to retain new knowledge. Next you'll move on to level 4 to analyze—break down information into parts—and level 5, where you evaluate new ideas, making decisions about them and judging them. As you reach the sixth, or highest, level, you create something new by combining information, concepts, and theories.

Figure 8.2 ▽ The Six Levels of Learning of Bloom's Taxonomy

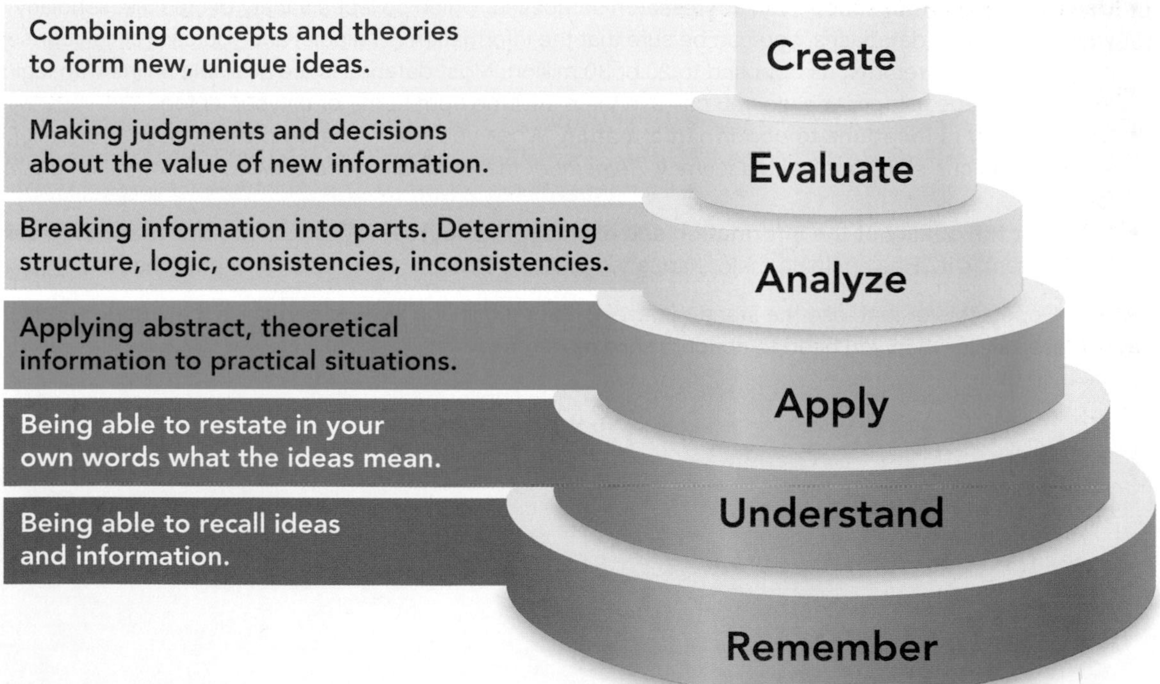

Combining concepts and theories to form new, unique ideas.
Create

Making judgments and decisions about the value of new information.
Evaluate

Breaking information into parts. Determining structure, logic, consistencies, inconsistencies.
Analyze

Applying abstract, theoretical information to practical situations.
Apply

Being able to restate in your own words what the ideas mean.
Understand

Being able to recall ideas and information.
Remember

Let's take a closer look at Bloom's Taxonomy by taking a concept you're likely to encounter in your first year of college—diversity—and matching your cognitive development of the concept to Bloom's taxonomy (Use the space on this page to take notes on how you would approach this task.):

Level 1 (Remember): Read a dictionary definition of the word *diversity*.

Level 2 (Understand): Explain the concept of diversity to another student without reading the dictionary definition.

Level 3 (Apply): Write about all the types of human diversity that exist within the student body at your college or university and possible categories of human diversity that are not represented there.

Level 4 (Analyze): Conduct two separate analyses to break down the issue into components or questions. The first analysis will look at why your institution has large numbers of certain types of students. The second analysis will consider why your institution has small numbers of other types of students.

Level 5 (Evaluate): Write a paper that combines your findings in level 4 and hypothesizes what components of your college or university culture either attract or repel certain students.

Level 6 (Create): In your paper, describe your institution's "diversity profile" and suggest new ways for your campus to support diversity.

If you pay close attention, you will discover that Bloom's taxonomy is often the framework that college instructors use to design classroom activities and out-of-class assignments. Be aware of how you use each of these levels to build your critical-thinking skills. No matter what the topic is, this framework will help move you to deeper understanding and an ability to apply what you learn to other situations and concepts. ■

Chapter Review

Steps to Success:
Thinking in College

○ **Understand what *critical thinking* means.** If you are not clear about this term, discuss it with another student, the instructor of this course, or a staff member in the learning center.

○ **Find ways to express your imagination and curiosity, and practice asking questions.** If you have the impulse to raise a question, don't stifle yourself. College is for self-expression and exploration.

○ **Challenge your own and others' assumptions that are not supported by evidence.** To help you better understand the position an individual may be taking, practice asking for additional information in a calm, polite manner that is not rejecting.

○ **During class lectures, presentations, and discussions, practice thinking from multiple points of view.** Start with your usual view toward the matter at hand. Then force yourself to imagine what questions might be raised by someone who has a different opinion

○ **Draw your own conclusions and explain to others what evidence you considered.** Don't assume that anyone automatically understands why you reached your conclusions.

○ **Join study groups or class project teams and work as a team member with other students.** When you are a member of a team, volunteer for roles that stretch you.

○ **Learn to identify false claims in commercials and political arguments.** Then look for the same faulty reasoning in people's comments you hear each day.

○ **Practice critical thinking not only in your academic work but also in your everyday interactions with friends and family.** Daily life presents many opportunities to flex your thinking muscles. When you think critically, your academic work is better and your relationships get stronger.

○ **Pay attention to how your instructors use Bloom's taxonomy to design classroom activities and out-of-class assignments.** Being aware of the level of thinking you're being asked to do will help you appreciate the progress you are making as a critical thinker.

Applying what you've learned . . .

Now that you have read and discussed this chapter, consider how you can apply what you have learned to your academic and personal lives. The following prompts will help you reflect on the chapter material and its relevance to you both now and in the future.

1. After reading this chapter, think of professions (for example, medicine, engineering, and marketing) in which problem solving and "thinking outside the box" are necessary. Choose one and describe why you think critical thinking is a necessary and valuable skill for that career.

2. In your opinion, is it harder to think critically than to base your arguments on how you feel about a topic? Why or why not? What are the advantages of finding answers based on your feelings? Based on critical thinking? How might you use both approaches in seeking answers?

Use Your Resources

GO TO ▷ Your course catalog and investigate some logic courses: If you need help developing your critical-thinking skills. For instance, check out your philosophy department's introduction to logic course. This course may be the single best one to take for learning critical-thinking skills.

GO TO ▷ The English department: If you need help in formulating logical arguments. Investigate courses that will help you develop the ability to formulate logical arguments and to avoid such pitfalls as logical fallacies.

GO TO ▷ Your student activities office or the speech or drama department: If you need help practicing your debating skills. Find out if your campus has a debate club/society or a debate team.

GO TO ▷ Your library and ask for help identifying works of literature such as _Twelve Angry Men_ by Reginald Rose (New York: Penguin Classics, 2006): If you would enjoy seeing examples from Hollywood showing how critical thinking applies to life situations. This work is a reprint of the original teleplay, which was written in 1954 and made into a film in 1958 (the film is available on DVD or you can stream it on Amazon Prime). The stirring courtroom drama pits twelve jurors against one another as they argue the outcome of a murder trial in which the defendant is a teenage boy. Although critical thinking is needed to arrive at the truth, all but one juror employ every possible noncritical argument to convince themselves of the defendant's guilt until the analysis of the lone holdout produces remarkable changes in the other jurors' attitudes.

GO TO ▷ The Internet: If you need more help with critical thinking. Google "help with critical thinking" for some valuable resources like those available through the Foundation for Critical Thinking. Evaluate your search results.

NOW... How do you measure up?

1. Even when people are irritating, it's important to try to listen to what they have to say.

   ○ Agree
   ○ Don't Know
   ○ Disagree

2. There can be more than one right answer to almost any question.

   ○ Agree
   ○ Don't Know
   ○ Disagree

3. It's important not to allow emotions to get in the way of making the right decision.

   ○ Agree
   ○ Don't Know
   ○ Disagree

4. Good thinkers listen to all sides of an argument before taking a position.

   ○ Agree
   ○ Don't Know
   ○ Disagree

How do your answers here compare to your responses to the quiz you took at the start of the chapter? Which sections of this chapter left a strong impression on you? What strategies for critical thinking have you started to use? Are they working? What other strategies will you commit to trying?

145
Information Literacy

147
Using the Library

149
Evaluating Sources

151
The Writing Process

Developing Information Literacy and Communication Skills

Domofon/Shutterstock

Your communication skills, especially the ability to write and speak clearly, persuasively, and confidently, will make a tremendous difference in how the rest of the world perceives you and how well you communicate throughout your life. In almost every occupation you will be expected to think, create, manage, lead, and communicate. To participate fully in the information age, you will also need to develop your information literacy skills: finding, evaluating, and using information that others have communicated through writing and speaking.

Information literacy is, first and foremost, the ability to manage the overwhelming amount of information available today. In addition to learning how to retrieve and select the best

resources to meet your needs, you will also learn how to synthesize and write or speak about the sources you have found. In assigned research projects, you will process information, pulling ideas and concepts together to create new information and ideas that other people can use.

Most people look at writing, speaking, and information literacy as tasks to be mastered and then forgotten. Nothing could be further from the truth. These are processes (step-by-step methods for reaching your final goal) that can help you create products (such as a final research paper, answers to an essay exam, or a presentation) throughout your education and career.

How do you measure up?

1. When searching online for information, it's important to select the most relevant resources, not just those that are first in a list on a search engine.
    ○ Agree
    ○ Don't Know
    ○ Disagree

2. In choosing resources for a major paper or research project, writers should avoid biased sources—those based on opinions that aren't backed up with solid evidence.
    ○ Agree
    ○ Don't Know
    ○ Disagree

3. Writing a draft and making revisions before submitting essays or major papers to college instructors will almost always improve the final grade.
    ○ Agree
    ○ Don't Know
    ○ Disagree

4. It is important to cite all sources accurately in a research paper.
    ○ Agree
    ○ Don't Know
    ○ Disagree

Review the items you marked "Don't Know" or "Disagree." Pay special attention to these topics in this chapter—you will find motivating strategies to develop in these areas. A follow-up quiz at the end of the chapter will prompt you to consider what you have learned.

The Early Bird Gets the A

△ **Analee Bracero**

When I was looking into going to college, Kean University in New Jersey had everything I wanted—a wide range of majors and lots of student activities. The college also has a good library system that allows me to conduct research both on and off campus.

Writing research papers in high school is much different from writing college research papers. In high school I usually got A's on my papers, so the D that I received on my first graded paper at Kean was a huge shock. I had waited until the day before to begin working on it, but I still thought it was good. But my instructor told me, "your paper reads like something that was written in a few hours at the last minute. And your bibliography cites Wikipedia more than the actual source material."

The instructor also pointed out a couple of places where I had copied material from a source without referencing it. "You're going to need to get your writing up to a college level. The best source of help for you will be the writing center, so make an appointment right away," the instructor told me. Now I start working on my papers early—as soon as I receive the assignment. I give myself plenty of time to do research in the library and online. Because I don't procrastinate, I can get help from the writing center without any last-minute stress. The strong grades I am earning prove that working this way pays off.

Not everyone arrives at college with the same expectations or the same high school preparation. As Analee's story illustrates, developing good habits for writing college research papers provides many benefits that can last throughout one's entire college experience, including less stress and better grades. What did Analee learn about the amount of time she should have spent on her paper? What could Analee do next to build on what she learned through this first assignment? What can you learn from Analee's story?

Information Literacy

Information literacy, a skill demanded by most twenty-first-century employers, is the ability to find, interpret, and use information to meet your needs. Information literacy requires that you also develop computer literacy, media literacy, and cultural literacy.

- **Computer literacy** is the ability to use electronic tools for conducting searches and for communicating and presenting to others what you have found and analyzed.

- **Media literacy** is the ability to think deeply about what you see and read through television, film, advertising, radio, magazines, and the Internet.

- **Cultural literacy** is having deep knowledge about the world around you—both past and present.

Learning to Be Information Literate

People are amazed at the amount of information available to them everywhere, especially online. What can we do about information overload? To become an informed and successful user of information, keep three basic goals in mind:

1. **Know how to find the information you need.** Once you have figured out where to look for information, you'll need to ask good questions and learn how to search information systems, such as the Internet, libraries, and databases.

2. **Learn how to interpret the information you find.** It is important to find information, but it is even more important to make sense of that information. What does the information mean? Is the information correct? Can the source be trusted?

3. **Have a purpose for collecting information and then put it to use.** Even the best information won't do much good if you don't know what to do with it. You should decide how to put your findings into an appropriate format, such as a research paper for a class or a presentation for a meeting.

In this chapter you'll explore ways to work toward each of these goals—doing so is really what college is all about.

Research—Information Literacy in Action

In the past you might have completed assignments that asked you to find a book, journal article, or Web page related to a particular topic. While finding information is an essential part of research, it's just the first step. Research is not just copying a paragraph from a book or putting together bits and pieces of information without adding any of your own comments. In fact, such behavior could easily be considered plagiarism, which could result in a failing grade or worse. You'll read more about plagiarism later in this chapter.

Research is a process that includes asking questions, collecting and analyzing data related to those questions, and presenting one or more answers. Good research is information literacy in action. If your instructor asks you to select and write about a topic, you might search for information about it, find multiple sources, select and organize a few, write a paper or prepare a presentation that cites your sources, draw conclusions of your own, and submit the final product. That's research—the conclusions that you make based on your research represent new information. It takes time to go through all the steps in doing good research. Some steps will be difficult, and you might be tempted to take shortcuts. However, learning to persist at these kinds of

△ **Stay Connected**
In today's world, information literacy is one of the most important skills a person can have. This means developing computer, media, and cultural literacy, along with learning how to find, interpret, and use information you need. Hero Images/Getty Images.

tasks in college will pay off in your career. You will find that the research and writing process becomes easier, and you will be more successful.

"Good research is information literacy in action."

Choosing, Narrowing, and Researching a Topic

Assignments that require the use of library materials will be a part of most of your classes. There are several ways to search for information, but before you start searching, you need to have a clear idea of what you're looking for.

Choosing a topic is often the hardest part of a research project. Your instructor may assign a general topic, but you'll probably want to narrow it down to a particular area that interests you. Imagine, for example, that you have been assigned to write a research paper on the topic of global warming. First, you will want to get an overview of this topic through Google or some other search engine. Once you've found basic information, you have a decision to make: What aspects of global warming will you research? You may realize that global warming includes many related sub-topics, and you can use this new information to create key words—words or phrases that tell an

online search engine what you're looking for. For example, for the topic "global warming," key words may include "climate change," "greenhouse effect," "ozone layer," "smog," or "carbon emissions." Even these terms will generate a large number of hits, and you will probably need to narrow your search even more. What you want are twelve or so focused and highly relevant hits on an aspect of global warming that you can use to write a well-organized research paper.

If you are having trouble coming up with key words, one place to begin your research is an encyclopedia, a book or an electronic database with general knowledge on a range of topics. You have probably used an encyclopedia recently without thinking about it: Wikipedia. A *wiki* is a type of Web site that allows many different people to edit its content. Many instructors feel that the information on Wikipedia is not reliable because anyone can change it; instead, they want students to use sources that have gone through a formal review process. Your instructors might even forbid Wikipedia; if so, avoid it altogether. Even if an instructor permits the use of Wikipedia, it's best to use it only as a *starting point* for your research. Do not plan on citing Wikipedia in your final paper.

Even with an understanding of various types of sources, it can be difficult to determine what exactly you need for your assignment. Figure 9.1 provides an overview of when to use different common research sources and gives examples of what you'll find in each source. ■

Figure 9.1 ▽ **Using Common Research Sources**
This chart differentiates the most common research sources. You will access these types of sources for classwork as well as your personal life.

INFORMATION TIME LINE		
Source	**When to access information**	**What it offers**
Newspapers (print and online)	Daily/hourly after an event	Primary-source, firsthand discussions of a current event, and of what happened at the time of the event; short articles
Magazines	Weekly/monthly after an event	Analysis by a journalist or reporter of an event days or weeks after it occurred; longer articles than in newspapers; informally credits sources; might include more interviews or research as well as historical context
Scholarly articles	Months after an event	In-depth analyses of issues; research-based scientific studies with formally credited sources, written and reviewed by experts; contains graphs, tables, and charts
Books	Months/years after an event	A comprehensive overview of a topic with broad and in-depth analyses

Using the Library

Libraries are no longer the cold, silent places that some of us remember. Today they are inviting and friendly, and so are the people who work in them. You can use libraries to read books and articles and to find online information and quiet spaces for study. Most libraries also have computers and printers that you can use to complete your assignments. Many libraries now also house tutoring and learning centers and have areas where you can grab a cup of coffee or a snack, socialize, relax, and work in groups.

Whenever you have research to do for a class, for your job, or for your personal life, visit a library in person or access it online. Although we might think that all valuable information can be found online, many resources are still stored in traditional print formats or in your college library database. A key component of being information literate is determining the kinds of sources you need to satisfy your research questions. Librarians at your college or university work with instructors to determine the kinds of materials that support their teaching. Most libraries have not only books but also government documents, microfilm, photographs, historical documents, maps, music, and films.

Of course, no one library can possibly own everything you might need or enough copies of each item, so groups of libraries share their materials with each other. If your college library does not have a journal or book that you need, or the item you need is checked out, you can use interlibrary loan, a service that allows you to request an item at no charge from another college or university library.

If it is difficult for you to get to your college library, you will still have off-campus, online access to library materials through a college-provided ID and password. You can also have online chats with librarians. To learn more, check out your library's Web site, or e-mail or phone the reference desk. Be sure to use the

△ **Library of the Future? No, the Present!**
College libraries are changing to learning commons as information goes digital and space for group work becomes a priority. This facility merges the library, information technology, and classrooms and contains multiple zones for individuals, small groups, and team-based learning. What does your college library offer?

handouts and guides that are available at the reference desk or online as well as tutorials and virtual tours that will help you become familiar with the collections, services, and spaces available at your library.

> ❝ Whenever you have research to do for a class, for your job, or for your personal life, visit a library in person or access it online. ❞

Library Resources

Many college-level research projects will require you to use a variety of sources to find information and do research. The most commonly used resources that college libraries offer are scholarly journals and periodicals.

Scholarly journals are collections of original, peer-reviewed research articles written by experts or researchers in a particular academic discipline. Examples are the *Journal of Educational Research* and the *Social Psychology Quarterly*. The term *peer-reviewed* means that other experts in the field read and evaluate the articles in the journal before it is published. You can find scholarly articles by using an online database that is organized by certain subject areas or your library's catalog and is accessible on or off campus. You may also be able to find some of the scholarly articles by using Google Scholar—a Web search engine that searches only within scholarly journal articles.

A periodical is a journal, magazine, or newspaper that is published multiple times a year. Scholarly journals are of course periodicals, but most periodicals are popular rather than scholarly. The articles in *Rolling Stone*, for instance, do not go through a peer-review process like the articles in scholarly journals. Magazines can be legitimate sources for your research, unless your assignment specifically

TRY IT!

FEELING CONNECTED ▷ **Is the Library a Thing of the Past?**

Students view the library differently. Some of them discover that the library is a great place to gather information, study, and relax. Others avoid the library and see no reason to use it. Is the library a necessary resource for learning in college? What do you think? What do your classmates think? Share your ideas in a discussion or a debate about the value of the library on today's college campuses.

requires all sources to be scholarly articles or books. Look back at Figure 9.1 for a breakdown of different types of sources.

Books are especially useful for research projects. Often students in introductory classes must write research papers on broad topics like the Civil War. While many scholarly articles have been written about the Civil War, they will not provide the kind of general overview of the topic that is available in books. Many books are also available electronically; some of these e-books can be easily accessed online. ▪

Evaluating Sources

The Internet makes research easier in some ways and more difficult in others. Through Internet search engines such as Google and Bing, you have immediate access to a great deal of free information, but many of the links will not take you to valid sources for serious research. The order of the search results can be misleading; it is determined not by the source's importance but by search formulas that depend both on popularity and whether someone pays for a source to be at the top of the list. Anyone can put up a Web site—a famous professor, a professional society, or a fifth grader.

Some students might at first be excited about receiving 243,000,000 hits from a Google search on global warming, but they may be shocked when they realize the information they find is not sorted or organized. Think carefully about the usefulness of the information based on three important factors: relevance, authority, and bias.

Relevance

The first thing to consider in looking at a possible source is whether it is relevant: Does it relate to your subject in an appropriate way? How well does it fit your needs? The answers to these questions depend on your research project and the kind of information you are seeking.

- **Is it introductory?** Introductory information is basic and elementary. It does not require background knowledge about the topic. Introductory sources can be useful when you're first learning about a subject.

- **Is it comprehensive?** Look for sources that consider the topic in depth and offer plenty of evidence to support the conclusions.

- **Is it current?** Give preference to recent sources, although older, primary sources can sometimes be useful.

- **Is it meaningful?** Use the "So what?" test: So what does this information mean? Why does it matter to my project?

Authority

Once you have determined that a source is relevant to your research project, make sure that it was created by someone qualified to write or speak on the subject. For example, a fifth grader would generally not be considered an authority, but if your topic is bullying in

◁ **The Ten-Minute Rule**
If you have been working hard trying to locate information for a research project for ten minutes and haven't found what you need, ask a librarian for help. Let the librarian know what searches you've tried, and he or she will be able to help you figure out new strategies to find the sources you need. In addition, the librarian can help you develop strategies to improve your research skills. Doing research without a librarian is like driving cross-country without using a map or GPS— technically, you can do it, but you might get lost along the way. Get to know at least one librarian as your go-to expert. Blend Images/Hill Street Studios/Getty Images.

elementary schools, a fifth grader's opinion might be exactly what you're looking for.

Determine whether your project calls for scholarly publications, magazines and newspapers, or both. Many journalists and columnists are extremely well qualified, and their work might be appropriate for your needs. But as a general rule, scholarly sources have more credibility than newspapers and magazines in a college research project (see Figure 9.1).

Bias

Research consists of considering and analyzing multiple perspectives on a topic and creating something new from your analysis. Signs of bias, such as overly positive or overly harsh language, hints of a personal agenda, or a stubborn refusal to consider other points of view, indicate that you should question the credibility and accuracy of a source. Although nothing is wrong with citing someone's particular point of view, as a researcher you will want to be aware that the bias exists. You may need to exclude strongly biased sources from your research. For example, if you are writing about climate change, you'll want to examine sources for evidence of political or personal agendas. The following questions can help you evaluate your sources:

- Who is the author?

- What is the author's goal in writing about this topic?

- Does the author present facts, personal opinions, or both?

- Does the author provide evidence that is based on other sources?

- What is the basis for the author's conclusions—sound evidence or personal opinion? ■

Synthesis and Sharing

You have probably heard the saying "Knowledge is power." But knowledge gives you power only if you use it to create a product—a piece of writing or a presentation. Consider your audience and how you will present the information. What do you hope to accomplish by sharing your conclusions? Make it a point to do something with the results of your research. Otherwise, why bother? You researched information to find the answer to a question. Now is the time to share that answer with others.

Many students construct a straightforward report that summarizes what they found, and sometimes that's enough. A more powerful report will include an analysis of the information. To do an analysis, first consider how the facts, opinions, and details you found from your different sources relate to one another. What do they have in common, and how do they differ? What conclusions can you draw from these similarities and differences? Essentially, what you're doing at this stage of any research project is synthesis, a process in which you put together parts of ideas to come up with a whole result. By accepting some ideas, rejecting others, combining related concepts, and pulling it all together, you'll create new information and ideas that other people can use. Your final paper or presentation will include analysis and synthesis of the sources you found through your research. Remember: You must clearly state which thoughts and ideas came from the sources you found, and which are yours.

The Writing Process

In college you are required to write often. Students have to write lab reports in science courses, reflection papers on what they read, and original essays. Like research, good writing takes practice, and it is always a good idea to ask for help. Here are some step-by-step guidelines for effective writing.

Steps to Good Writing

The writing process typically includes the following three steps:

1. Prewriting

2. Drafting

3. Revising

Let's look more closely at each one of these steps.

Step 1: Using prewriting to discover what you want to say.

Prewriting is a powerful process for discovering ideas you didn't know you had. It simply means writing things down as they come to mind without consciously trying to organize your thoughts, find exactly the right words, or think about structure. Sometimes called freewriting, prewriting can involve filling a page, whiteboard, or screen with words, phrases, or sentences. Prewriting also helps you avoid the temptation to try to write and edit at the same time.

When you prewrite, you might notice that you have more ideas than you can fit into one paper, and this is very common. Prewriting helps you figure out what you really want to say as you make connections between different ideas.

Step 2: Drafting.

When you have completed your research with the help of your librarian, gathered a lot of information sources and ideas, and done some prewriting, it's time to move to the drafting stage. Before you start writing your draft, you need to organize all the ideas you generated in the prewriting step and form a thesis statement, a short statement that clearly defines the purpose of the paper (see Figure 9.2).

Most students find that creating an outline helps them organize their thoughts, resulting in a clear structure from the thesis to the conclusion (see Figure 9.3 for an example). Once you've set the structure for your paper and added analysis and synthesis of your research findings, you'll be well on your way to a final draft. If you have chosen the thesis carefully, it will help you check to see that each sentence relates to

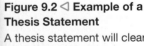

Figure 9.2 ◁ **Example of a Thesis Statement**
A thesis statement will clearly and succinctly express the purpose of your paper.

Thesis: Napoleon's dual personality can be explained by examining incidents throughout his life.

1. Explain why I am using the term "dual personality" to describe Napoleon.

2. Briefly comment on his early life and his relationship with his mother.

3. Describe Napoleon's rise to fame from soldier to emperor. Stress the contradictions in his personality and attitudes.

4. Describe the contradictions in his relationship with Josephine.

5. Summarize my thoughts about Napoleon's personality.

6. Possibly conclude by referring to opening question: "Did Napoleon actually have a dual personality?"

your main idea. When you have completed this stage, you will have the first draft of your paper in hand.

Step 3: Revising. The key to good writing is rewriting or revising, which is taking a good piece of writing and making it great. Revising is usually the step in the writing process that takes the most time. After you draft your paper, read it through once, twice, or more. You may need to reorganize your ideas, cut unnecessary words, rewrite some sentences or paragraphs, or use stronger words.

After you revise your paper, put it aside for at least a day and then reread it. Distancing yourself from your writing for a while allows you to see it differently later. You will probably find more grammatical and spelling errors that need to be corrected and problems with organization that need revising. You will make your writing stronger as a result.

It also might help to ask a classmate or someone in the writing center to review your paper. Once you have talked with your reviewers about their suggested changes, it will be your decision to either accept or reject them. At this point, you are ready to finalize your writing and turn in your paper. Reread the paper one more time, and double-check spelling and grammar.

> ❝ Like research, good writing takes practice, and it is always a good idea to ask for help. ❞

Figure 9.3 ▽ Example of an Outline
An outline is a working document; you do not need a complete outline to begin writing. Note how this author has a placeholder for another example; she has not yet decided which example from her research to use.

Outline for Napoleon Paper

   I. Thesis—Napoleon's dual personality can be explained by examining incidents in his life

  II. Dual Personality

     a. What is it?

     b. How does it apply to Napoleon?

 III. Napoleon's Rise to Fame

     a. Contradictions in his personality and attitudes

       i. Relationship with Josephine

      ii. Example #2 (to come)

 IV. Summary of my thoughts about Napoleon's personality

  V. Conclusion

     a. Restate and answer thesis

       i. Yes, he had a dual personality because:

         1. Josephine

         2. Example #2

Time and the Writing Process

Many students turn in poorly written papers because they skip the first step (prewriting) and the last step (rewriting/revising) and make do with the middle one (drafting). The best writing is usually done over an extended period of time, not as a last-minute task.

When planning the amount of time you'll need to write your paper, make sure to add enough time for the following:

- Doing more than a single "round" of revising as part of the writing process

- Asking your instructor for clarification on the assignment and for examples of papers that have received good grades. Some instructors will be willing to review a draft of your paper before you turn in the final version.

- Seeking help from a librarian and staff and trained peers in the writing center or learning center

- Narrowing or expanding your topic, which might require finding some new sources

- Balancing other assignments and commitments

- Dealing with technology problems

△ **Write. Review. Revise.**
Good writers spend more time revising and editing their written work than they spend writing the original version. Never turn in your first draft; spend the necessary time to reread and improve your work.
© Radius Images/Corbis.

Knowing Your Audience

Before you came to college, you probably spent much more time writing informally than writing formally. Think about all the time you've spent writing e-mails, texts, and tweets. Now think about the time you've spent writing papers for school. The informal style that you use in writing an e-mail, text, or post is not the style you'll use in writing a formal research paper. When you write research papers or essays in college, you should assume that your audience includes instructors and other serious students who will make judgments about your knowledge and abilities based on your writing. You should not be sloppy or casual when writing a formal paper.

TRY IT!

MANAGING TIME ▷ Is It Worth Some Extra Time to Improve Your Writing?

Think for a minute about your writing process—the steps you go through when you write a major paper. Do you rush through or skip the prewriting or revising stage to save time? Would you produce a better product by spending more time, especially in revising and polishing your writing? On your next research paper, devote the right amount of attention to each step of the writing process, and based on the quality of the paper and the grade you earn, decide whether it was worth it.

Citing Your Sources

If you include material written by others in an essay or research paper, remember that you must include a complete citation, a reference that enables a reader to locate the material you have used. Citing your sources serves many purposes. Source citations show your audience that you have based your conclusions on good, reliable evidence. They also provide a starting place for anyone who would like more information about the topic or is curious about how you reached your conclusions. Most important, citing your sources is the simplest way to avoid plagiarism—taking another person's ideas or work and presenting them as your own. Some students consider plagiarizing because they think that doing so will help them get a better grade. Because plagiarism is a problem on all college campuses, instructors are now using electronic systems such as Turnitin (turnitin.com) to identify passages in student papers that have been plagiarized. Because plagiarism is a form of cheating, students who are caught plagiarizing are likely to face severe penalties. These penalties might include a failing grade on the assignment, a failing grade in the course, or even expulsion from the college or university.

Your instructors will tell you about their preferred method for citation: footnotes, references in parentheses included in the text of your paper, or endnotes. If you're not given specific guidelines or if you simply want to be sure that you do it right, use a handbook or writing style manual. One standard manual is the *MLA Handbook for Writers of Research Papers,* published by the Modern Language Association (mlahandbook.org). Another is the *Publication Manual of the American Psychological Association* (apastyle.org). You can also download MLA and APA apps on your mobile devices from Google Play or iTunes. ■

> ❝ Citing your sources is the simplest way to avoid plagiarism. ❞

TRY IT!

MAKING DECISIONS ▷ Which Way Will You Go?

At some point in their college experience, many students will be tempted to take a shortcut on a written assignment by "borrowing" a paper from the Internet or from another student or copying information written by others without an appropriate citation. These actions, defined as plagiarism, will put your college degree and chances for employment at risk. Make a decision now to avoid plagiarism by remembering these two basic rules:

1. If you use somebody else's exact words, you must give that person credit.

2. If you use somebody else's ideas, *even if you use your own words to express those ideas,* you must give that person credit.

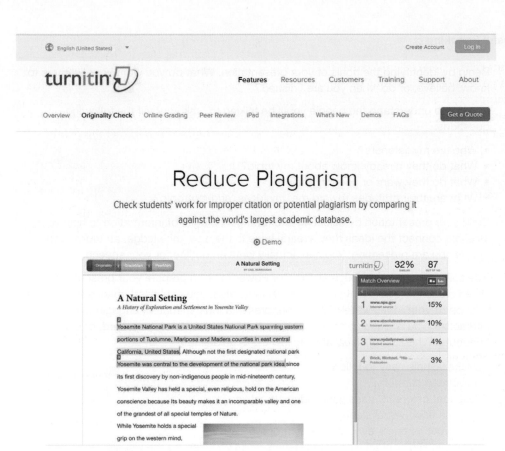

At the Podium: Speaking in Public

What you have learned in this chapter about writing also applies to public speaking—both are processes that you can learn and master, and each results in a product. Since the fear of public speaking is very common—more common, studies show, than the fear of death—you might be thinking along these lines: What if I plan, organize, prepare, and practice my speech, but my mind goes completely blank, I drop my note cards, or I say something totally embarrassing? Remember that people in your audience have been in your position and will understand your anxiety. Your audience wants you to succeed. Just be positive, rely on your wit, and keep speaking. Just as there is a process for writing a paper, there is a process for developing a good speech. The guidelines in Table 9.1 can help you improve your speaking skills and lose your fear of speaking publicly.

△ **Speak with Confidence**
If you follow the guidelines to successful speaking, you will be able to deliver a meaningful presentation that clearly informs your audience about a topic that matters to them. © Hill Street Studios/Blend Images/Corbis.

Table 9.1 ▽ **Steps to Successful Speaking**

1: Clarify your objective.	Begin by identifying the goals of your presentation. What do you want your listeners to know, believe, or do when you are finished?
2: Understand your audience.	In order to understand the people you'll be talking to, ask yourself the following questions: • Who are my listeners? • What do they already know about my topic? • What do they want or need to know? • What are their attitudes toward me, my ideas, and my topic?
3: Organize your presentation.	Build your presentation by selecting and arranging blocks of information to help your listeners connect the ideas they already have to the new knowledge, attitudes, and beliefs you are presenting. You can actually write an outline for your speech.
4: Choose appropriate visual aids.	Use software programs, such as Prezi or PowerPoint, to prepare your presentations. When creating PowerPoint slides or Prezi templates, you can insert images and videos to support your ideas while making your presentations animated, engaging, and interactive. You might also choose to prepare a chart, write on the board, or distribute handouts. When using visual aids, follow these guidelines: • Make visuals easy to follow. • Proofread carefully. • Use font colors to make your slides attractive. • Explain each visual clearly. • Give your listeners enough time to process visuals. • Maintain eye contact with your listeners while you discuss the visuals. Don't turn around and address the screen. Remember that a fancy slide show can't make up for lack of careful research or sound ideas.

5: Prepare your notes.	Memorize the introduction and conclusion of your speech, and then use a carefully prepared outline to guide you in between.
	Practice in advance. Because you are speaking mainly from an outline, your choice of words will be slightly different each time you give your presentation, with the result that you will sound prepared but natural.
	Try using note cards; number them in case you accidentally drop the stack on your way to the front of the room.
6: Practice your delivery.	Practice your delivery before an audience: a friend, your dog, even the mirror. If you ask a practice audience (friends or family) to give you feedback, you'll have some idea of what changes you might want to make.
	Practice your presentation aloud several times to control your anxiety.
	Consider making an audio or video recording of yourself on your cell phone or tablet to hear or see your mistakes.
	Use eye contact and smile.
7: Pay attention to word choice and pronunciation.	As you reread your presentation, make sure that you have used the correct words to express your ideas.
	Get help ahead of time with words you aren't sure how to pronounce.
	Try your best to avoid *like, um, uh, you know,* and other fillers.
8: Dress appropriately.	Dress appropriately. Leave the baseball cap, T-shirt, and tennis shoes at home.
	Don't overdress, but do look professional.
9: Request feedback from someone in your audience.	After you have completed your speech, ask a friend or your instructor to give you some honest feedback.
	Pay attention to suggestions for ways you can improve.

TRY IT!

SETTING GOALS ▷ **Developing Confidence in Public Speaking**

Do you enjoy public speaking? Are you an anxious or a confident speaker? What do you usually do to become more comfortable when speaking in front of a group? Make a list of your strategies and be prepared to discuss them with your classmates. Set a goal to seek opportunities to develop your public speaking skills. You'll be glad you did. At many points in college and in your career, you'll need to speak in front of others, so get motivated to seize chances to practice.

" Your audience wants you to succeed. "

Chapter Review

Steps to Success:
Developing Information Literacy
and Communication Skills

○ **Work to learn "information literacy" skills.** These skills include the abilities to find, evaluate, and use information.

○ **Become comfortable in your campus library, and get to know your college librarians.** Their primary function is to help you find the information you need.

○ **Accept that research projects and papers are part of college life.** Learn how to do them well. Doing so will teach you how to "research" the information you'll need after you've finished college.

○ **Become familiar with as many new electronic sources as possible.** You must be able to do research and seek the information you need in ways beyond Google or Wikipedia.

○ **When you use the ideas of others, be sure to give them credit; then create your own unique synthesis and conclusions.** Someday you will create your own "intellectual property," and you will want others to give you credit for your ideas.

○ **Take the time and effort to develop your writing and speaking skills.** Effective writing and speaking are skills for success in college and in life after college.

○ **Understand the differences between formal and informal communication.** When you are in doubt about what's appropriate, use a more formal writing style.

○ **Learn and practice the three distinct stages of writing: prewriting, drafting, and revising.** Going through each stage will improve the finished product.

○ **Learn and practice the steps to effective speaking.** These steps are presented in Table 9.1.

Applying what you've learned . . .

Now that you have read and discussed this chapter, consider how you can apply what you have learned to your academic and personal lives. The following prompts will help you reflect on the chapter material and its relevance to you both now and in the future.

1. It is important to get familiar with all the resources in your campus library. Think about a book that you love that was turned into a movie (for example, the *Twilight* or *Hunger Games* series). Search your library catalog to find the print copy and an e-book version. See if the library has it as an audiobook or in a language other than English. Find the DVD and soundtrack in your library's media collection, or see if you can download the music. Take a moment to appreciate what is available at your campus library!

2. Before reading this chapter, had you considered the differences between writing an exam response and writing a blog post or a response to someone on Facebook? Think about your online communications in the past week. Can you say for certain that you knew exactly who your audience was each time? Did you send or post anything that could be misinterpreted or read by someone outside your intended audience? What advice about online communications would you give to other students?

Use Your Resources

GO TO ▷ Your instructor: If you need help understanding his or her expectations for a writing assignment.

GO TO ▷ The library: If you need help working on an assignment. Head over to the reference desk and talk with a librarian about the assignment you are working on.

GO TO ▷ The writing center: If you need help finding effective writing and research tools.

GO TO ▷ The departments of speech, theater, and communications: If you need help finding resources and specific courses to help you develop your speaking skills.

GO ONLINE TO ▷ Purdue University's Online Writing Lab (http://owl.english.purdue .edu/owl/resource/584/02): If you need help with documenting print or electronic sources or with understanding forms of citation.

GO ONLINE TO ▷ Plain Language.gov (plainlanguage.gov/howto/guidelines /FederalPLGuidelines/index.cfm): If you need help with converting government jargon into plain language.

GO ONLINE TO ▷ Toastmasters International's public speaking tips (https://www .toastmasters.org/Resources/Public-Speaking-Tips): If you need help developing your public speaking skills.

NOW... How do you measure up?

1. When searching online for information, it's important to select the most relevant resources, not just those that are first in a list on a search engine.

   ○ Agree
   ○ Don't Know
   ○ Disagree

2. In choosing resources for a major paper or research project, writers should avoid biased sources—those based on opinions that aren't backed up with solid evidence.

   ○ Agree
   ○ Don't Know
   ○ Disagree

3. Writing a draft and making revisions before submitting essays or major papers to college instructors will almost always improve the final grade.

   ○ Agree
   ○ Don't Know
   ○ Disagree

4. It is important to cite all sources accurately in a research paper.

   ○ Agree
   ○ Don't Know
   ○ Disagree

How do your answers here compare to your responses to the quiz you took at the start of the chapter? Which sections of this chapter left a strong impression on you? What strategies for developing information literacy, writing, and speaking have you started to use? Are they working? What other strategies will you commit to trying?

LaunchPad
macmillan learning

10

163
Personal Relationships

165
The Ties That Bind: Family

167
Connecting with Others in a Digital Age

169
Thriving in Diverse Environments

173
Connecting through Involvement

Connecting with Others in a Diverse World

WunderfulPixel/Shutterstock

LaunchPad
macmillan learning

To access the LearningCurve study tool, Video Tools, and more, go to *LaunchPad Solo for College Success*. **macmillanhighered.com/ collegesuccessmedia**

What does success in college have to do with connecting with others? Very simply, the quality of the relationships you develop and maintain in college will have an important effect on your success.

Not only will you develop relationships with students who look, act, and think like you, but you will also have the opportunity to get to know other students whose life experiences and worldviews are different. A college or university serves as a microcosm of the real world—a world that requires us all to live, work, and socialize with people from diverse ethnic, cultural, and economic groups. In few real-world settings do members of these different groups interact in such close proximity as they do on a college campus.

You will also maintain relationships with members of your family and friends from your community, although those relationships may change in some ways. It will be especially important for you to keep the lines of communication open with family members to increase their understanding of your college experience.

How do you measure up?

1. One of the best parts of college is getting to know people who are different from me in terms of ethnicity, religion, or life experience.
   - ○ Agree
   - ○ Don't Know
   - ○ Disagree

2. Family members can be an important source of support for first-year students.
   - ○ Agree
   - ○ Don't Know
   - ○ Disagree

3. It will be beneficial for me to select at least one college course that exposes me to other cultures.
   - ○ Agree
   - ○ Don't Know
   - ○ Disagree

4. Being involved in college life outside of class will probably help me get a good job after graduation.
   - ○ Agree
   - ○ Don't Know
   - ○ Disagree

Review the items you marked "Don't Know" or "Disagree." Pay special attention to these topics in this chapter—you will find motivating strategies to develop in these areas. A follow-up quiz at the end of the chapter will prompt you to consider what you have learned.

△ **Frank Lee**

Finding Help When You Least Expect It

Last week during Professor Velez's office hours I went to visit her with some questions about the lecture. I noticed a photo of two people who looked like her mother and father, and we ended up having a really interesting talk about our families. Professor Velez told me that she was the first person in her family to go to college. It was a surprise for me to learn that at first her parents were suspicious about her psychology major and the whole idea of college and were afraid for her to leave home. I told her that I have been having a lot of trouble dealing with my family since I came to college—especially my mother. She has been calling me every day and trying to tell me what courses I should take, how much I should study, what my major should be, and even what time I should go to bed.

Professor Velez said she understood why I was frustrated. "I know you wish your parents would let you make your own decisions, but remember that they really care about you and want you to have a great experience. Perhaps if you call them every few days and tell them what's going on in your life, they will call you less often." I decided to follow her suggestion. My mom was really surprised when I called her yesterday. I spent about thirty minutes telling her everything that was happening to me, and I promised to call again over the weekend. I'm keeping my fingers crossed that she'll let me make the calls from now on.

What challenges do college students face when they move away from their family? What are some strategies for maintaining communication with your family while still making your own decisions? What did Frank learn from Professor Velez that will help him in the future?

Personal Relationships

One of the best things about going to college is meeting new people. In fact, scholars who study college students have found that students learn as much—or more—from other students as they learn from instructors. Although not everyone you meet in college will become a close friend, you will likely find a few special relationships that may even last a lifetime. Some relationships will be with people who have a background that is different from yours.

Roommates

For students whose college experience involves living in a residence hall or other off-campus housing, adjusting to a roommate can be a significant transition. Although it's tempting to room with your best friend from high school, that friend might not make a good roommate for you. In fact, many students lose friends by rooming with them. A roommate doesn't have to be a close friend, just someone with whom you can share your living space comfortably. Often, a roommate is someone you might not have selected if you had been given a choice, but you find that sharing a living space works well. Many students end up developing a lasting relationship with someone who at first was a total stranger. Some students, however, end up with an exasperating acquaintance they wish they'd never met.

It's important for roommates to establish in writing their mutual rights and responsibilities. Many colleges provide contract forms that you and your roommate might find useful if things go wrong. If you have problems with your roommate, talk them out promptly. Speak directly—politely, but plainly. Conflicts with roommates provide good opportunities to practice communication skills and can help build emotional intelligence. If the problems persist, or if you don't know how to talk them out, ask your residence hall adviser for help. Working through issues such as roommate challenges helps build resilience. In your life, you will inevitably have conflicts with others that you will have to navigate.

◁ **Group Selfie**
The memories you create with your college friends will stay with you forever. © William Perugini/ Shutterstock.

"One of the best things about going to college is meeting new people."

Romantic Relationships

You may already be in a long-term committed relationship, or you might have your first serious romance with someone you meet on campus. Given that college allows you to meet people from different backgrounds who share common interests, you might find it easier to meet romantic partners in college than it ever was before. Whether you commit to one relationship or you keep yourself open for meeting others, you'll grow and learn about yourself and those with whom you become involved. One type of involvement you should definitely avoid is a romantic relationship with an instructor or someone who supervises you at your job. When a romantic partner has power over your grades or your employment status, you are setting yourself up for potential trouble down the road.

If you are thinking about getting married or entering a long-term commitment, consider this: Studies show that the younger you are when you marry, the lower your odds are of enjoying a successful marriage. It is important not to marry before both you and your partner are certain who you are and what you want.

Breakups

Breaking up is hard, but if it's time to end a relationship, do it calmly and respectfully. Explain your feelings and talk them out. If you don't get a mature reaction, take the high road; don't join someone else in the mud.

Almost everyone has been rejected or "dumped" at one time or another. Let some time pass, be open to emotional support from your friends and family, and, if necessary, visit your college counselor or a chaplain. These professionals have assisted many students through similar experiences, and they can be there for you as well. ∎

The Ties That Bind: Family

Almost all first-year students, no matter their age, are connected to other family members. Your family might be a spouse and children, a partner, or your parents and siblings. The relationships that you have with family members can be a source of support throughout your college years, and it's important to do your part to maintain these relationships.

If you come from a cultural background that values family relationships and responsibilities above everything else, you will also have to work to balance your home life and college. In some cultures, if your grandmother or aunt needs help, that might be considered just as important—or more important—than going to class or taking an exam.

If you are living at home with one or more family members, you may have to bargain for time and space to study. This can be especially tough if you have children who are demanding your attention or if you are living in a small space, and you might be forced to study after others have gone to sleep. Unless you have to study at home so that you can provide care for family members, you might want to find a study space on campus or at a nearby public library, especially before an upcoming test or exam.

Negotiating the demands of college and family can be difficult. However, most college instructors will be flexible with requirements if you have genuine problems with meeting a deadline because of family obligations. It's important that you explain your situation to your instructors; don't expect them to be able to guess what you need. As the demands on your time increase, it's also important that you talk with family members to help them understand your role and responsibilities as a student.

Marriage and Parenting during College

While marriage and parenting can coexist positively with being a college student, meeting everyone's needs—your own, your spouse's,

◁ **Sweet Success**
Whether you are single or have a spouse or partner, being a parent while being a college student is one of the most challenging situations you can face. Find other students who have children so that you have a support system—it can make all the difference. You may not believe it now, but you are functioning as an important role model for your children. They will learn from you that education is worth striving for, even in the face of many obstacles. © Paul Barton/Corbis.

your children's—is not easy. If you are married, whether or not you have children, you need to become an expert at time management. If you do have children, make sure you find out what resources your college offers to help you with child care.

Sometimes going to college can create conflict between you and your spouse or partner as you take on a new identity and new responsibilities. Financial problems are likely to put extra pressure on your relationship, so both you and your partner have to work hard at paying attention to each other's needs. Be sure to involve your spouse and children in your decisions. Bring them to campus at every opportunity, and let your spouse (and your children, if they are old enough) read your papers and other assignments. Finally, set aside time for your partner and your children just as carefully as you schedule your work and your classes.

Relationships with Parents

Your relationship with your parents will never be quite the same as it was before you began college. On the one hand, you might find it uncomfortable when your parents try to make decisions on your behalf, such as choosing your major, determining where and how much you work, and setting rules for what you do on weekends. On the other hand, you might find that it's hard to make decisions on your own without talking to your parents first. While communication with your parents is important, don't let them make all your decisions. Your college can help you draw the line between which decisions should be yours alone and which decisions your parents should help you make. Many college students are living in blended families, so more than one set of parents is involved in their college experience. If your father or mother has remarried, you might have to negotiate with both family units.

During this period of transition, a first step in establishing a good relationship with your parents is to make sure the lines of communication are open. They might have concerns about your safety and well-being—you will understand these concerns better when you become a parent yourself. Your parents may be worried that you'll get hurt in some way. They might still see you as young and innocent, and they don't want you to make the same mistakes that they might have made or to experience dangerous situations that have been publicized in the media. They might be concerned that your family values or cultural values will change or that you'll never really come home again, and for some students that is exactly what happens.

Remember, though, that parents generally mean well even if their good intentions aren't always expressed in productive ways. Most of them love their children and want to protect them, even if their children have grown up. To help your parents feel more comfortable with your life in college, try setting aside regular times to update them on how things are going for you. Ask for and consider their advice. You don't have to take it, but your parents will likely appreciate the chance to give it, and thinking about your parents' suggestions can be useful as you weigh the many factors that will help you make decisions.

Even if you're successful in establishing appropriate boundaries between your life and your parents' lives, it's hard not to worry about what's happening at home, especially when your family is in a crisis. If you find yourself in the midst of a difficult family situation, seek help from your campus's counseling center or from a chaplain. And whether or not your family is in crisis, if they are not supportive, reach out to others who can offer the emotional support that you need. With your emotional needs satisfied, your reactions to your real family will be much less painful. ■

Connecting with Others in a Digital Age

So much of our communication with others occurs through e-mail, text and photo messaging, mobile apps, and posting on social networking sites. Online communication enables us to connect with others, whether we're forming new friendships or romantic relationships or maintaining established ones. Online communication also gives us a broad sense of community.

Social networking sites and apps such as Facebook, Twitter, Instagram, Vine, Viber, Telegram, WhatsApp, and Snapchat are popular with college students; it's likely that you use sites and apps such as these throughout the day to keep up with your friends. While social media outlets have both positives and negatives, one thing is certain: As students enter college, most do not carefully examine what they share through social media. Online statements, posts, and messages can have a strong impact, so you should be careful about everything you put into public view. Today it is common for many employers to check job applicants' online images before they offer them jobs. Given how often we use technology to communicate with others, it becomes critically important to use it properly. When you do, you are strengthening, and not weakening, your relationships. Here are some helpful suggestions for improving online communication.[1]

1. **Match the seriousness of your message to your communication medium.** Know when to communicate online versus offline. *Online* is best for transmitting quick reminders or messages that require time and thought to craft. Texting a friend to remind her of a coffee date that you've already set up likely makes good sense—calling or reminding her in person is a bit disruptive. E-mail may be best when dealing with problematic people or trying to resolve certain types of conflicts. That's because you can take time to think and

△ **Devices, Devices, Everywhere**
These days, wherever you look you see people on their various devices. While digital devices offer ways to connect with others, consider how devices are limiting our abilities to build relationships. © sturti/iStock.

carefully draft and revise your responses before sending them—something that isn't possible in a brief text message or during face-to-face interactions (see number 5 on following page).

Offline, and ideally face-to-face interaction, is better for sharing personal information such as news of health issues or for in-depth, lengthy, and detailed explanations of professional or personal problems or important relationship decisions. Many people still expect important news to be shared in person, even though online communication is being used more and more for big announcements. Most of us, though, would be startled if our spouse revealed a long-awaited pregnancy through e-mail, or if a friend disclosed a serious illness through a text message.

2. **Don't assume that online communication is always more efficient.** If your message needs a quick decision or answer, a phone call or a face-to-face conversation may be better.

[1] Adapted from Steven McCornack, *Reflect & Relate: An Introduction to Interpersonal Communication*, 3rd ed., pp. 24–27. © 2013 Bedford/St. Martin's. Boston, MA.

Use online communication if you want the person to have time to respond. Issues that may cause an emotional reaction are more effectively and ethically handled in person or over the phone, but opt for online communication to allow someone time to respond. If your message needs a quick decision or answer—like deciding when to meet for lunch—a phone call or a face-to-face conversation may be better. Often a one-minute phone call or a quick face-to-face exchange can save several minutes of texting and can prevent waiting for a response to an e-mail.

3. **Presume that your posts are public.** You may be thinking of the laugh you'll get from friends when you post the funny picture of yourself drunkenly hugging a houseplant on Instagram. But would you want family members, future in-laws, or potential employers to see the picture? Even if you have privacy settings on your personal page, what's to stop friends from downloading your photos and posts and distributing them to others? Keep this rule in mind: Anything you've sent or posted online can potentially be seen by anyone. Follow this rule: If you wouldn't want a message to be seen by the general public, don't post it or send it online.

4. **Remember that your posts are permanent.** Assume that what goes online or is shared through a mobile app lives on forever, despite claims to the contrary of some sites and apps. Old e-mails, photos, videos, tweets, blogs, you name it—all of these may still be accessible years later. As just one example, everything you have ever posted on Facebook is stored on the Facebook server, even if you delete it. And Facebook legally reserves the right to sell your content, as long as the company first deletes personally identifying information (such as your name). Think before you post.

> ## If you wouldn't want a message to be seen by the general public, don't post it or send it online.

5. **Practice the art of creating drafts.** Get into the habit of saving text and e-mail messages as drafts, then revisiting them later and editing them as needed for appropriateness, effectiveness, and ethics. Don't feel pressured to answer an e-mail immediately. Taking time to respond will result in a more competently crafted message. Because online communication makes it easy to flame, many of us impetuously fire off messages that we later regret.

6. **Protect your online identity.** Choose secure passwords for Web sites of financial institutions like banks or credit card companies, your social networking sites, and course sites where your grades might be listed. Limit the amount of personal information available on your social media profiles, ratchet up your security settings, and accept friend requests only from people you know.

7. **Exercise caution and common sense when online correspondence turns into a face-to-face meeting.** Keep in mind that some people tell lies on their profiles and posts. Select a public meeting place, and be sure a friend, family member, or roommate knows about your plans. ■

TRY IT!

FEELING CONNECTED ▷ Gone but Not Forgotten

How many of your high school friends are with you every day, and how many of them are at another college or university or back at home? While you will make lots of new friends in college, you'll also want to keep up with friends from the past. It's easy to do that with all the available online communication methods. And don't miss your high school reunions — they're a special opportunity to connect with your memories and see how far you and your friends have come.

Thriving in Diverse Environments

So far in this chapter, you have learned about various ways to connect with others while in college and also about how being in college changes many of the relationships in your life. A logical next step is to increase your awareness of differences and similarities among people, which is an important component of your ability to connect with others and to build and maintain healthy relationships. Colleges and universities attract students with different backgrounds; the ethnicity, cultural background, economic status, and religion of college students may vary widely on your campus. These differences provide many opportunities for students to experience diversity.

Diversity is the difference in social and cultural identities among people living together. Through self-assessment, discovery, and open-mindedness, you can begin to understand your perspectives on diversity. This work, although difficult at times, will add to your educational experiences, personal growth, and development. Thinking critically about your personal values and belief systems will allow you to have a greater sense of belonging and to make a positive contribution to our multicultural society.

Stereotyping: Why We Believe What We Believe

Many of our beliefs are the result of our personal experience. Others are a result of a *stereotype*, a generalization—usually exaggerated or oversimplified and often offensive—that is used to describe or distinguish a group. A negative experience with members of a particular group may result in the stereotyping of people in that group. We may acquire stereotypes about people we have never met before or may have accepted a stereotype without even thinking about questioning it. Children who grow up in an environment in which dislike and distrust of certain types of people are openly expressed might adopt these judgments even if they have had no interaction with those being judged.

◁ **Expand Your Worldview**
How has going to college changed your experience with diversity? Are you getting to know people of different races or ethnic groups? Do your classes have both traditional-aged and returning students? Are you seeking out people who are different from you and sharing personal stories and worldviews? © 2/Ocean/Corbis.

MAKING DECISIONS ▷ Resist Prejudice

All of us have been guilty of stereotyping people at some point in our lives. College is a good time to challenge your prejudices—beliefs or opinions you hold that are based not on reason or actual experience but on someone's ethnicity, religion, sexual orientation, political viewpoint, or other defining characteristic. The first step is to be aware of these prejudices. Then decide to challenge these prejudices by getting to know people as individuals, rather than making assumptions about them because they are members of certain groups. Spending time with people who view the world differently than you do will contribute to your college experience and help you avoid stereotyping.

Try to avoid developing exaggerated feelings of superiority or inferiority. What matters now is not what you had or didn't have before you came to college; what matters is what you do in college. You have more in common with other students than you think. Now your individual efforts, dreams, courage, determination, and ability to stay focused can be your success factors.

> " You have more in common with other students than you think. "

Other Differences You Will Encounter in College

When we hear the word *diversity*, most of us immediately think of differences in race or ethnic group. But you will experience many other kinds of human difference during your years in college.

Age. Although some students enter college around age eighteen, others choose to enter or return to college in their thirties and beyond. Age diversity in the classroom gives everyone the opportunity to learn from others who have different life experiences. Many factors come into play when after entering college, students stop out for a period of time, and then reenter.

Economic status. The United States is a country of vast differences in wealth. This considerable economic diversity can be either a positive or a negative aspect of college life. On the positive side, you will be exposed to, and can learn from, students who present you with a wide range of economic differences. Meeting others who have grown up with either more or fewer opportunities than you did is part of learning how to live in a democracy.

Religion. Many students come to college with deeply held religious views. Some will create faith communities on campus. Their religions will be not only those with a common Judeo-Christian heritage but also Islam, Hinduism, and Buddhism. Learning about different faith perspectives is another way you can explore human difference.

Some students and instructors may consider themselves atheists or agnostics, either denying or doubting the existence of a divine creator. Whatever *your* religious views may be, it is important that you respect the views of others. Learning more about world religions can help you better understand your own faith perspective.

Learning and physical challenges. Although the majority of college students have reasonably average learning and physical abilities, the numbers of students with physical or learning challenges are rising on most college campuses, as are the services that are available to them. Physical challenges can include hearing impairment, visual impairment, paralysis, or specific disorders such as cerebral palsy or multiple sclerosis. As discussed earlier in this book, many students have some form of learning disability that makes college work a challenge.

A person with a physical or learning challenge wants to be treated just as you would treat anyone else—with respect. If a student with such a challenge is in your class, treat him or her as you would any student; too much eagerness to help might be seen as an expression of pity.

If you have, or think you might have, a learning disability, visit your campus learning center for a diagnosis and advice on getting extra help for learning problems. Unlike in high school, college students with disabilities need to inform the appropriate office if they require accommodations.

Sexuality. The word *sexuality* refers to the people to whom you are romantically attracted. You are familiar with the terms *gay, straight, homosexual, heterosexual, bisexual, queer* or *questioning*, and *transgender*. In college, you will likely meet students, staff members, and instructors whose sexual orientation may differ from yours. While some people are lucky enough to come from welcoming environments, for many students college is the first time they have been able to openly express their sexual identity. Sexual orientation can be difficult to talk about, and it is important that you respect all individuals with whom you come in contact. Check to see if your campus has a center for the lesbian, gay, bisexual, transgender, and queer/questioning (LGBTQ) community. Consider going to hear some speakers, and expand your worldview.

Creating a Welcoming Environment on Your Campus

Colleges are working to provide a welcoming and inclusive campus environment for all students. Because of acts of violence, intimidation, and stupidity occurring on campuses, college administrations have established policies against any and all forms of discriminatory actions, racism, and insensitivity. Many campuses have adopted zero-tolerance policies that prohibit verbal and nonverbal harassment as well as hate crimes such as physical assault, vandalism, and intimidation. If you have been the victim of a racist, insensitive, or discriminatory act, report it to the proper authorities.

Whatever form these crimes might take on your campus, it is important to examine your thoughts and feelings about their occurrence. Ask yourself: Will you do something about it, or do you think it is someone else's problem? Commit to becoming involved in making your campus a safe place for all students. ■

TRY IT!

SETTING GOALS ▷ Make a New and Different Friend

College will give you the opportunity to expand your horizons. And if you want college to be more than a repeat of high school, you have to be willing to motivate yourself to branch out, to try new things, and to meet new people. Sometimes it's easy to stay in the same rut because it feels comfortable, but college is about making new friends and broadening your worldview. Learning about the views and experiences of others can motivate you to both explore human differences and look for what we all have in common. Set a goal of befriending someone who you think is different from you based on what you observe. Pay attention to what other students say in class, and get an idea of which students think differently from you and hold different values. Strike up a conversation with one of these students, and find out more about his or her background and what the two of you have in common in spite of your differences. Is this person as different from you as you originally thought? What have you learned about the assumptions you make about people?

Connecting through Involvement

A college or university can seem to be a huge and unfriendly place, especially if you went to a small high school or grew up in a small town. Getting involved in campus life will help you feel comfortable in your new environment, enrich your college experience, and help you make friends, so make sure to take advantage of student activities on your campus. Getting involved is not difficult, but it will take some initiative on your part. Consider your interests and choose some activities to explore. You might be interested in joining an intramural team, performing community service, running for a student government office, or getting involved in a structured campuswide club or organization. Some clubs are related to professions, while others are related to general interests.

While involvement is the key, it's important to strike a balance between finding a niche where you are immediately comfortable and challenging yourself to have new and different interactions with others. Having an open mind and experiencing diversity will prepare you for changes in the workforce that you'll experience in coming years. Also, challenge yourself to learn about various cultural groups in and around your college and home community, and participate in campus ethnic and cultural celebrations to learn about unique traditions, ideas, and viewpoints.

Almost every college has numerous organizations you can join; usually, you can check them out through activity fairs, printed guides, open houses, Web sites, Facebook pages, and so on. If a particular organization interests you, consider attending one of the organization's meetings before you decide to join. Find out what the organization is like, what the expected commitment is in terms of time and money, and whether you feel comfortable with the members. Students who become involved with at least one organization are more likely to complete their first year and remain in college.

TRY IT!

MANAGING TIME ▷ How Involved Is Too Involved?

How many clubs and organizations have you joined? Do you think you are too involved in campus activities? As you develop your term schedule, include your out-of-class activities and obligations. If you are spending more time participating in extracurricular activities than studying, you probably should cut back, at least for the first year. And if you think you are not involved enough, try to find an extracurricular opportunity that interests you and fits into your schedule.

Be careful not to overextend yourself when it comes to campus activities. Although it is important to get involved, joining too many clubs or organizations will make it difficult to focus on any one activity and will interfere with your studies. Future employers will see a balance in academics and campus involvement as a desirable quality in prospective employees. Don't fall into the trap of thinking that more is better. In campus involvement, as in many things, quality is much more important than quantity.

> " Students who become involved with at least one organization are more likely to complete their first year and remain in college. "

Connecting by Working

One of the best ways to develop meaningful relationships on your campus is to get an on-campus job, either through the federal work-study program or directly through the college. Generally, your on-campus supervisors will be much more flexible than off-campus employers in helping you balance your study demands and your work schedule. You might not make as much money working on campus as you would in an off-campus job, but the relationships that you'll develop with influential people who care about your success in college and who will write those all-important reference letters make on-campus employment well worth it. Consider finding a job related to your intended major. For instance, if you are a pre-med major, you might be able to find on-campus work in a biology or chemistry lab. That work could help you gain knowledge and experience as well as make connections with faculty experts in your field.

If an on-campus job is not available or you don't find one that appeals to you, an off-campus job can allow you to meet new people in the community. If you already had a job before starting college, talk to your employer about the new demands on your time. Also keep in mind that some employers offer tuition assistance in certain circumstances; ask whether any such opportunities are available to you.

Wherever you decide to find a job, it's important that you limit work to a reasonable number of hours per week. Although some students have to work to pay their tuition or living expenses, many college students work too many hours just to support a certain lifestyle. Be careful to maintain a reasonable balance between work and study. Don't fall into the trap of thinking, I can do it all. Too many college students have found that trying to do it all means not doing anything well.

Connecting through Community Service

As a first-year student, one way to support causes important to you and expand your experience with diversity is to consider volunteering for a community service project such as serving the homeless at a soup kitchen or helping build or renovate homes for needy families. Your campus's division of student affairs might have a volunteer or community service office that offers other service opportunities such as working with elementary school students who are learning to read, tutoring in an after-school program, participating in a campus cleanup, or working in a local animal shelter. You can also check Volunteer Match (volunteermatch.org) for opportunities in your area. Simply enter your zip code and, if you wish, key words to help you find volunteer work in your field of interest. ■

Connecting the College Experience to Career Success

Your college experience will help prepare you for many situations you will encounter in the workplace. If you have already held a job, you probably already have an idea of how working relates to being a good student. For instance, just as instructors have expectations of you, so will your employer or supervisor. Just as you have to be in class on time, you will need to be on time for work. But although cutting class occasionally without notifying anyone does not usually have serious consequences, such behavior in the workplace will likely get you fired. Your instructors expect you to work on your own and show initiative. Similarly, your supervisor expects you to complete assigned tasks and will be impressed when you go above and beyond your specific work responsibilities to develop new ideas and plans that benefit the company or organization.

The opportunities you have to develop relationships in college, especially with those who are different from you, will help you in the workplace, which is becoming more globally diverse. As you get experience working with diverse individuals in college, you will learn to appreciate the ways that different people with different backgrounds approach the same task. Just as you might participate in a study group on campus, your job will likely place you in a team with other employees who have to negotiate differences and produce a single product or outcome. Group experiences of any kind while you're in college—clubs, organizations, student government, and study groups—will help prepare you to work in teams in the workplace.

Communicating clearly and respectfully is a skill that you will develop in college and will also practice on the job. When you're in college, you may face conflict with an instructor, a friend or roommate, or a family member. And as you pursue your career, conflicts may arise with supervisors, coworkers, a spouse or partner, or even your children. Basic rules apply: Discuss your perspective respectfully and thoughtfully rather than exchanging angry e-mails or engaging in a shouting match. Try to see the situation from the other person's point of view, and if possible, negotiate your differences.

At this stage in your life, you probably have a sense of your ethics—your morals or sense of right and wrong—but have you considered your work ethic? A work ethic refers to the moral principles or values people apply to their jobs, such as honesty, a sense of responsibility, diligence, and determination to do one's best. College provides opportunities to practice and strengthen these values, and they will serve you well in your chosen career. In so many ways, college is a training ground for full-time employment. It also represents a time and a place where you can clarify your sense of life purpose — a purpose that will connect your interests, your relationships, and your values. Remember, the more effort you put into your college experience, the more success awaits.

Chapter Review

Steps to Success:
Connecting with Others in a Diverse World

○ **Be open to new relationships.** College may be a great time for you to test out serious relationships, including romantic ones.

○ **Don't hesitate to get help from your campus counseling center.** When counselors are asked, "What is the most common type of problem you help students address?" the answer is "relationships."

○ **Work to have a good relationship with your family during the college years.** Family members have your best interests at heart, and college is a time to become closer to them while also setting boundaries.

○ **Get involved.** Join other students in groups sponsored by your educational institution. Students who are involved are more likely to graduate from college than those who are not. Getting involved is fun, easy, free, and rewarding, and employers will be interested in your extracurricular activities.

○ **Look for the right on- or off-campus job.** Working during college is a good thing, depending on where you work, how much you work, and what you do. Get help on this important decision from your adviser and career center.

○ **Consider performing some kind(s) of service during college.** By doing so, you will develop meaningful relationships that will help you clarify your career choice.

Applying what you've learned . . .

Now that you have read and discussed this chapter, consider how you can apply what you have learned to your academic and personal lives. The following prompts will help you reflect on the chapter material and its relevance to you both now and in the future.

1. If you are not already involved in on-campus activities and clubs, visit your college's Web site or activities office to learn more about the kinds of clubs, organizations, service-learning opportunities, sports teams, and volunteer work that are offered. Find at least one activity that seems interesting to you and learn more about it. When does the group meet and how often, and how many students are involved?

2. Check out some of your fellow students' profiles on Facebook or Twitter. What kinds of personal information do they share? What kinds of issues are they writing about? Do they use the privacy settings that are available? Do you think that it is important for college students to be careful about the kinds of information they post on social networking sites? Why or why not?

Use Your Resources

GO TO ▷ **The counseling center:** If you need help thinking and talking about your relationships and making the most appropriate decisions. It is normal to seek such assistance. This kind of counseling is strictly confidential (unless you are a threat to yourself or others) and usually is provided at no charge, which is a great benefit.

GO TO ▷ **A campus chaplain:** If you need help from a member of the clergy in dealing with a relationship problem. Many public and private colleges have religiously affiliated chaplains, most of whom have specialized training in pastoral counseling. They also organize and host group activities in campus religious centers that you might want to take advantage of.

GO TO ▷ **Student organizations:** If you need help getting into a small group with other students who share the same interests with you.

GO ONLINE TO ▷ **The University of Chicago's Student Counseling Virtual Pamphlet Collection (www.dr-bob.org/vpc/):** If you need help finding Web sites devoted to relationship problems. Browse among the many links to see whether any information applies to you.

GO ONLINE TO ▷ **The Community Toolbox's chapter, "Cultural Competence in a Multicultural World" (http://ctb.ku.edu/en/table-of-contents/culture/cultural-competence/culture-and-diversity/main):** If you need help finding a good resource for becoming culturally competent. The Community Toolbox, a public service of the University of Kansas, is a free online resource for those working to build healthier communities and bring about social change. Its mission is to promote community health and development by connecting people, ideas, and resources.

GO ONLINE TO ▷ **Diversity and Democracy (www.aacu.org/diversitydemocracy):** If you need help finding resources related to civic learning and democratic engagement, global learning, engagement with diversity, and social responsibility.

GO ONLINE TO ▷ **Teaching Tolerance (www.tolerance.org):** If you need help accessing resources for dealing with discrimination and prejudice both on and off campus.

NOW... How do you measure up?

1. One of the best parts of college is getting to know people who are different from me in terms of ethnicity, religion, or life experience.

   ○ Agree
   ○ Don't Know
   ○ Disagree

2. Family members can be an important source of support for first-year students.

   ○ Agree
   ○ Don't Know
   ○ Disagree

3. It will be beneficial for me to select at least one college course that exposes me to other cultures.

   ○ Agree
   ○ Don't Know
   ○ Disagree

4. Being involved in college life outside of class will probably help me get a good job after graduation.

   ○ Agree
   ○ Don't Know
   ○ Disagree

How do your answers here compare to your responses to the quiz you took at the start of the chapter? Which sections of this chapter left a strong impression on you? What strategies for connecting with others have you started to use? Are they working? What other strategies will you commit to trying?

LaunchPad
macmillan learning

11

181
Living on a Budget

185
Understanding Financial Aid

189
Achieving a Balance between Working and Borrowing

191
Managing Credit Wisely

Managing Money

To access the LearningCurve study tool, Video Tools, and more, go to *LaunchPad Solo for College Success*. **macmillanhighered.com/ collegesuccessmedia**

Whether we like it or not, we can't ignore the importance of money. Money is often symbolically and realistically the key ingredient to independence and even, some people have concluded, to a sense of freedom. You probably know of instances in which money divided a family or a relationship or seemed to drive someone's life in a direction that person would not have taken otherwise. Money can also affect people's specific academic goals, causing them to select or reject certain academic majors or degree plans.

Sometimes parents will insist that students major in a field that is more likely to yield a good job and a good salary. Given the cost of college today, these attitudes are understandable.

Although your primary goal in college should be to achieve a strong academic record, the need for money can be a significant distraction, making it more difficult to complete your degree. Sometimes, in their attempt to survive financially, students will overuse credit cards and get themselves in serious financial trouble. Educators recognize that not understanding personal finances can hinder a student's progress, and mandatory personal finance classes are now being added in high schools and are available as options at some colleges. The purpose of this chapter is to provide basic information and suggestions so that money issues will not be a barrier to your success in college. There are sources of financial assistance through loans, grants, and work-study programs, and this chapter will help you develop a strategy for investigating your options. Think of this chapter as a summary of needed financial skills; if you want more information, consider taking a personal finance class at your college or in your community.

How do you measure up?

1. A budget should guide how much money I spend each month.

- ○ Agree
- ○ Don't Know
- ○ Disagree

2. I know how many courses I have to take to receive or maintain financial aid.

- ○ Agree
- ○ Don't Know
- ○ Disagree

3. I understand the disadvantages of working too many hours a week off campus.

- ○ Agree
- ○ Don't Know
- ○ Disagree

4. I am working to build a good credit score while I'm in college.

- ○ Agree
- ○ Don't Know
- ○ Disagree

Review the items you marked "Don't Know" or "Disagree." Pay special attention to these topics in this chapter—you will find motivating strategies that will help you develop in these areas. A follow-up quiz at the end of the chapter will prompt you to consider what you have learned.

Eating Your Words

△ **Jeff Zisa**

My first two years at college, it was easy to figure out my budget, because so many of my expenses were fixed. But this year I have a car and an off-campus apartment, so I decided to get off the meal plan and buy my own food.

"This is a bad idea," said my mother when I told her of my plan. "What are you going to eat?"

"Stuff I cook," I said. "It'll be cheaper in the long run. All my roommates and I are taking turns."

We did take turns, for the first week or so. Sam made pizza. Nick made burritos. I made my famous spaghetti. Occasionally, we made more pizza or spaghetti. Then classes started and sports and clubs kicked in, and I guess no one really had time to go to the grocery store anymore. In fact, it was hard to even eat a bowl of cereal in the morning because we were always out of milk. It got to the point where we ate out all the time, and even the cheapest meal out costs $10. So within months I had to call and tell my parents that I'd maxed out my credit card, drained my bank account, and run up over $200 in penalties—all on food.

"I know I should have kept track of what I was spending," I admitted. "It just added up so fast."

"See, I warned you," my mother said. "You learned a painful lesson." An ominous pause followed. "So . . . what kind of job are you planning to get?"

Why is it so important to track your spending in college? What steps could Jeff take to manage his money more carefully? Going to college may give some students their first experience of living on a budget, or they may already be very good at living within their means. Some students make it a habit to track their income and expenses precisely, but other students seem to be unaware of how much money they are spending. If they run out, which they often do, they rely on credit cards to get them to the end of the month. Getting in the habit of spending more money than you have can sabotage not only your college experience but also your life after college.

Living on a Budget

Face it: College is expensive, and most students have limited financial resources. Not only is tuition a major cost, but day-to-day expenses can also add up quickly. No matter what your financial situation, a budget for college is a must. Although a budget might not completely eliminate debt after graduation, it can help you become realistic about your finances so that you will have a basis for future life planning.

A budget is a spending plan that tracks all sources of income (such as student loan disbursements and money from parents) and expenses (like rent and tuition) during a set period of time (such as a week or a month). Creating and following a budget will allow you to pay your bills on time, cut costs, put some money away for emergencies, and finish college with as little debt as possible.

Creating a Budget

A budget will condition you to live within your means, put money into savings, and possibly invest down the road. Here are a few tips to help you get started.

Gather income information. To create an effective budget, you need to learn more about your income and your spending behaviors. First, determine how much money is coming in and when. Sources of income might include a job, your savings, gifts from relatives, student loans, scholarship dollars, or grants. List all your income sources, making note of how often you receive each type of income (weekly or monthly paychecks, quarterly loan disbursements, one-time gifts, etc.) and how much money you can expect each time. Knowing when your money is coming in will help you decide how to structure your budget. For example, if most of your income comes in on a monthly basis, you'll want to

> " No matter what your financial situation, a budget for college is a must. "

create a monthly budget. If you are paid every other week, a biweekly budget might work better.

Gather expense information for your college or university. Your expenses will include tuition; residence hall fees if you live on campus; and the costs of books and course materials, lab fees, and membership fees for any organizations you might join. Some institutions offer a separate January or May term. Although your tuition for these one-month terms is generally covered in your overall tuition payment, you would have extra expenses if you wanted to travel to another location in the United States or abroad.

Gather information about living expenses. First, get a "reality check." How do you *think* that you are spending your money? To find out for sure where your money is going and when, track your spending for a few weeks—ideally, for at least a full month— in a notebook or in a table or spreadsheet. The kinds of expense categories you should consider will vary depending on your situation. If you are a full-time student and you live with your parents or other family members, your living expenses won't be the same as those of a student living in a campus residence hall or in an off-campus apartment. If you are a returning student holding down a job and have a family of your own to support, you will calculate your expenses differently.

Whatever your situation, keeping track of your expenses and learning about your spending behaviors are important habits. Consider which of the following expense categories are relevant to you:

- Rent/utilities (electricity, gas, water)
- Cell phone / cable / Internet / Wi-Fi
- Transportation (car payment, car insurance, car repairs, gas, public transportation)
- Child care
- Groceries
- Medical expenses (prescriptions, doctor visits, hospital bills)
- Clothing/laundry
- Entertainment (dining out, hobbies, movies)
- Personal grooming (haircuts, toiletries)
- Miscellaneous (travel, organization dues)

Be sure to recognize which expenses are fixed and which are variable. A *fixed expense* is one that will cost you the same amount every time you pay it. For example, your rent is a fixed expense because you owe your landlord the same amount each month. A *variable expense* is one that may change. Your textbooks are a variable expense because the number and cost of them will be different each term.

Find out how you are doing. Once you have a sense of how your total income compares to your total weekly or monthly expenses, you can get a clearer picture of your current financial situation.

Make adjustments. Although your budget might never be perfect, you can strive to improve it. In what areas did you spend much more or much less than expected? Do you need to reallocate funds to better meet the needs of your current situation? Be realistic and thoughtful in how you spend your money, and use your budget to help meet your goals, such as planning for a trip or getting a new pair of jeans.

TRY IT!

MAKING DECISIONS ▷ **Miscellaneous Expenses**

Trying to get a handle on your "miscellaneous" expenses can be a challenge. Make a decision to write down everything you purchase over a two-week period, and see how many of those expenses don't fit in any of the categories listed on pages 180–81. Which of your miscellaneous expenses really are necessary, and which aren't? The unnecessary expenses are places to reduce money you spend. Make some tough choices to cut back, and start immediately. Track your spending for another two weeks. Can you tell the difference?

Whatever you do, don't give up if your bottom line doesn't turn out to be what you expected. Be resilient and get back on track. Budgeting is a lot like dieting; you might slip up and eat a pizza (or spend too much buying one), but all is not lost. If you stay focused and flexible, your budget can lead you to financial stability and independence.

Cutting Costs

Once you have put together a working budget and have tried it out and adjusted it, you're likely to discover that your expenses still exceed your income. Don't panic. Simply begin to look for ways to reduce those expenses. Here are some tips for saving money in college.

Recognize the difference between your needs and your wants. A *need* is something you must have. For example, tuition and textbooks are considered *needs*. Your *wants* are goods, services, or experiences that you wish to purchase but could reasonably live without. For example, concert tickets and mochas are *wants*. Your budget should always provide for your *needs* first.

Use low-cost transportation. If you live close to campus, consider whether you need a car. Take advantage of lower-cost options such as public transportation or biking to class to save money on gasoline and parking. If you live farther away, check to see whether your institution hosts a ride-sharing program for commuter students, or carpool with someone in your area.

Seek out discount entertainment options. Take advantage of discounted or free entertainment through your college. Most institutions use a portion of their student fees to provide affordable entertainment options such as discounted or free tickets to concerts, movie theaters, sports events, or other special activities.

Embrace secondhand goods. Use online resources such as Craigslist and Freecycle.org and thrift stores such as Goodwill to expand your wardrobe, purchase extras such as games and sports equipment, or furnish and decorate your room, apartment, or house.

Avoid unnecessary fees. Making late payments on credit cards and other bills can lead to expensive fees and can lower your credit score (which in turn will raise your interest rates). Note payment due dates carefully on your calendar to avoid this type of costly mistake. ∎

△ **Go Vintage**
Saving money doesn't mean you have to deprive yourself. Shopping at thrift stores for your clothes or apartment furnishings is a fun, affordable way to get one-of-a-kind pieces and not break the bank. © ANDREW WINNING/Reuters/Corbis.

SETTING GOALS ▷ **Your Personal Budget: There's an App for That**

Technology can really help you when it comes to keeping track of your money—knowing how much you have, how much you need, and whether there are any problems with transactions moving through your accounts. Use one of the many tools available to develop a budget for this term. Don't put it off! Unexpected financial problems can be a major source of stress and can sabotage your academic progress, so use your desire to avoid these kinds of problems as motivation to take control of your income and your expenses now. Try Bankrate's Student Budget Calculator (bankrate.com/calculators/smart-spending/college-student-budget-calculator.aspx), or check with your bank or credit union about available online services such as free online access to your accounts, so you can deposit funds, make purchases, transfer funds, and receive deposit or withdrawal notifications via your cell phone or e-mail. Many banks can also send you electronic notifications of these transactions, so you are always aware of how much money is currently in your account and when activity occurs that will affect your

account. These services allow you to review your account information, which will motivate you to make better decisions about when and how you use your money. And check out some of these cool apps:

- **Mint (mint.com).** A Web site and phone app, Mint allows you to combine information from all your financial accounts in one place, so you can see how much money you have in investments, income, loans, and payments. While it is not a bank, it does allow you to see your whole financial picture at once.
- **PayPal Mobile (paypal.com).** This app allows you to spend money and allows other people to give you money, including money you earn from part-time jobs, gigs, or monetary gifts from friends or family members.
- **Pocket Budget (mapeapps.com).** This app helps you manage your personal finances with easy ways to track your expenses and income and ideas to improve your cash flow.

Unexpected Benefits of Being Good with Money

You may be wondering why we included a chapter in this text about managing your money, which might seem to be "none of our business." You might wonder how this aspect of college is related to academic success. Well, we have worked with college students for decades. We have watched many of them experience major money problems and, as a result, get in serious financial trouble with a bank or credit card company, develop a poor credit rating that will follow them for many years, lose their motivation for academic work, and ultimately struggle to achieve their life and career goals. Occasionally, money problems are out of a student's control; but more often, they result from poor money management.

How you manage money while you're in college will affect the rest of your life. This is true whether you have a generous allowance from your family or no financial help at all. You might know students who often "hit people up" for money. These students are probably wasting money and will still be wasting money when they are in their thirties, forties, and fifties. You might also know students who are frugal, tracking virtually every penny they spend. These students may actually save money while they're in college, and this habit of saving will be with them throughout their lives. Which group are you in? And how important is it, really?

As it turns out, your ability to manage money is likely to affect your job prospects. A 2012 survey of employers conducted by the Society of Human Resource Management found that 53 percent[1] run credit checks on all or some potential new hires. Especially when there is competition for a job, employers may be looking at not only your academic qualifications or your experience, but also your ability to manage money. This is especially true if you are applying for a job in a bank, a brokerage house, the government, or other financial institutions where the potential exists for fraud and embezzlement.

Here is the bottom line: If you develop the habit of budgeting and money management while you're a college student, it will pay off for the rest of your life, no matter how much or how little money you ultimately have. But if you are in the habit of wasting money now, you might always waste it, and this may be a sign to a potential employer that you lack a sense of personal responsibility. Practice now by developing good budgeting strategies; don't let money management be a lifelong struggle for you.

[1] http://www.shrm.org/research/surveyfindings/articles/pages/creditbackgroundchecks.aspx

Understanding Financial Aid

Few students can pay the costs of college tuition, academic fees, books, room and board, bills, and random expenses without some kind of help. Luckily, financial aid—student loans, grants, scholarships, work-study programs, and other sources of money to support your education—is available to help cover your costs.

Types of Aid

While grants and scholarships are unquestionably the best forms of aid because they do not have to be repaid, the federal government, states, and colleges offer many other forms of assistance, such as loans, work-study opportunities, and cooperative education. A student loan is a form of financial aid that must be paid back with interest.

Grants are funds provided by the government to help students pay for college and do not need to be repaid. They are given to students based on their financial needs. Some grants are specific to a particular academic major. Grants are awarded by the federal government, state governments, and the educational institutions themselves. Students meet academic qualifications for grants by being admitted to a college and maintaining grades that are acceptable to the grant provider.

A scholarship is money from your college or another source that supports your education and does not have to be repaid. Some scholarships are need-based—that is, they are awarded on the basis of both talent and financial need. *Talent* can refer to your past accomplishments in the arts or athletics, your potential for future accomplishments, or even where you are from. Some colleges and universities place importance on admitting students from other states or countries. *Need* in this context means the cost of college minus a federal determination of what you and your family can afford to contribute toward that cost. Your institution might provide scholarships from its own resources or from individual donors. Donors themselves sometimes stipulate characteristics of scholarship recipients, such as age or academic major.

> ❝ Few students can pay the costs of college tuition, academic fees, books, room and board, bills, and random expenses without some kind of help. ❞

Other scholarships are known as merit scholarships. These are based on talent as defined above but do not require you to demonstrate financial need. It can be challenging to match your talent with merit scholarships. Most of them come through colleges and are part of the admissions and financial aid processes, which are usually described on the college's Web site. Web-based scholarship search services are another good source to explore. Be certain that the Web site you use is free, will keep your information confidential unless you release your name, and will send you a notice (usually through e-mail) when a new scholarship that matches your qualifications is posted. Also be sure to ask your employer, your family's employers, and social, community, or religious organizations about any available scholarships.

Work-study means that students who receive financial aid can also have part-time jobs to earn extra money if their aid amount is not enough to cover all their education costs. Students receive work-study notices as part of the overall financial aid notice and then can sign up to be interviewed for work-study jobs. Although some work-study jobs are relatively menial, the best options provide experience related to your academic studies while allowing you to earn money for college. Your salary is based on the skills required for a particular position and the hours involved. Keep in mind that you will be expected to accomplish specific tasks while on duty, although some supervisors might permit you to study during any downtime. Work-study positions give you the opportunity to develop and test out some or all components of your personal work ethic such as honesty, personal initiative, sense of responsibility, discipline, and willingness to work in a team toward a common goal.

Cooperative (co-op) education allows you to alternate a term of study (a semester or quarter) with a term of paid work. Engineering co-op opportunities are among the most common, and the number of co-op programs in health care fields is growing. Colleges make information about co-ops available through admissions and academic departments.

Navigating and Qualifying for Financial Aid

The majority of students need help in paying for college, and various types of financial aid are available: scholarships, grants, loans, and

paid employment. Financial aid professionals refer to this combination as a *package.*

Financial aid seems complex because it can come from so many different sources. Each source may have a different set of rules about how to receive the money and how not to lose it. The financial aid office at your college can help you find the way to get the largest amount of money that doesn't need to be repaid, the lowest interest rate on loans, and work possibilities that fit your academic program. Do not overlook this valuable campus resource. It is the best place to begin looking for all types of financial assistance.

Most financial assistance requires some form of application. The application used most often is the Free Application for Federal Student Aid (FAFSA). All students should complete the FAFSA by the earliest submission deadline among the colleges they are considering. The FAFSA Web site (https://fafsa.ed.gov/) is very

△ **Show Me the Money**
Don't let the paperwork scare you away. If you're not already receiving financial aid, be sure to investigate all the available options. And remember that your institution may also offer scholarships or grants that you don't have to repay. © Riza Liu/PSU Vanguard.

informative. If additional forms are also required, such as the College Board's PROFILE form (http://student.collegeboard.org/css-financial-aid-profile) or individual scholarship applications, they will be listed in colleges' financial aid or admissions materials or by organizations that offer scholarships.

Read *Steps to Qualify for Financial Aid*, which outlines the steps you must take to qualify for most scholarships and grants, especially those sponsored by the federal government or state governments. The amount of financial aid you receive will depend on the cost of your academic program and what you or your family can pay as determined by the FAFSA. The cost includes average expenses for tuition and fees, books and supplies, room and board, transportation, and personal expenses. The financial aid office will subtract from that cost the amount you and your family are expected to pay. In some cases that amount can be as little as zero. Financial aid is designed to make up as much of the balance or "need" as possible.

How to Keep Your Funding

If you earn average or better grades, complete your courses each term, and finish your program or degree on time, you should have no trouble maintaining your financial aid. It's a good idea to check with the financial aid office before you drop classes to make sure you will not lose any aid.

Some types of aid, especially scholarships, require that you maintain full-time enrollment and make satisfactory academic progress. Dropping or failing a class might jeopardize all or part of your financial aid unless you are enrolled in more credits than the minimum required for financial aid. For full-time financial aid that minimum is often defined as twelve credit hours per term. If you initially enrolled in fifteen credit hours and dropped one three-hour course, your aid should not change. Even so, talk with a financial aid counselor before making the decision to drop a course, just to be sure. Remember that, although the financial aid office is there to serve you,

Steps to Qualify for Financial Aid

1. Enroll half-time or more in a certificate or degree program at one of the more than 4,500 colleges and universities certified to distribute federal financial aid. A few aid programs are available for less than half-time study; check with your department or college.

2. Complete the FAFSA. The first FAFSA you file is intimidating, especially if you rush to complete it right before the deadline. Completing the FAFSA in subsequent years is easier because you only need to update items that have changed. To make the process easier, get your personal identification number (PIN) a few weeks before the deadline. This PIN will be the same one you'll use throughout your college career. Try to do the form in sections rather than tackling all of it at once. Most of the information is basic: name, address, driver's license number, and things you will know or have in your personal files and records. For many undergraduates the financial section will require your own and your parents' information from tax materials. However, if you are at least twenty-four, are a veteran, or have dependents, you do not need to submit your parents' tax

information. If you are married, your spouse's tax information will be needed.

3. Complete the College Board PROFILE form if your school or award-granting organization requires it. Review your college's admission information, or ask a financial aid adviser to determine whether this form is required.

4. Identify any additional applications that are required. These are usually scholarship applications with personal statements or short essays. The organizations, including the colleges that are giving the money, will provide instructions about what is required. Most have Web sites with complete information.

5. Follow instructions carefully, and submit each application on time. Financial aid is awarded from a fixed pool of funds. Once money is awarded, there is usually none left for those who file late.

6. Complete the classes for which you were given financial aid with at least a minimum grade point average as defined by your academic department or college or the organization that provided you the scholarship.

you must take the following steps to be your own advocate.

- **File for financial aid every year.** Even if you don't think you will receive aid for a certain year, you must file annually in case you become eligible in the future.

- **Meet all filing deadlines.** Students who do not meet filing deadlines risk losing aid from one year to the next.

- **Talk with a financial aid officer immediately if you or your family experiences a significant loss** (such as the loss of a job or the death of a parent or spouse). Don't wait for the next filing period; you might be eligible for funds for the current year.

- **Inquire every year about criteria-based aid.** Many colleges and universities have grants and scholarships for students who meet specific criteria. These might include grants for minority students, grants for students in specific academic majors, and grants for students from single-parent families.

- **Inquire about campus jobs throughout the year,** as these jobs might be available at any time, not just at the beginning of the term.

If you do not have a job and want or need to work, keep asking.

- **Consider asking for a reassessment of your eligibility for aid.** If you have reviewed your financial aid package and think that your circumstances deserve additional consideration, you can ask the financial aid office to reassess your eligibility. The office is not always required to do so, but the request might be worth your effort. ∎

TRY IT!

SETTING GOALS ▷ Exhaust All Avenues

Learn about possible sources of financial support on your campus in addition to those you may already be receiving. The best single source for this information is your institution's financial aid office. You may also want to check with your employer (if you work off campus), your parents' employers, houses of worship, and civic organizations such as the Rotary or Kiwanis club in your hometown.

Achieving a Balance between Working and Borrowing

After you have determined your budget, decided what (if anything) you can pay from savings, and taken your scholarships and grants into consideration, you may find that you still need additional income. Each term or year, you should decide how much you can work while maintaining good grades and how much you should borrow from student loans.

Advantages and Disadvantages of Working

The majority of students today find that a combination of working and borrowing is the best way to gain experience, finance college, and complete their educational goals on time. Paid employment while you are in college has benefits beyond the money you earn. Having a job in a field related to your major can help you develop a credential for graduate school and make you more employable later because it shows you have the capability to manage several priorities at the same time. Working while you are in college can help you determine whether a particular career is what you will really want after you graduate. And students who work a moderate amount (fifteen or twenty hours per week) typically get better grades than students who do not work at all.

However, it's almost impossible to get great grades if you work full-time while also trying to be a full-time student. Some first-year students prefer not to take a job while they're making adjustments to a new academic environment. You might find that you're able to work some terms but not others while you are a student. And family obligations or challenging classes can sometimes make the added burden of work impractical or impossible.

Part-time off-campus jobs that relate to your major or career plan are hard to come by. You'll likely find that most part-time employment has little or no connection to your career objectives. A better option may be to seek a job on campus. In addition to the feeling of connectedness that on-campus jobs often offer, students who work

on campus develop relationships with instructors and staff members who can help them negotiate the academic and social sides of campus life and make plans for the future. While off-campus employers are often unwilling to allow their student employees time off for study and exam preparation, college employers will want you to put your studies and exam preparation first. The downside to on-campus employment is that you'll likely earn less than you would in an off-campus job, but if success in college is your top priority, the upside of working on campus outweighs the downside.

Student Loans

Although you should be careful not to borrow yourself into a lifetime of debt, avoiding loans altogether could delay your graduation and your progress up the career ladder. For most students some level of borrowing is both necessary and prudent.

The following list provides information about the most common types of student loans. The list reflects the order in which you should apply for and accept loans to get the lowest interest rates and best repayment terms.

- **Subsidized federal student loans** are backed by the government, which pays the loan interest on your behalf while you are enrolled in undergraduate, graduate, or professional school.

FEELING CONNECTED ▷ Search Party

When job searching, you probably want to find the best-paying job possible. Earning money while you're in college provides income to help with your expenses, and hopefully you are getting in the habit of budgeting. Remember, too, that the ideal job will not only pay well but also move you toward your long-term career objectives. Connect with other students in your class who need or want to find jobs. Investigate what on-campus and part-time off-campus jobs are available for students, and share ideas for searching for jobs that make sense considering the competing responsibilities of work, college, and other personal and family commitments. Compare the wages, hours, and working conditions of available jobs. Share leads. Share your perspectives with one another and with your whole class.

> ❝ Your education is the most productive investment you can make for your future and that of your family. ❞

These loans require at least half-time enrollment and a submitted FAFSA application.

- **Unsubsidized federal student loans** may require that you make interest payments while you are enrolled. If not, the interest is added to the amount you owe; this is called *capitalization.*

- **Parent Loan for Undergraduate Students (PLUS) loans** are applied for and owed by parents but disbursed directly to students. The interest on PLUS loans is usually higher than the interest on federal student loans but lower than that on private loans. Parents who apply must provide information on the FAFSA.

- **Private student loans** are offered through banks and credit unions. Private loans often have stricter credit requirements and higher interest rates than federal loans do, and interest payments on private loans begin immediately.

Student loans are a very important source of money for college, but like paid employment, loans should be considered carefully. Loans for costs such as textbook purchases and tuition fees are good investments. Loans for a more lavish lifestyle are likely to weigh you down in the future. As one wise person put it, if by borrowing you live like a wealthy graduate while you're a student, you'll live like a student after you graduate. Student loans can be a good way to begin using credit wisely, a skill you are likely to need throughout your life. ■

Plan for the Future

It's never too early to begin thinking about how you will finance your life after graduation and whether you will begin working immediately or pursue a graduate or professional degree. Your work, whether on or off campus, will help you make that decision. Here are some tips that will help you plan now for your future.

- **Figure out your next step—more education or work?** If you are working on campus, get to know faculty or staff members and seek their advice about your future plans. If you are working off campus, think carefully about whether your current job is one that you would want to continue after you graduate. If not, keep your options open and look for part-time work in a field that more closely aligns with your career plans or long-term educational objectives.

- **Keep your address current with the registrar.** Even when you have finished your degree or program, and especially if you stop classes for a term, alert the registrar of any changes in address. This is doubly important if you have a student loan; you don't want to get a negative report on your credit rating because you missed information about your loan.

- **Establish a savings account.** Add to it regularly, even if you can manage to deposit only a few dollars a month. The sooner you start, the greater your returns will be.

Your education is the most productive investment you can make for your future and that of your family. Research shows that the completion of programs or degrees after high school increases earnings, opens up career options, leads to greater satisfaction in work, results in more engaged citizenship such as voting and community service, and greatly increases the probability that your children will go on to college. Although college is a big investment of time and money, it's an investment you'll be glad you made.

Managing Credit Wisely

When you graduate, you will leave your institution with two significant numbers. The first is your grade point average (GPA), which represents the level of academic success you attained while in college. The second, your credit score, is a numerical representation of your fiscal responsibility. Although this second number might be less familiar to you than the first, it could be a factor that determines whether you get your dream job, regardless of your GPA. In addition, twenty years from now you're likely to have forgotten your GPA, while your credit score will be more important than ever.

Your credit score is derived from a credit report that contains information about accounts in your name. These accounts include credit cards, student loans, utility bills, cell phones, and car loans, to name a few. This credit score can determine whether or not you will qualify for a loan (car, home, student, etc.), what interest rates you will pay, how much your car insurance will cost, and your chances of being hired by certain organizations. Even if none of these things are in your immediate future, now is the time to start thinking about your credit score.

Although using credit cards responsibly is a good way to build credit, acquiring a credit card has become much more difficult for college students. In May 2009, President Barack Obama signed legislation that prohibits college students under the age of twenty-one from obtaining a credit card unless they can prove that they are able to make the payments or unless the credit card application is cosigned by a parent or guardian.

Understanding Credit

Even if you can prove that you have the means to repay credit card debt, it is important for you to thoroughly understand how credit cards work and how they can both help and hurt you. Simply put, a credit card allows you to buy something now and pay for it later. Each month you will receive a statement listing all purchases you made with your credit card during the previous thirty days. The statement will request a payment toward your balance and will set a payment due date. Your payment options will vary: You can pay your entire balance, pay a specified portion of the balance, or make only a minimum payment, which may be as low as $10.

Beware: If you pay only the minimum required, the remaining balance on your card will be

◁ **In Case of Emergency**
Having a credit card for emergencies is a good practice. Circumstances that might warrant the use of credit include paying critical expenses to care for yourself or your family, dealing with an auto accident, an unforeseen medical expense, or traveling on short notice to handle a crisis. But remember that spring break is *not* an emergency. © Britt Erlanson/cultura/ Corbis.

charged a finance fee, or interest charge, causing your balance to increase before your next bill arrives even if you don't make any more purchases. Paying the minimum payment is almost never a good strategy and can add years to your repayment time. In fact, assuming an 18 percent interest rate, if you continually pay only $10 per month toward a $500 credit card balance, it will take you more than seven years to pay it off! And you'll pay an extra $431 in interest, almost doubling the amount you originally charged.

Avoid making late payments. Paying your bill even one day late can result in a finance charge of up to $30, and it can raise the interest rate not only on that card but also on any other credit accounts you have. If you decide to use a credit card to build credit, you might want to explore the automated online payment options that are available to you. Remember that the payment due date is the date that the payment should be received by the credit card lender, not the date that you send it.

If you decide to apply for a credit card while you're in college, remember that it should be used to build credit and for emergencies. Credit cards should not be used to fund a lifestyle that you cannot otherwise afford or to buy wants (see the section *Living on a Budget* in this chapter). If you use your credit card just once a month and pay the balance as soon as the bill arrives, you will be on your way to a strong credit score in just a few years.

> ❝ Credit cards should not be used to fund a lifestyle that you cannot otherwise afford. ❞

Debit Cards

Although you might wish to use a credit card for emergencies and to establish a good credit rating, you might also look into the possibility of applying for a debit card (also called a checkcard). The big advantage of a debit card is that you don't always have to carry cash and thus don't run the risk of losing it. Because the amount of your purchases will be limited to the funds in your bank account, a debit card is also a good form of constraint on your spending.

The only real disadvantage is that a debit card provides direct access to your checking account, so it's very important to keep your card in a safe place and away from your personal identification number (PIN). The safest way to protect your account is to commit your PIN to memory. If you lose your debit card or credit card, notify your bank immediately. ■

◁ **Don't Let This Happen to You**

The 2013 comedy *Identity Thief* tells the story of an identity-theft victim (played by Jason Bateman) who confronts the thief (played by Melissa McCarthy). In the movie the victim answers questions about vital personal information in a phone call that he did not initiate—a big no-no—and his life is turned upside down. If identity theft happens to you, it's not so funny. Bob Mahoney/©Universal/courtesy Everett Collection.

Frequently Asked Questions about Credit Cards and Identity Theft

- **I have a credit card with my name on it, but it is actually my parents' account number. Is this card building credit for me?** No. You are considered an authorized user on the account, but your parents are the primary account holders. To build credit, you must be the primary account holder or at least a joint account holder.

- **I have a credit card and am the primary account holder. How can I resist abusing it?** Use your credit card to help you build credit by making small charges and paying them off each month. Stick to two expense categories only, such as gas and groceries, and don't make any exceptions unless you have an emergency.

- **I choose the "credit" option every time I use my debit card. Is this building credit for me?** No. Using the credit function of your debit card is more like writing an electronic check because you are still taking money directly out of your checking account. Even if your debit card has a major credit card (Visa, MasterCard, etc.) logo on it, it is not building credit for you.

- **I have a few store credit cards (Target, Best Buy, etc.). Are these accounts included on my credit report?** Yes. However, though they will affect your credit score, store credit cards do not carry as much weight as major credit cards (Visa, MasterCard, etc.). It is OK to have a few store credit cards, but a major credit card will do more to help you build credit.

- **Where can I apply for a major credit card?** A good place to begin is your bank or credit union. Remember that you might have to prove your ability to make payments in order to obtain a card. Use your credit card to build credit by making small charges and paying them off each month.

- **If one credit card will help me build credit, will several build my credit even more?** Research shows that there is no benefit to having more than two major credit cards. And even if you're able to pay the required monthly amounts, having too many accounts open can make you appear risky to the credit bureaus determining your credit score.

- **What if I forget and make a late payment? Is my credit score ruined?** Your credit report reflects at least the past seven years of activity but puts the most emphasis on the most recent two years. In other words, the farther you get from your mistakes, the less impact they will have on your credit score. There is no quick fix for improving a credit score, so beware of advertisements that say otherwise.

- **If building credit is a wise decision, what's so bad about using credit cards to buy some things that I really want but can't afford right now?** It is not wise to use credit cards to purchase things that you cannot afford. Living within your means is always the way to go.

- **What is identity theft?** In this insidious and increasingly common crime, someone assumes your identity, secretly opens up accounts in your name, and has the bills sent to another address.

- **How can I protect myself from identity theft?** *Be password savvy.* The more sensitive the information, the stronger your password should be. Aim for passwords with eight to fourteen characters, including numbers, both uppercase and lowercase letters, and, if allowed, a few special characters like @ and #. Never use an obvious number like your birthday or wedding anniversary. Don't use the same username and password for every site. Change the password to your online credit card or bank account at least once a year. If you must keep a written record of your usernames and passwords, keep the list in a secure place at home, not in your wallet. *Beware of scams.* Lots of them are out there. Don't make yourself vulnerable. A few tips: Research a company or organization before submitting your résumé. Do not transmit personal information (social security number, bank details, credit or debit card numbers, passwords, etc.) through e-mail. Doing so could put you at risk of identity theft. Don't answer questions about vital personal information over the phone if you didn't originate the call. Don't reply to e-mails, pop-ups, or text messages that ask you to reveal sensitive information. Don't send sensitive data by e-mail. Call instead and deal only with businesses you trust. Never click on links in unsolicited e-mails or paste URLs or lines of code into your browser bar. If an offer sounds too good to be true—like a huge line of credit at 0 percent interest—it probably is.

- **Where can I get my credit report?** You can keep an eye on your credit report by visiting the free (and safe) Web site www.annualcreditreport.com at least once a year. Regularly reviewing your credit history pays off in major ways. It alerts you to any new accounts that might have been opened in your name. It also lets you catch unauthorized activity on accounts that you've closed or haven't used lately. Everyone is entitled to one free credit report a year from each of the three major credit bureaus.

Chapter Review

Steps to Success: Managing Money

○ **Make financial literacy a key college success skill.** Financial literacy is a specialized form of information literacy.

○ **Create a budget and then live within it.** Remember that it's your budget, tailor-made by and for you.

○ **Act on some of the suggestions offered in this chapter for cutting your costs.** For most college students, cutting costs is even more important than increasing their income.

○ **Learn as much as you can about the different types of financial aid.** Find out what is offered to U.S. college students and by your particular college, even though the term has already started. It's never too late to take advantage of these opportunities.

○ **Consider the pros and cons of working while in college.** If you do plan to work, consider how much and where you will work. Realize that students who borrow money and attend college full-time are more likely to attain their degrees than those who use a different strategy.

○ **Remember that you will finish college with two key numbers: your GPA and your credit score.** Potential employers will be checking your transcripts *and* your credit reports.

○ **Learn the strategies in this chapter for wise credit card management.** College is a time to learn how to use credit wisely.

○ **Protect yourself from identity theft.** Be password savvy and avoid scams.

○ **Take advantage of help offered on your campus to learn financial management skills.** You can't help it if you didn't learn these skills before; you may not have had any money to manage!

Applying what you've learned . . .

Now that you have read and discussed this chapter, consider how you can apply what you have learned to your academic and personal lives. The following prompts will help you reflect on the chapter material and its relevance to you both now and in the future.

1. Sometimes planning for the future is hard. Why not start small? Describe at least two things you can do each week to save money. For example, using public transportation when possible can help reduce the expense of owning a car.

2. Money can be a difficult subject to talk about, and sometimes it seems easier not to worry about it. Ask yourself some hard questions. Do you spend money without much thought? Do you have a lot of debt and not much to show for it? Describe what you want your financial picture to look like.

Use Your Resources

GO TO ▷ **Your institution's financial aid office:** If you need help understanding financial aid opportunities and how to apply for scholarships.

GO TO ▷ **Your local United Way office:** If you need credit counseling. Many communities have credit counseling agencies within the local United Way.

GO TO ▷ **Your college's student affairs office:** If you need help finding programs on money management. These programs are often offered in residence halls or through the division of student affairs.

GO TO ▷ **The business school or the division of continuing education:** If you need help finding a course in personal finance. Check your college catalog or Web site, or call the school or division office.

GO TO ▷ **The counseling center:** If you need help managing money problems that are related to compulsive shopping or gambling.

GO TO ▷ **Your campus library or bookstore:** If you want additional print resources about money management. A good book to look for is Susan Knox's *Financial Basics: A Money-Management Guide for Students* (Columbus: Ohio State University Press, 2004).

GO ONLINE TO ▷ **The Budget Wizard (budget.cashcourse.org):** If you want to use a free, secure budgeting tool from the National Endowment for Financial Education (NEFE).

GO ONLINE TO ▷ **The Free Application for Federal Student Aid (https://fafsa.ed.gov):** If you want to access the online application for federal student aid. You can set up an account, complete the application electronically, save your work, and monitor the progress of your application.

GO ONLINE TO ▷ **FastWeb (FastWeb.com):** If you are interested in using a free scholarship search service and discovering sources of educational funding you never knew existed.

GO ONLINE TO ▷ **Bankrate (bankrate.com):** If you are interested in unbiased information about the interest rates, fees, and penalties associated with major credit cards and private loans. This site also provides calculators that let you determine the long-term costs of different kinds of borrowing.

NOW... How do you measure up?

1. A budget should guide how much money I spend each month.

   ○ Agree
   ○ Don't Know
   ○ Disagree

2. I know how many courses I have to take to receive or maintain financial aid.

   ○ Agree
   ○ Don't Know
   ○ Disagree

3. I understand the disadvantages of working too many hours a week off campus.

   ○ Agree
   ○ Don't Know
   ○ Disagree

4. I am working to build a good credit score while I'm in college.

   ○ Agree
   ○ Don't Know
   ○ Disagree

How do your answers here compare to your responses to the quiz you took at the start of the chapter? Which sections of this chapter left a strong impression on you? What strategies for managing money have you started to use? Are they working? What other strategies will you commit to trying?

199
Understanding Wellness

208
Maintaining Sexual Health

210
Alcohol and Other Substances

Staying Healthy

Fenton one/Shutterstock

The first year of college can be one of life's most interesting and challenging transitions. Much of what you experience will be new—new friends, new freedoms, and new responsibilities. You will notice that many students use sensible and healthy coping strategies to handle the transition to college successfully. They watch what they eat and drink, exercise regularly, and get enough sleep. However, some students go in the opposite direction; they stay up late, drink too much, smoke, overeat, or engage in risky sexual behaviors. Many students gain weight during the college years, and much of that weight gain happens in the first year.

This chapter explores the topic of staying healthy, which includes taking care of your mind, body, and spirit; making healthy choices; and achieving balance. The college experience shouldn't only be about studying; it's also important to spend time with friends and enjoy the freedom and all the activities your college has to offer. But the freedoms you experience in college bring challenges and risks, and your success in college will depend on your ability to make sensible decisions about your personal habits and behaviors.

![LaunchPad macmillan learning]

To access the LearningCurve study tool, Video Tools, and more, go to *LaunchPad Solo for College Success.* **macmillanhighered.com/ collegesuccessmedia**

How do you measure up?

1. When I feel overwhelmed, I deal with my stress in healthy ways, like exercising or taking control of my schedule to make time to tackle my top priorities.

   ○ Agree
   ○ Don't Know
   ○ Disagree

2. Exercising regularly will help me manage my weight and stay fit.

   ○ Agree
   ○ Don't Know
   ○ Disagree

3. I have adequate information about sex and contraception.

   ○ Agree
   ○ Don't Know
   ○ Disagree

4. I know the difference between responsible and irresponsible alcohol use.

   ○ Agree
   ○ Don't Know
   ○ Disagree

Review the items you marked "Don't Know" or "Disagree." Pay special attention to these topics in this chapter—you will find motivating strategies to develop in these areas. A follow-up quiz at the end of the chapter will prompt you to consider what you have learned.

△ **Ariela Gavi**

Denise Lett/Shutterstock.

Some People Make It Look So Easy

Week 5 at college: My roommate, Julia, slips on a pair of elegant heels with the air of a movie star. To look at perfect Julia, you would never guess she has a complex life—taking fifteen credits, playing on the field hockey team, and working part-time in the math department, all while maintaining a 3.8 GPA.

"Why so bummed out?" she says. "C'mon, get dressed."

Julia and I share a major in business administration. We both have part-time academic jobs. Sadly, the similarities end there.

"How do you always manage to channel Sofía Vergara?" I ask her. "Look at me: I'm like someone who's been hiding in a Dunkin' Donuts warehouse." It's not much of an exaggeration: I'm so stressed out by school and work that I've embraced every donut or sweet roll that I can get my hands on. I no longer fit into anything in my wardrobe that doesn't involve an elastic waist. The weight gain then makes me more stressed. I can't sleep. I feel totally disorganized.

Julia shifts a basket of dirty laundry from my bed and sits down beside me. "Don't be silly," she says sympathetically.

"I just don't know how you get everything done and stay so Zen," I tell her. "I feel like I'm running as fast as I can just to keep up."

What can Ariela learn from Julia? What steps could Ariela take to manage stress better? Why is it important for students to eat properly, get regular exercise, and maintain a regular sleep schedule? Do you have more in common with Ariela or Julia? What strategies do you use to stay healthy? When do you slip up?

Understanding Wellness

Wellness is a concept that encompasses the care of your mind, body, and spirit. Wellness involves making healthy choices and achieving balance throughout your life. It includes reducing stress in positive ways, keeping fit, fostering your spirituality, deepening your self-knowledge, maintaining good sexual health, and taking a safe approach to alcohol and other drugs—assuming that you are of legal age to consume them.

Take this short quiz. As you consider each question, rate yourself on a scale of 1 to 5, with 1 being "never" and 5 being "always."

1. Are you able to manage your stress successfully? _____

2. Do you eat a wide range of healthy foods? _____

3. Do you exercise at least once a day? _____

4. Do you get seven or more hours of sleep each night? _____

5. Do you say "no" to others in order to manage your obligations? _____

6. Do you seek help from friends, family, or professionals when you need it? _____

7. Are you in control of your sexual health? _____

8. Do you avoid abusing alcohol, tobacco, or other substances? _____

9. Do you live a balanced life? _____

In what areas did you mark 4 or 5? _____
_____
_____

In what areas did you mark 1 or 2? _____
_____
_____

As you read the following preview of the nine components of wellness, pay special attention to the areas that you scored as 1 or 2.

1. **Stress management.** Occasional stress is a normal reaction to being a new college student. Recognize when your stress level is getting out of control, and seek help before stress gets in the way of your academic performance.

2. **Diet and nutrition.** Eating fast food will often increase your cholesterol and your weight. Substitute water for diet sodas, and opt for fresh, unprocessed foods.

3. **Exercise.** Exercising helps relieve stress and control weight. If you don't have time to work out every day, start with a smaller goal of three or four times a week.

4. **Sleep.** Going without sleep will negatively affect your overall health and ability to perform academically. Seven or eight hours of sleep per night can significantly improve your ability to handle stress.

5. **Saying "no" when you need to.** In order to manage your obligations, sometimes you have to say "no" to friends or even family. Know what your priorities are and stick to them.

6. **Seeking help for emotional problems.** If your emotions are out of control, if you are feeling depressed, or if you are becoming anxious about what's happening in your life, consider talking to a friend or family member or seeing a professional counselor.

7. **Sexual health.** Be sure that you practice safe sex. Understand the resources available to you when you have questions or problems.

8. **Substance abuse.** During your college years you will encounter substances like alcohol, tobacco, and drugs. Be sure you know the laws that govern the use of these substances in your state. If you are of legal age, remember that moderation is key. Are you a smoker? If so, quit now. There is no such thing as a safe level of smoking.

9. **Balance.** Wellness is about mind, body, and spirit. When you take care of all aspects of your personal wellness, it will be easier for you to handle problems when they develop.

Managing Stress to Maintain Wellness

Everyone experiences stress at one time or another—it's a normal part of being a human being—but the level of stress that affects college students can undermine their ability to succeed academically. Consider the level of stress you feel today. Rate your current stress level on a scale of 1 to 5, with 1 being "little or no stress" and 5 being "extremely stressed."

My current stress level: _____

If your stress level is 3 or higher, describe the symptoms of stress that you are experiencing.

_____

_____

Can you identify *why* you are feeling this level of stress?

_____

_____

If your stress level is 1 or 2, what accounts for your low level of stress?

_____

_____

Is the stress rating you gave yourself consistent most of the time, or does it fluctuate from day to day? If you have a high level of stress almost every day, you should seek some assistance from a counselor or health professional.

Stress has many sources, but two are prominent: life events and daily hassles. Life events are occurrences that represent major adversity, such as the death of a parent, spouse, partner, or friend. Researchers believe that an accumulation of stress from life events, especially if many occur over a short time period, can cause physical and mental health problems. Daily hassles are the minor irritants that you experience every day, such as losing your keys, having three tests on the same day, quarreling with your roommate, or worrying about money.

When you are stressed, your breathing becomes rapid and shallow; your heart rate increases; the muscles in your shoulders, forehead, neck, and chest tighten; your hands become cold or sweaty; your hands and knees may shake; your stomach becomes upset; your mouth goes dry;

△ **Nothing but Blue Skies**
When you are feeling stressed, take a moment to breathe. This strategy sounds simple, but it gets overlooked. Focusing on inhaling and exhaling slowly and picturing a serene scene like a blue sky or a sunny beach can help slow your heart rate and calm you down. You might also picture yourself succeeding at the task that is currently stressing you out. Breathing and visualization techniques can be powerful tools. Filipe Frazao/Shutterstock.

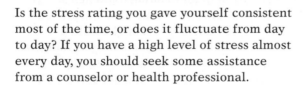

TRY IT!

MAKING DECISIONS ▷ **Are You About to Lose It?**

Are you so stressed out that you can't concentrate or study, or maybe you're irritable with your roommate or best friend for no good reason? Have you always been this way, or is stress something new? Whatever your history with stress, now is the time to make a decision to learn more about it and get it under control. A first step is to read the material to the left and apply these strategies. A second step might be to develop an exercise regimen that includes yoga. Meditation is another tried-and-true stress-reduction technique. Give yourself a couple of weeks, and if your stress level is still high, seek external help from your college counseling center. By reducing or eliminating your stress and worry, you can improve your academic performance and even your relationships with others.

and your voice may sound strained. Over time, stress can develop into a number of chronic health issues.

Stress also causes psychological changes. You might experience confusion, trouble concentrating, memory lapses, and difficulty solving problems. As a result of stress, you may also make decisions that you regret later. High stress levels can lead to anger, anxiety, depression, fear, frustration, and irritability, which might cause you to lose sleep. These stress-related changes can turn into more serious psychological ailments such as depression or panic attacks.

The best starting point for handling stress is to be in good physical and mental shape. When you pay attention to your body and mind, you can recognize the signs of stress before they become uncontrollable and then modify your lifestyle as needed. Identify the parts of your life that do not work well, make plans for change, and then carry out the plans. For example, if you are stressed because you are always late for classes, get up ten minutes earlier. If you get nervous when you talk to a certain negative classmate before a test, avoid that person. Learn test-taking skills so that you can manage test anxiety. If doing poorly on a test causes you to give up or become depressed, develop your resilience and belief in yourself.

Another way to take control of your lifestyle is by knowing your limits and making priority lists. This might mean saying "no" to friends or family members who distract you from your tasks and obligations. It is OK to say "no," and you don't have to feel guilty about it. You will have obligations from clubs, classes, and friends, and you will have to work hard to manage all these obligations and still maintain good grades.

The Importance of Good Nutrition

What you eat and drink connects to your overall health, well-being, and stress. Eating a lot of junk food will reduce your energy level. When you can't keep up with your work because you're slow or tired, you will experience more stress.

SETTING GOALS ▷ **Use Stress to Your Advantage**

Do you get stressed before an exam or graded presentation? Some level of stress might motivate you to do well, but a high stress level can have the opposite effect. The next time you are stressed before a test or presentation, note how you feel, both physically and mentally. Are you more energized and more alert? Or does your stress negatively affect your concentration or self-confidence? Set a goal to manage your stress so that it helps, not hurts, your preparation and performance.

Caffeine is probably the best example of a common substance that is linked to high stress levels. College students, like many adults, use caffeine to enhance their productivity. Caffeine helps increase alertness and reduce fatigue if used moderately. Up to 400 milligrams (mg) of caffeine a day appears to be safe for most adults. That's roughly the amount of caffeine in four cups of coffee, ten cans of cola, or two "energy shot" drinks.[1] However, too much caffeine can cause nervousness, headaches, irritability, upset stomach, and sleeplessness—all symptoms of stress. Monitor and limit your daily use of caffeine, especially if you consume energy drinks. Using coffee or energy drinks when you're cramming for exams, or even to get through the day, can become a crutch. Find other sources of energy, like jogging or power napping.

Many of us find that gaining weight is really easy; a few days of donuts, pizza, and soft drinks can pack on unexpected pounds. Losing weight, even a small amount, is far more difficult. Let's face it—food is one of life's greatest pleasures, and having the self-discipline to say "no" to a giant piece of birthday cake is difficult. Weight gain will also reduce your energy and interest in exercise.

If you are gaining weight and losing energy, what can you do about your eating habits? It might not be easy at first, but if you start making small changes, you can build toward a new way of eating. You will not only feel

[1] "Caffeine: How Much Is Too Much?," Mayo Clinic, accessed January 13, 2016, www.mayoclinic.org/caffeine /ART-20045678?p=1.

better but also be healthier and probably happier. Here are some commonsense suggestions:

- Limit snacks to healthy options such as fruit, vegetables, yogurt, hummus, and small portions of nuts, like pistachios, almonds, cashews, or walnuts.

- Be careful about fad diets. Before using diet pills or beginning a diet regimen such as the Paleo, Atkins, or South Beach diet, check with your physician. These diets might cause you to miss essential nutrients, especially if you are an athlete. Changing your portion sizes can be a first step toward weight loss.

- Drink plenty of water. Drinking 64 ounces of water a day helps flush your system, keep your skin healthy, and manage your weight. A rule of thumb: To keep hydrated, drink water before and after a workout and between meals.

- Add variety to your meals. Cafeterias offer options, and the most important strategy is to eat a meal that includes protein, vegetables, grains, salad, and fruit. Stay away from fried and sugary foods. A good reference is

ChooseMyPlate.gov, shown in Figure 12.1. Watch your portion sizes. Avoid large, jumbo, or king-size fast-food items and all-you-can-eat buffets.

- Eat a healthy breakfast! Your brain will function better if you eat a power-packed meal first thing in the morning. Try oatmeal, smoothies, eggs, and foods high in protein.

- Always read the nutrition label on packaged foods; look for the number of grams of fat, sugars, protein, carbohydrates, and sodium. Sodium (table salt) will make you retain water, which increases your weight and can possibly increase your blood pressure. Do not let items marketed as "nonfat/low-fat" options fool you. Often, these products contain chemicals and by-products that are worse for you than their full-fat counterparts.

- If possible, take time to cook your own food, bring your lunch, and pack your own snacks. Preparing your own meals and snacks is almost always healthier and more cost-effective than eating out or buying snack food.

Figure 12.1 ▷ MyPlate Eating Guidelines

In 2011 the federal government introduced the MyPlate icon to replace the Food Guide Pyramid. ChooseMyPlate.gov provides tips and recommendations for healthy eating and for understanding the plate's design.

Source: USDA.

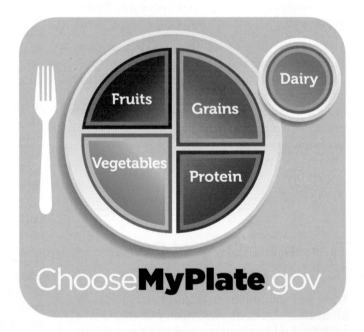

12 Staying Healthy

Risky Eating Habits

Although we advise you to think about what you eat each day, we also advise you not to overthink your diet. Remember that the key to good health is achieving balance, and an obsession with how much you eat may be a sign that things are out of balance. Over the last few decades, an increasing number of both male and female college students have developed eating disorders such as anorexia nervosa (an extreme fear of gaining weight), bulimia (overeating followed by self-induced vomiting or laxative use), or binge eating (compulsive overeating long past the feeling of being full).

Anyone who is struggling with an eating disorder should seek immediate medical attention. Eating disorders can be life-threatening if they are not treated by a health care professional. Contact your student health center or the National Eating Disorders Association (nationaleatingdisorders.org or 1-800-931-2237) to find a professional in your area who specializes in treating eating disorders.

◁ **A Serving Is a Slice, Not an Entire Pizza**
Have you ever found yourself staring at the remains of a pizza and realizing that your eating is out of control? Start to rein yourself back in. Pick up some healthy snacks. Throw out half-eaten bags of chips. Give yourself an extra half hour in the morning to walk or jog. It's never the wrong time and never too late to take better care of yourself, and no step in the right direction is too small. © Image Source/Corbis.

Exercising to Maintain Wellness

Exercise is an excellent stress-management and weight-management technique and the best way to stay fit. Whether it's walking to class, going to the campus recreation center, or going for a bike ride, it is important to be active every day. Choose activities that you enjoy so that you look forward to your exercise time and make it a regular part of your routine.

Besides doing wonders for your body, aerobic exercise keeps your mind healthy. When you do aerobic exercise, your body produces hormones called beta-endorphins. These natural narcotics cause feelings of contentment and happiness and help manage anxiety and depression. Your mood, energy level, sleep, and sense of competence will improve with regular aerobic exercise. Think about ways to combine activities efficiently. Leave your car at home and walk or ride a bike to class. If you drive, park at the far end of the parking lot to get in extra steps. Go to the gym with a friend, and ask each other study questions while you're on the treadmills. Take the stairs whenever possible. Wear a pedometer, and aim for a certain number of steps each day. Play organized sports or use your campus fitness center. Remember that exercise is most effective if you make it part of your day-to-day life.

Another way to monitor your weight-management progress during exercise is to be aware of your body mass index (BMI). Knowing your BMI is a good way to understand your optimum range. According to the U.S. Centers for Disease Control and Prevention (CDC), BMI is calculated by dividing your weight by your, height and provides an effective way to screen for health issues. Calculate your BMI by going to this Web site and entering your height and weight: nhlbi.nih.gov/health/educational/lose_wt/BMI/bmicalc.htm. As you will note, a BMI under 18.5 is "underweight," 18.5 to 24.9 is "normal," 25 to 29.9 is "overweight," and 30 or higher is "obese."

Use Technology to Stay Fit

We all want to be healthy and look fit, but we live in a world that makes us inactive and presents us with convenient but unhealthy food options. Many of us spend lots of time in front of television and computer screens. Even when we aren't watching a particular show or presentation, we view videos on our phones, at the gas pump, in restaurants, or while we wait for the elevator. When we are bored, we have game systems and games on our phones that often keep us sitting in one spot. It seems like we are in front of digital screens almost twenty-four hours a day. So instead of letting technology make you a couch potato, how can you use it to help you become and stay fit?

First, learn how to filter out the fiction. When it comes to fitness and nutrition, there's a lot of conflicting advice and bad information out there, and more than a few scams. Zero in on a few reputable, well-vetted sources of information. You can find everything from healthy menu plans to yoga training to fitness tips on the following Web sites:

- fitday.com
- fitness.com
- primusweb.com/fitnesspartner
- livestrong.com
- mensfitness.com

- nutritiondata.self.com
- weightwatchers.com

You can also download health-related phone apps such as FitStar, Argus, Human, Fooducate, Diet Point Weight Loss, HealthyOut Guide, and SparkPeople.

Go an extra step by using your electronic calendar to send periodic alerts to your cell phone throughout the day to take breaks or work out. When you are studying, working, or attending classes, it is very easy to forget to give your body time to be active. You don't necessarily have to change clothes or go to the gym. Sometimes all it takes is a brisk walk or fifteen minutes of stretching and relaxed breathing to reset your body and your mind.

If you want to stay healthy, but hours sitting in front of a computer are getting in your way, enlist technology to get you moving. Make some of the time you spend in front of a screen active time. Clear some floor space, and use YouTube or online services like Netflix to stream workout programs. Video gaming systems like Xbox also let you enjoy real-life workouts in the virtual world. Try Dance Dance Revolution or virtual baseball, bowling, boxing, golf, or tennis. While you're at it, get your roommates or family members to join in.

Getting Enough Sleep to Maintain Wellness

Getting adequate sleep is another way to protect yourself from stress. According to a 2013 Gallup poll, almost 50 percent of individuals aged eighteen to twenty-nine get less than the recommended seven hours of sleep per night.[2] Lack of sleep can lead to anxiety, depression, and academic problems. Research has shown that students who stay up late partying or pull all-nighters studying earn lower grades.[3] Try the following suggestions to establish better sleep habits:

- Avoid daytime naps that last more than thirty minutes.

- Try reading or listening to a relaxation tape before going to bed.

- Exercise during the day.

- Get your clothes, school materials, and food together for the next day before you go to bed.

- Sleep in the same room and bed every night.

- Stick to a regular weekday schedule for going to bed and getting up.

△ **Catch Some Z's**
When you aren't getting enough sleep, you cannot do your best. A brief nap of twenty minutes or so can revive you when you're feeling tired during the day. Establish good sleeping habits and grab opportunities for power naps when you can. © Randy Faris/Corbis.

[2] http://www.gallup.com/poll/166553/less-recommended-amount-sleep.aspx
[3] http://www.aasmnet.org/articles.aspx?id=2327.

Emotional Health

Your emotional or mental health is an important component of your overall wellness. Particularly in the first year of college, some students have difficulty establishing positive relationships with others, dealing with pressure, or making wise decisions. Other students are optimistic and happy and seem to believe in their own abilities to address problems successfully. Your ability to deal with life's challenges is based on your emotional intelligence (EI).

Depression. Depression is one of the most common psychiatric disorders in the United States. According to the National Institute of Mental Health, an estimated 17 million adult Americans suffer from depression during any one-year period.[4] College students are at especially high risk for both depression and suicide because of the major life changes and high stress levels some of them experience.

Depression is not a weakness; it is an illness that needs medical attention. Feelings of depression are often temporary and may be situational. A romantic breakup, a disappointing grade, or an ongoing problem with another person can create feelings of despair. Although most depression goes away on its own, if any of the following symptoms last for more than two weeks, it is important to talk to a health care provider.

- Feelings of helplessness and hopelessness
- Feeling useless, inadequate, bad, or guilty
- Self-hatred, constant questioning of one's thoughts and actions
- Loss of energy and motivation
- Loss of appetite
- Weight loss or gain
- Difficulty sleeping or excessive need for sleep
- Loss of interest in sex
- Difficulty concentrating for a significant length of time

Suicide. The CDC reports that students aged fifteen to twenty-four are more likely than any other age group to attempt suicide.[5] Most people who commit suicide give a warning of their intentions. The following are common indicators of someone's intent to commit suicide:

- Recent loss and inability to let go of grief
- Change in personality—sadness, withdrawal, indifference
- Expressions of self-hatred
- Change in sleep patterns
- Change in eating habits
- A direct statement about committing suicide (e.g., "I might as well end it all")
- A preoccupation with death

If you or someone you know threatens suicide or displays any of these signs, it's time to consult a mental health professional. Most campuses have counseling centers that offer both one-on-one sessions and support groups for students, usually for free.

Finally, remember that there is no shame attached to having high levels of stress, depression, anxiety, or suicidal tendencies. Unavoidable life events or physiological imbalances can cause such feelings and behaviors. Proper counseling, medical attention, and in some cases prescription medication can help students cope with depression and suicidal thoughts.

Cyberbullying. In recent years cyberbullying has increased, not just in grade school and high school, but also on college campuses. Experts define cyberbullying as "any behavior performed through electronic or digital media by individuals or groups who repeatedly communicate hostile or aggressive messages intended to inflict harm or discomfort on others."[6] According to a recent study, the prevalence of cyberbullying among college

[4] http://www.apa.org/topics/depress/recover.aspx

[5] http://www.cdc.gov/ViolencePrevention/pdf/Suicide-DataSheet-a.pdf

[6] P. K. Smith et al., "Cyberbullying: Its Nature and Impact in Secondary School Pupils," *Journal of Child Psychology and Psychiatry* 49, no. 4 (2008): 375–76.

◁ **Difficulty Coping**
Many events in life can trigger feelings of despair. Know the signs of depression. If you or someone you care about seems to be having trouble, reach out. College campuses have resources to help.
© Wavebreak Media Ltd/Veer/Corbis.

populations ranges from 10 to 28.7 percent.[7] These may seem like low numbers, but cyberbullying can go unreported because of embarrassment or privacy concerns. Recently, tragic cyberbullying stories that have resulted in the victim's clinical depression or suicide have been reported.

Cyberbullying is a serious issue and a crime that harms individuals in many ways. It should be dealt with immediately. If you or someone you know has experienced cyberbullying, report it as soon as possible. These foundations and resources are available to help students report cyberbullying:

- U. S. Government Web site (stopbullying.gov)

- Megan Meier Foundation (meganmeierfoundation.org)

- National Crime Prevention Council (ncpc.org) ■

[7] Carlos P. Zalaquett and SeriaShia J. Chatters, "Cyberbullying in College: Frequency, Characteristics, and Practical Implications," *SAGE Open* (January–March 2014): 1–8, http://sgo.sagepub.com/content/4/1/2158244014526721.

Maintaining Sexual Health

Survey data reported in 2015 by the American College Health Association found that about 66 percent of traditional-age college students reported having intercourse in the previous twelve months.[8] Whether or not you are sexually active, it can be helpful to consider your sexual values and whether sex is right for you at this time in your life. If you decide to become sexually active, you should adopt strategies for avoiding the unwanted consequences of unprotected sex.

Communicating about Safe Sex

Communication is the most important aspect of sexual relationships. You and your partner must share your needs, backgrounds, and how to be safe. Without communication, intentions can get confused and emotions can become muddled. Here are some communication strategies:

- **Discuss testing for sexually transmitted infections (STIs).** Make sure both partners have been tested recently. The rule of thumb for a sexually active person is to get tested at least once a year, and after any unprotected encounter.

- **Share expectations.** Partners should talk about what they expect from the sexual encounter. Partners should be clear about their comfort level and what they want from the experience.

- **Use protection.** Protecting yourself and your partner from unwanted consequences—pregnancy or the transmission of STIs—is important, and so is communicating about protection ahead of time. Do you and your partner have what you need, or does one of you need to buy it? One encounter can change your entire life, so make sure you are prepared.

- **Communicate in "I" statements.** "I" statements help facilitate open communication. When you use "I" statements, you accept responsibility for your feelings, and you do not accuse or threaten each other. A statement like "I feel like we need to explore our options" is more useful than "You don't know what you're talking about."

8 http://www.acha-ncha.org/docs/NCHA-II_WEB_SPRING_2015 _UNDERGRADUATE_REFERENCE_GROUP_EXECUTIVE _SUMMARY.pdf

Avoiding Sexually Transmitted Infections

You can avoid STIs and unwanted pregnancies by abstaining from sex entirely. Many college students choose this option, finding that masturbation is a reasonable alternative to sex with a partner.

If you are having sex with a partner, you're more likely to avoid STI transmission if you have only one partner. Whether you're monogamous or not, you should always protect yourself by using a condom or being sure your partner uses one.

In addition to being a contraceptive, a condom can help prevent the spread of STIs—including human immunodeficiency virus (HIV) and human papillomavirus (HPV)—during anal, vaginal, and oral intercourse. The most up-to-date research indicates that condoms are very effective at both preventing the transmission of STIs and preventing pregnancy when used correctly and consistently when you have sex. Note that only latex rubber condoms and polyurethane condoms—not lambskin or other types of natural membrane condoms—provide this protection. Use a water-based lubricant such as K-Y Jelly rather than an oil-based lubricant, which can cause a latex condom to break.

In recent years the number of STIs on college campuses has increased dramatically, faster than other illnesses on campuses today. Approximately 5 to 10 percent of visits by U.S. college students to college health services are for the diagnosis and treatment of STIs. HPV, a sexually transmitted infection that is closely linked to cervical cancer, is the most common STI.[9] In fact, the CDC estimates that 79 million Americans are currently infected with HPV. Gardasil, a vaccine that became available in 2006, provides protection for both men and women against the strains of HPV that cause genital warts, anal cancer, and cervical cancer. For more information about this vaccine or to receive the three-injection series, contact your college or university health services or your local health care provider.

9 http://www.cdc.gov/std/hpv/stdfact-hpv.htm

Using Birth Control

Sexually active heterosexual students have to take steps to prevent unwanted pregnancies. The best method of contraception is any method that you use correctly and consistently each time you have intercourse. Always discuss birth control with your partner so that you both feel comfortable with the option you have selected.

Remember, birth control only protects against pregnancy. Use condoms for protection against STIs, in addition to your chosen method of pregnancy prevention. What if the condom breaks or you forget to take your birth control pill? Emergency contraceptive pills can reduce the risk of pregnancy. According to the Planned Parenthood Federation of America,[10] if emergency contraceptive pills are taken within five days (120 hours) after unprotected intercourse, they can significantly reduce the risk of pregnancy. ■

[10] https://www.plannedparenthood.org/learn/morning-after-pill-emergency-contraception

Protecting Yourself and Others against Sexual Assault and Violence

Sexual assault on college campuses is a problem that has existed for many years. Everyone is at risk for becoming a victim of sexual assault, but the majority of victims are women. The results of a recent study conclude that during their first year in college, one in seven women will have experienced incapacitated assault or rape (under the influence of alcohol or drugs) and nearly one in ten will have experienced forcible assault or rape.[11] According to statistics, more than 80 percent of these survivors will be assaulted or raped by someone they know[12]—and most will not report the crime. Alcohol is a factor in nearly 75 percent of the incidents.[13]

Interventions to reduce sexual violence on campus are urgently needed. In 2013 the federal government instituted an initiative called the Campus Sexual Violence Elimination (SaVE) Act. The act mandates that all colleges and universities must provide sexual assault, violence, and harassment education to students. The Campus SaVE Act provides an amendment to the Clery Act of 1990, which the federal government implemented after a college student, Jeanne Clery, was raped and killed. The Clery Act required postsecondary institutions to report sexual crimes and related statistics. As always, the victim's identity must remain confidential in such reports. You can find out more about the Campus SaVE Act by visiting campussaveact.org, contacting your campus security or public safety office, or contacting your student judicial office. It is always up to the survivor to decide how he or she would like to proceed after a sexual assault has occurred.

Whether sexually assaulted by an acquaintance or by a stranger, a survivor can suffer long-term traumatic effects as well as depression, anxiety, and even suicide. Many survivors blame themselves, but the only person at fault for a sexual assault is the perpetrator. If you are a survivor of sexual assault, regardless of whether you choose to report it to the police, it is useful to seek help by contacting a counselor, a local rape crisis center, the campus public safety or police department, student health services, women's student services, or a local hospital emergency room. Here are some steps you can take to help a sexual assault survivor:

- Remain empathetic and nonjudgmental.
- Keep information private and ensure the survivor's confidentiality.
- Listen.
- Ask the survivor how he or she would like to proceed—discuss options like contacting campus police or the campus counseling center.
- Seek out advice from a professional on how to help the survivor.
- Stay in touch and follow up to see if the survivor is getting the help he or she needs.

Many sexual assaults on college campuses happen early in the first term. Moving to college can bring you into contact with new people and new places that are unfamiliar and may be unsafe. You should have a heightened sense of awareness when going to social events in your first few months on campus. Always take a friend with you, bring your cell phone, carefully monitor what you are drinking, trust your intuition, and be sure to become familiar with your surroundings so you know how to leave or get help if needed. If you observe a sexual assault or a potential sexual assault, make your presence known. Don't be a bystander; intervene in any way you can. Create a distraction, and if you need help, ask for help.

[11] Kate B. Carey et al., "Incapacitated and Forcible Rape of College Women: Prevalence across the First Year," *Journal of Adolescent Health* 56 (2015): 678–80, http://i2.cdn.turner.com/cnn/2015/images/05/20/carey_jah_proof.pdf.
[12] Christopher P. Krebs et al., "The Campus Sexual Assault (CSA) Study," (report prepared for National Institute of Justice, 2007), https://www.ncjrs.gov/pdffiles1/nij/grants/221153.pdf.
[13] Meichun Mohler-Kuo et al., "Correlates of Rape While Intoxicated in a National Sample of College Women," *Journal of Studies on Alcohol* 65, no. 1 (2004): 37–45, http://www.jsad.com/doi/10.15288/jsa.2004.65.37.

Alcohol and Other Substances

In this section our purpose is not to make judgments but to warn you about the ways in which irresponsible use of substances can have a negative impact on your college experience and your life. In today's world it is easy to obtain substances, both legal and illegal, that can cause serious harm to your health and well-being. For college students tobacco, alcohol, and marijuana are the substances most commonly used and abused.

The Use and Abuse of Alcohol

In college many students will encounter alcohol. Of course, there are legal age restrictions on consuming alcohol and you should not drink alcohol if you are under age twenty-one. If you decide to consume alcohol, you can still make

△ **Consider the Consequences**
This party looks like fun. But if you drink too much, you may find yourself hooking up with someone you hardly know. What started off as a good time could end up being your worst nightmare. © 2/Ocean/Corbis.

responsible decisions by using the harm-reduction approach. The following are some simple harm-reduction approaches to consuming alcohol.

- **Slow down drinking.** One way to maintain a "buzz"—the euphoric sensation you experience from drinking—is by drinking one beer per hour or less. Pacing yourself and limiting your drinks help prevent you from attaining a high blood alcohol content (BAC) level.

- **Eat while you drink.** Sometimes eating while you consume alcohol helps slow down your drinking and slows down the processing of alcohol. Body weight and gender play a large role in this as well.

- **Drink water.** Alcohol dehydrates your body, so it is important to drink plenty of water while consuming alcohol.

- **Designate a driver before you go out.** Walking is always a better option than driving a vehicle, but if you are going to take a vehicle to a destination where you will drink, designate a sober driver before you leave.

Many college students report having to help a drunken friend; therefore, it's important that all students learn about the effects of alcohol consumption. Alcohol can turn drinkers and nondrinkers into victims. You might have heard news reports about college students who died or were seriously or permanently injured as a result of one incidence of excessive drinking.

People experience the pleasurable effects of alcoholic beverages as the alcohol begins to affect the brain. How fast you drink makes a difference, too. Drinking more than one drink an hour may cause a rise in BAC because the body is absorbing alcohol faster than it can eliminate it. And popular home remedies for sobering up, like drinking coffee or water or taking a cold shower, don't work.

Driving is measurably impaired even at BAC levels lower than the legal limit of .08. In fact, a safe level for most people may be half the legal limit, or .04. As BAC levels climb past .08, people become less coordinated and less able to exercise good judgment. Most people become severely uncoordinated at BAC levels higher than .08 and may begin falling down, slurring their speech, and, if driving, unable to maintain lane position and brake appropriately[14].

Most people pass out or fall asleep when their BAC level is above .25. At BAC levels higher than .30, most people will show signs of severe alcohol poisoning, such as an inability to wake up, slowed breathing, a fast but weak pulse, cool or damp skin, and pale or bluish skin; they need medical assistance immediately. ■

[14] http://www.cdc.gov/motorvehiclesafety/impaired_driving/bac.html

Tobacco and Marijuana

Tobacco is a legal drug that contains nicotine, a highly addictive substance, and is the cause of many serious medical conditions, including heart disease, lung disease, and some forms of cancer. One concern that particularly relates to college students is *social smoking*. This term describes smoking by students who do so only when hanging out with friends, drinking, or partying. Most college students feel they will be able to give up their social smoking habit once they graduate, but some find that they have become addicted to cigarettes.

You may have noticed advertisements for electronic cigarettes (e-cigarettes or e-cigs) or seen them in stores. E-cigarettes are battery-operated products designed to deliver nicotine, flavors, and other chemicals in the form of vapor. Vaping, the term for using e-cigarettes, has not been fully studied, so consumers currently don't know the potential risks.

A final reason for smokers to quit, and for others never to start, is the out-of-pocket cost, which varies by state. A pack-a-day smoker spends more than $1,500 annually on cigarettes (ranging from $1,662 in Missouri where cigarettes are cheapest to $3,674 in New York where cigarettes are most expensive). A pack-a-day smoker over the course of a lifetime will have spent more than $84,000 on cigarettes (from $84,754 in Missouri to $187,379 in New York).[15] Contact your campus health center for more information about quitting.

Recently, Colorado, Washington, Oregon, Alaska, and Washington, DC, became the first places in the United States to legalize recreational marijuana use for individuals twenty-one years or older. It is still not legal in other states or federally, however. College students sometimes get caught with marijuana, and as with tobacco, there are health risks associated with smoking it. Some impacts of marijuana use include an increase in anxiety, paranoia, short-term memory loss, and depression. In addition, much like tobacco, marijuana smoke increases your risk for lung cancer.

[15] https://wallethub.com/edu/the-financial-cost-of-smoking-by-state/9520/#main-annual

Chapter Review

Steps to Success:
Staying Healthy

○ **Understand that wellness is about your body, mind, and spirit.** These components can influence each other and can, in turn, affect your success in college.

○ **Remember that managing stress is a key college success strategy.** College, with its many demands, increases stress. Use the strategies from your college success course to learn how to reduce stress in college and beyond.

○ **Appreciate the role that your emotional health plays in your overall wellness, and recognize the warning signs of depression in yourself and others.** Remember that depression can negatively affect your college experience. It's important for any student who is depressed to seek help from the campus counseling center.

○ **Consider the powerful connections between things you control through your decisions.** Make good decisions concerning diet, exercise, sleep, your schedule, and your stress levels.

○ **Practice making good decisions about sexual health.** Make wise choices to protect yourself against unwanted pregnancy and sexually transmitted infections. Learn to communicate about sex, and work to develop and maintain respectful relationships.

○ **Learn about sexual assault.** Know how to define sexual assault, what laws are in place to protect victims, and what you should do if you witness a sexual assault.

○ **Practice moderation in using alcohol and other legal drugs.** Successful students can have a good time in college without letting alcohol or marijuana use interfere with their academic success or personal health. Contrary to prevalent stereotypes, it is not the norm for students to abuse these substances.

○ **Learn about the costs of smoking in your state.** Not only will you spend a lot of money purchasing tobacco products, but you will also have a higher likelihood of developing significant and costly health problems than if you don't smoke.

Applying what you've learned . . .

Now that you have read and discussed this chapter, consider how you can apply what you have learned to your academic and personal lives. The following prompts will help you reflect on the chapter material and its relevance to you both now and in the future.

1. Identify one area in your life in which you need to make changes to become healthier. How do you think becoming healthier will improve your performance in college? What are the challenges you face in becoming healthier?

2. If you could make only three recommendations to an incoming first-year college student about managing stress in college, what would they be? Use your personal experience and what you have learned in this chapter to make your recommendations.

Use Your Resources

GO TO ▷ The counseling center: If you need help with anxiety and stress. Professionals here will offer individual and group assistance and lots of information. Remember that their support is confidential, and you will not be judged.

GO TO ▷ The campus health center or online to Planned Parenthood Federation of America (www.plannedparenthood.org): If you need help with STI prevention or birth control. You should be able to receive treatment for an STI as well.

GO TO ▷ Health education and wellness programs: If you need help with problems and challenges with alcohol or other drugs or with sexual decision making. Student peer health educators who are trained and supervised by professionals can provide support. Taking part in such peer leadership is also a great way to develop and practice your own communication skills.

GO TO ▷ Campus support groups: If you need help dealing with problems related to excessive alcohol and drug use, abusive sexual relationships, and other issues.

GO ONLINE TO ▷ Go Ask Alice! (goaskalice.columbia.edu): If you need advice about health issues related to being in college. This Web site, sponsored by Columbia University, has answers to many health questions.

GO ONLINE TO ▷ The American Institute of Stress (stress.org): If you need help combating stress.

GO ONLINE TO ▷ The Academy of Nutrition and Dietetics (eatright.org) or Shape Up America! (www.shapeup.org): If you need help finding information on healthy eating and nutrition.

GO ONLINE TO ▷ The National Eating Disorders Association (nationaleatingdisorders.org): If you want to learn more about online screening, treatment, and support for an eating disorder that you or someone you care about is struggling with.

GO ONLINE TO ▷ The American Cancer Society (cancer.org): If you want to learn more about the health effects of tobacco.

NOW... How do you measure up?

1. When I feel overwhelmed, I deal with my stress in healthy ways, like exercising or taking control of my schedule to make time to tackle my top priorities.
   - ○ Agree
   - ○ Don't Know
   - ○ Disagree

2. Exercising regularly will help me manage my weight and stay fit.
   - ○ Agree
   - ○ Don't Know
   - ○ Disagree

3. I have adequate information about sex and contraception.
   - ○ Agree
   - ○ Don't Know
   - ○ Disagree

4. I know the difference between responsible and irresponsible alcohol use.
   - ○ Agree
   - ○ Don't Know
   - ○ Disagree

How do your answers here compare to your responses to the quiz you took at the start of the chapter? Which sections of this chapter left a strong impression on you? What strategies for staying healthy have you started to use? Are they working? What other strategies will you commit to trying?

LaunchPad
macmillan learning

LaunchPad Solo for College Success is a great resource. Go online to master concepts using the LearningCurve study tool and much more. **macmillanhighered.com/collegesuccessmedia**

13

217
Careers and the New Economy

219
Self-Exploration in Career Planning

221
Exploring Your Interests

225
Planning for Your Career

226
Getting Experience

229
Job Search Strategies

232
Skills Employers Seek

Considering Majors and Careers

Introwizi/Shutterstock

LaunchPad
macmillan learning

To access the LearningCurve study tool, Video Tools, and more, go to *LaunchPad Solo for College Success*. **macmillanhighered.com/ collegesuccessmedia**

College is a time for gaining academic knowledge and exploring career opportunities with the goal of developing from a student into a productive member of the global economy. However, you don't have to be sure about your academic and career goals as you begin or return to college. Rather, you can use your first classes and even your first year of college to explore your interests and see how they might connect to various academic programs. You may discover interests and opportunities you never imagined.

Depending on your academic strengths, you can major in almost anything. As this chapter emphasizes, how you integrate your classes with extracurricular pursuits and work experiences will prepare you for a first career—or, if you have been in the labor force for some time, for advancement in your current job or even a new career. Try a major that you think you will like or that you feel drawn toward, and see what develops. But keep an open mind, and don't pin all your hopes for finding a career on that major alone. Your selection of a major and a career ultimately has to fit with your overall life goals, purposes, values, and beliefs. This chapter provides you with tips and resources for career planning. Visiting your college career center can help you build on the information in this chapter.

How do you measure up?

1. The world economy is changing, and how it changes will probably affect my job prospects.
   - ○ Agree
   - ○ Don't Know
   - ○ Disagree

2. There is no guarantee that anyone's first career choice will be permanent.
   - ○ Agree
   - ○ Don't Know
   - ○ Disagree

3. I know my strengths and interests and how they might influence my career choice.
   - ○ Agree
   - ○ Don't Know
   - ○ Disagree

4. One of the most important things college students can do in the first year is visit the campus career center.
   - ○ Agree
   - ○ Don't Know
   - ○ Disagree

Review the items you marked "Don't Know" or "Disagree." Pay special attention to these topics in this chapter—you will likely find new ways of thinking about these questions. A follow-up quiz at the end of the chapter will prompt you to consider what you have learned.

Build Your Résumé from Day One

△ **Brett Kossick**

Monkey Business Images/Shutterstock.

"I really admire your focus," said Dr. Woloshyn, my academic adviser, when I dropped by his office to talk about my course schedule. Many people study a whole gamut of things until they settle on a major and don't specialize until graduate school. That's so not me.

"I've wanted to be an engineer for as long as I can remember," I said. "So I'm a little confused about the courses you suggested—Business Writing? Multicultural Communications? I plan to work in robotics, not marketing."

"Oh, really?" Dr. Woloshyn asked with a curious smile. Then he leaned forward on his desk. "Brett, didn't you tell me that you have an internship with a leading technology corporation this summer? Did anyone tell you what you would be doing there?"

"Not really," I said. "They just said I'd be helping out in different divisions of the company, depending on what they need."

"Right," said Dr. Woloshyn. "And is there a chance you might like to work there after you graduate?"

"Are you kidding? That would be my dream job."

"Good. So, let's think about it: Some divisions of the company might be working on new business proposals and will value a gifted writer. Some might be working on projects involving media companies, investment bankers, schools, or even foreign governments. They will need people who work well in a team structure. Some divisions might be working on new apps or software applications, which means—"

"That the classes you're suggesting make a lot of sense," I cut in. We grinned at each other as I stood up. "Thanks, Professor. I guess I'll go register now."

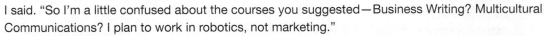

As Brett's story shows, college students should keep in mind how they plan to use their degree and begin building the skills that employers seek. What is your ideal job? How can you develop yourself as the ideal employee for that job? What kinds of skills do you need to develop as a college student? Can expertise in writing, critical thinking, and teamwork help you achieve your goals?

Careers and the New Economy

For some people the reason for attending college is to get a good job. For others the reason is to fulfill the dream of getting a college education, which helps students not only get better jobs but also become effective leaders.

Over the past few years the global economy has experienced extreme ups and downs, but the employment situation for college graduates is beginning to improve. Unemployment rates for bachelor's degree holders vary by major but average about 8 percent. This rate is much lower than the unemployment rate for people without a college degree.[1] The good news is that employers will likely hire many college students in the next few years. Economic uncertainty is a reality, and although earning a college degree is one of the best ways for you to increase your chances of being employed, it is important to make decisions about your major and career path based on information about yourself and the long-term demands of the job market.

Characteristics of Today's Economy

Today's economy has characteristics that are new and quite different from those of previous years—it is global, innovative, without boundaries, ever changing, and social. The most motivated and successful college students will work hard to understand these characteristics, and will consider them carefully as they make decisions that relate to their futures. As we take a look at each characteristic, think about the potential impact on the program of study and possible career path you are envisioning for yourself.

- **It's global.** Many corporations are multinational; they look for cheap labor, capital, and resources both within and outside the United States. Competition on a global level

presents challenges for American workers. College graduates in the United States now compete for jobs with others around the world.

- **It's innovative.** The economy has always depended on creativity to generate consumer interest in new products and services. As a leader in innovation, the United States needs college graduates who are creative and imaginative.

- **It's without boundaries.** You might be an accountant and find yourself working with the public relations division of your company, or you might be a nurse who does staff training. The ability to work outside of traditional boundaries will be essential to your professional success.

- **It's ever changing.** In the future new jobs in nearly every industry will demand more education and training. Therefore the most important skill you need to learn in college is how to keep learning throughout your life.

- **It's social.** Technology has allowed us to stay constantly connected in our personal and business lives; however, it has also decreased face-to-face social interactions. Employers rank the following abilities as the most important skills or qualities they look for in job candidates: the ability to work in teams; the ability to make decisions and solve problems; the ability to plan, organize, and prioritize work; and the ability to verbally communicate with people inside and outside the organization.[2] In this world of ever-increasing technology advancements, skills that come from face-to-face interaction with others are top assets that organizations look for when hiring new employees.

These characteristics of the economy—that it is global, innovative, without boundaries, ever changing, and social—should provide a roadmap for you as you make decisions throughout your college experience.

---

[1] Libby Sander, "New Graduates' Unemployment Rates – That Predictable Summer Surge," *The Chronicle of Higher Education*, August 13, 2013, http://chronicle.com/article/In-New-Graduates-Unemployment/141093/

[2] National Association of Colleges and Employers, *Job Outlook 2014* (Bethlehem, PA: National Association of Colleges and Employers, 2013).

Building the Right Mindset for the Future

Even after you have landed a job, you will be expected to continue learning and developing yourself. Whether you are preparing to enter a career for the first time or to change careers after many years on the job, keep in mind the following:

- **A college degree does not guarantee employment.** Consider what it will be like competing for jobs with hundreds of other men and women earning the same degree as you and graduating from college at the same time. With a college degree, however, more opportunities, financial and otherwise, will be available to you than if you did not have a degree. For those who pursue a degree and complete it, the reward is considerable. Just because you want to work for a certain organization or in a certain field, though, doesn't mean that job will be available when you graduate.

- **You are more or less solely responsible for your career.** Career development is a lifelong process, controlled only by you. Many employers offer some degree of training, but the ultimate task of creating a career path is yours. Students who realize they are responsible for managing their careers actively throughout their lifetime will be more successful and more satisfied than those who think someone else will manage things for them.

- **To advance your career, you must accept the risks that accompany employment and plan for the future.** Organizations grow or downsize in response to economic conditions, so you must do your best to prepare for the unexpected. Lifelong learning will help keep you employable and can provide you with many opportunities, regardless of the economy.

- **A first career choice might not be permanent.** College students often view the choice of a career as a major, permanent decision. However, a career is based on your professional development decisions over a lifetime. There is no one right occupation; rather, there are many career choices you might find satisfying.

△ **Thinking Things Through**
When you're asked about your plans for employment after college, do you have a response? Do you feel clueless? If so, you're not alone. Many students come to college without firm career plans. This chapter will give you some new ways to think about your career choices. Your experiences in college will help you make thoughtful decisions about your future. Blend Images/Getty Images.

Now the good news: Hundreds of thousands of graduates find jobs every year, even in difficult economic times. When the economy is tough, it might take them longer to get where they want to be, but persistence pays off. If you start preparing now and continue to do so while in college, you'll have time to build a portfolio of academic and other learning experiences (such as on-campus clubs and groups, internships, work-study jobs) that will enhance your career profile. ■

❝ Hundreds of thousands of graduates find jobs every year, even in difficult economic times. ❞

Self-Exploration in Career Planning

Are you confident in your skills and abilities? Do you know what you want or can accomplish? How well you know yourself and how effectively you can do the things you need to do are central to your success not only as a student but also as a person. Self-exploration is the process of gathering information about yourself in order to make informed decisions. Factors that can affect your career choices include your values, skills, aptitudes, personality, life goals and work satisfaction, and interests. Learning about these factors is an important step in career planning.

Values

Your values, formed through your life experiences, are those things you feel most strongly about. For career planning, values generally refer to what you most want in a career in terms of how you want to live. For example, some people value job security, money, and a regular schedule. Others value flexibility, excitement, independence, variety, and particular work environments, such as the outdoors.

Knowing your personal wishes and needs in relation to your values is important. You might find that what you value most is not money but rather the chance to work for a specific cause or the opportunity to have a particular lifestyle. In general, being aware of what you value is important because a career choice that is closely related to your core values is likely to be the best one for you.

" Good career exploration begins with considering what you like to do and relating that to your career choices. "

Skills

The ability to do something well can usually be improved with practice. You may bring different skills to different situations, and it is important to know both your strengths and your weaknesses. Skills typically fall into three categories:

1. **Personal.** Some skills come naturally or are learned through experience. Examples of these are honesty, punctuality, teamwork, self-motivation, and conflict management.

2. **Workplace.** Some skills can be learned on the job; others are gained through training in a specific area. Examples include designing Web sites, bookkeeping, and providing customer service.

3. **Transferable.** Some skills gained through previous jobs, hobbies, or everyday life can be transferred to another job. Examples include planning events, motivating others, paying attention to detail, and organizing workspaces.

By identifying your skill set, you can turn your current skills into career possibilities. During the college years, build your strengths and develop your weaker skills. Whether in or out of class, find ways to practice what you are good at doing and get help with what you need to improve.

Aptitude

Aptitude is your natural or acquired proficiency in a particular area, which makes it easier for you to learn or to do certain things. Shine a light on your aptitudes and discover a path in which your strengths become your best intellectual assets.

Personality

Your personality makes you who you are and can't be ignored when you make career decisions. The quiet, orderly, calm, detail-oriented person will probably make a different work choice than the aggressive, outgoing, argumentative person. The Myers-Briggs Type Indicator, one of the best-known and most widely used personality inventories, is one of several assessments that can help you understand how you make decisions, perceive the world, and interact with others.

Life Goals and Work Satisfaction

Every person defines success and satisfaction differently, and the process of defining them is complex and personal. Two factors can change how we feel about our success and satisfaction: achieving our life goals and being satisfied with our work. If your values are not in line with the values of the organization where you work, you might be in for trouble.

Interests

Your interests, developed from birth, will help shape your career path. Good career exploration begins with considering what you like to do and relating that to your career choices. For example, because you enjoyed writing for your high school paper, you might be interested in writing for the college newspaper with an eye on entering a career in journalism. Or you might enroll in Psych 101 because of your interest in human behavior and realize halfway through the course that psychology is not what you imagined and that you have no desire to become a psychologist. Because your interests are unique to you, you are the only person who can determine what you want to do in the future. ■

◁ **A Passion for Helping People?**
Do you enjoy working with the public? Are you interested in helping sick people? Do you want to work in a health-related field? Does a career in the health professions align with your values, interests, and personality? If you are not sure, you might want to reconsider your plans. © Jose Luis Pelaez Inc/Blend Images/Corbis.

Exploring Your Interests

Most students want their academic major to lead directly to a career, although this doesn't always happen. Most academic advisers would agree with this advice: Try a major you think you'll like and that makes sense given your values, strengths, aptitudes, skills, personality, goals, and interests, and see what develops. Take advantage of available self-assessments to help you learn more about yourself.

John Holland, a psychologist at Johns Hopkins University, developed a number of tools and concepts that can help you organize the various dimensions of yourself so that you can identify potential career choices (see Table 13.1). Holland suggests that people are separated into six general categories based on differences in their interests, skills, values, and personality characteristics—in short, their preferred approaches to life. Holland's system organizes career fields into the same six categories. Career fields are grouped according to what they require of a person (the skills and personality characteristics most commonly associated with success in those fields) and what rewards they provide (the interests and values most commonly associated with satisfaction). As you view Table 13.1, highlight or note characteristics that you believe you have as well as those that are less closely matched.

Your career choice ultimately should involve a complex assessment of the factors that are most important to you. Holland created a hexagonal model (see Figure 13.1) that shows the relationship between the personality types and environments. The closer the types, the closer the relationships among the career fields; the farther apart the types, the more different the career fields are from each other. Notice that the personality types closest to each other are more alike than those farther away. If you compare the personality types opposite each other on the hexagon, this is most evident. For example, read the descriptions for Enterprising and Investigative. You will see that they are virtually the opposite of each other. On the other hand, Realistic and Conventional are fairly close. The same holds true with work environments. Conflict arises in relationships between personality types and career fields that are far apart from each other—in other words, mismatched.

Holland's model can help you address the questions surrounding career choice in two ways. First, you can begin to identify many career fields that are consistent with what you know about yourself. Once you have identified potential fields, you can use the career center at your college to get more information about these fields, such as the daily activities for specific jobs, the interests and abilities required, the preparation required for entry, the working conditions, the salary and benefits, and the employment outlook. Second, you can begin to identify the harmony or conflicts in your career choices. Doing so will help you analyze the reasons for your career decisions and help you be more confident as you make choices.

Throughout this book, you have been introduced to a variety of self-assessments designed to provide a clearer picture of who you are as an individual. These assessments are tools that can help you in the career exploration process. Never think that you have to make a decision based on the results of only one assessment. Career choices are complex and involve many factors; furthermore, career decisions are reversible. It is important not only to take time to talk your interests over with a career counselor but also to shadow individuals in the occupations that interest you. Obtaining a better understanding of the skills, commitment, and opportunities related to an occupation will help you make informed decisions about your own career choices. ∎

" You can gain an edge over other job seekers by researching career fields that interest you. "

Figure 13.1 ▽ Holland's Hexagonal Model of Career Fields

This model shows the relationship between personality types and career fields. The closer the types, the closer the relationship. Read the descriptions in Table 13.1, and think of people you know in the career fields listed. Do you think that their personality characteristics reflect the descriptions in the table?

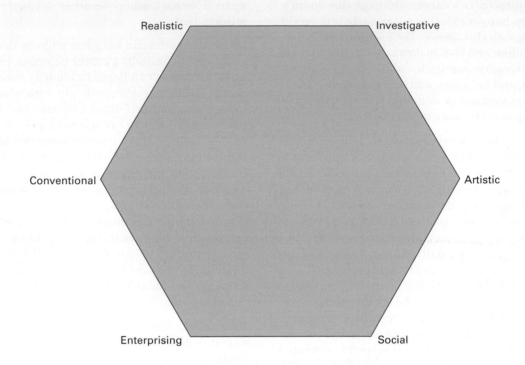

TRY IT!

FEELING CONNECTED ▷ Where Do You Fit in the Holland Model?

After you have read about and discussed the Holland model, decide where you belong: Which of the six types is most like your personality? After you decide whether you are mostly Realistic, Investigative, Artistic, Social, Enterprising, or Conventional, find others in your class who have the same type. Get together in a small group and talk about your characteristics and how they link to your career goals. Share ideas about part-time jobs or campus clubs and organizations that will give you an opportunity to expand your interests.

Diving into Career Research

In the world of business, anything older than six months is considered ancient. Today, information about industries—career fields—and the companies that represent them is essential for anyone who wants to get a sense of how careers are trending, what the coolest sectors are, which college majors are in or out, where the money is, and who's hiring. The more knowledge you have, the better your chances are of making a good career decision. You can gain an edge over other job seekers by researching career fields that interest you.

If you have no idea where to begin your research, start with a tried-and-true comprehensive resource and follow these steps.

Step 1. Figure out which career fields interest you. Visit O*NET OnLine (onetonline.org) and use the Find Occupations option on the page to begin your search. Search occupations by key word, or choose from the following occupational categories:

- **Bright Outlook.** These are occupations that are new and emerging, are expected to grow rapidly in the next several years and to have large numbers of job openings.
- **Career Cluster.** These are occupations in the same field of work that require similar skills. You can use Career Clusters to help focus your education plans toward obtaining the necessary knowledge, competencies, and training for success in a particular career.
- **Green Economy Sector.** These are occupations in fields related to environmental protection and sustainable energy.

- **Industry.** These are broad groups of businesses or organizations with similar activities, products, or services.
- **Job Family.** These are groups of occupations based on skills, education, training, credentials, and work performed.
- **Job Zone.** These zones group occupations into one of five categories based on levels of education, experience, and training necessary to perform the job.
- **STEM Discipline.** These are occupations that require education in science, technology, engineering, and mathematics (STEM) disciplines.

Step 2. Continue your research to identify your desired role within the field that interests you most.

Step 3. Identify companies or organizations of interest within a larger career field. The federal government alone, for example, has approximately 575 departments and agencies. Because you have so many choices, this part of your research depends on your own expectations and wants.

Step 4. Do research on each individual employer of interest. How well does the organization pay compared to others in the same career field? Does this employer require long hours or frequent travel? Set up an informational interview to talk to people who are already working within the organization.

See these other helpful resources to do additional career research:

Market Research	marketresearch.com
Wall Street Journal	exccutivelibrary.com/Research.asp
First Research	firstresearch.com/Industry-Profiles.aspx
Market Watch	marketwatch.com/tools/industry
Hoovers	hoovers.com
Occupational Outlook Handbook	bls.gov/ooh/
Indeed.com	indeed.com
Job.com	job.com
JobBank USA	jobbankusa.com
LinkedIn	LinkedIn.com
Simply Hired	simplyhired.com
USA Jobs	usajobs.gov
Volunteer Match	volunteermatch.org

Table 13.1 ▽ Holland Personality and Career Types

Category	Personality Characteristics	Career Fields
Realistic (R)	These people describe themselves as concrete, down-to-earth, and practical doers. They exhibit competitive/assertive behavior and show interest in activities that require motor coordination, skill, and physical strength. They prefer situations involving action solutions rather than tasks involving verbal or interpersonal skills, and they like taking a concrete approach to problem solving rather than relying on abstract theory. They tend to be interested in scientific or mechanical areas rather than the arts.	Environmental engineer, electrical contractor, industrial arts teacher, navy officer, fitness director, package engineer, electronics technician, Web designer
Investigative (I)	These people describe themselves as analytical, rational, and logical problem solvers. They value intellectual stimulation and intellectual achievement, and they prefer to think rather than to act and to organize and understand rather than to persuade. They usually have a strong interest in physical, biological, or social sciences. They are less apt to be people oriented.	Urban planner, chemical engineer, bacteriologist, flight engineer, genealogist, laboratory technician, marine scientist, nuclear medical technologist, obstetrician, quality-control technician, computer programmer, environmentalist, physician, college professor
Artistic (A)	These people describe themselves as creative, innovative, and independent. They value self-expression and relating with others through artistic expression and are also emotionally expressive. They dislike structure, preferring tasks involving personal or physical skills. They resemble investigative people but are more interested in the cultural or the aesthetic than the scientific.	Architect, film editor/director, actor, cartoonist, interior decorator, fashion model, graphic communications specialist, journalist, editor, orchestra leader, public relations specialist, sculptor, media specialist, librarian, reporter
Social (S)	These people describe themselves as kind, caring, helpful, and understanding of others. They value helping and making a contribution. They satisfy their needs in one-to-one or small-group interaction using strong speaking skills to teach, counsel, or advise. They are drawn to close interpersonal relationships and are less apt to engage in intellectual or extensive physical activity.	Nurse, teacher, social worker, genetic counselor, marriage counselor, rehabilitation counselor, school superintendent, geriatric specialist, insurance claims specialist, minister, travel agent, guidance counselor, convention planner
Enterprising (E)	These people describe themselves as assertive, risk taking, and persuasive. They value prestige, power, and status and are more inclined than other types to pursue such objectives. They use verbal skills to supervise, lead, direct, and persuade rather than to support or guide. They are interested in people and in achieving organizational goals.	Banker, city manager, FBI agent, health administrator, judge, labor arbitrator, salary and wage administrator, insurance salesperson, sales engineer, lawyer, sales representative, marketing manager
Conventional (C)	These people describe themselves as neat, orderly, detail oriented, and persistent. They value order, structure, prestige, and status and possess a high degree of self-control. They are not opposed to rules and regulations. They are skilled in organizing, planning, and scheduling and are interested in data and people.	Accountant, statistician, census enumerator, data processor, hospital administrator, insurance administrator, office manager, underwriter, auditor, personnel specialist, database manager, abstractor/indexer

Source: Table 13.1 and Figure 13.1 reproduced by special permission of the Publisher, Psychological Assessment Resources, Inc., 16204 N. Florida Ave., Lutz, FL 33549. From *The Self-Directed Search Professional User's Guide* by John L. Holland, PhD. Copyright © 1985, 1987, 1994, 1997. Further reproduction is prohibited without permission from PAR, Inc.

Planning for Your Career

The process of making a career choice begins with creating a career plan, and college is a good time to start, if you haven't already. Here are some important steps to take:

- **Visit the career center.** From helping you choose a major and career direction to getting an internship to helping you understand which careers will require a graduate degree, the career center is a valuable source of guidance. Attend workshops on advanced résumé writing, internship placement, interviewing, and other job search skills. Participate in mock interview activities to improve your interviewing skills. Take advantage of what your institution's career professionals have to offer.

- **Explore the career center Web site.** You'll find listings for part- and full-time positions, internships, cooperative (co-op) programs, and seasonal employment. You'll also find on-campus interviewing opportunities for internships and for full-time employment after graduation.

- **Attend your college's career fairs.** Employers in the area visit your campus to hire students. Get to know more about the employers who hire graduates in your major, and check your career center Web site for the dates of upcoming career fairs. Some career fairs may be specific to disciplines such as health care, information technology, or business.

- **Take as many self-assessments as possible.** Talk to a career counselor about your skills, aptitudes, interests, and career plans. Research possible occupations that match your skills, interests, and academic major.

- **Take a variety of classes, and pay attention to your grades.** College gives you the opportunity to get exposure to various knowledge areas. Remember, though, that employers and graduate schools want candidates with good grades.

- **Network.** Connect with instructors, family members, and friends to find contacts in your fields of interest so that you can learn more about those areas. Spend the summer completing internship, service-learning, and co-op experiences.

- **Build communication skills.** The ability to communicate verbally with persons inside and outside an organization is an important attribute that employers seek in new graduates. You should take every available opportunity to practice communicating, whether through classroom presentations, group work, leadership, or employment opportunities.

- **Improve your computer skills.** Today's college students have never been more technologically savvy, but not all technology experience is equal. As you begin to make decisions about your career path, explore and become familiar with technologies used in your field. Take advantage of the computer courses and workshops your college offers.

- **Create and monitor your digital footprint.** Have you Googled yourself lately? Do you like what you see online? Would an employer? Make sure nothing inappropriate is posted about you on Facebook, Instagram, Twitter, or other social media sites.

- **Visit work environments in person.** Explore career options through informational interviews (interviewing to find out more about a career) and job shadowing (observing someone at work—with his or her permission).

- **Get a job.** Many students already have jobs when they enter college. Holding a job, especially one related to your major or to a course you are taking, can enhance your classroom learning. Even a part-time job will develop your skills and might help you make decisions about what you like—and don't like—in a work environment.

You might complete these steps at a different pace or in a different order than your friends do, and that's OK. What you want is to develop your qualifications, make good choices, and take advantage of opportunities on and off campus to learn more about your career preferences. Keep your goals in mind as you select courses and look for employment, but also keep an eye out for special opportunities. The route you think you want to take might change as you do. ■

Getting Experience

Developing a career plan, getting a handle on your interests, and doing industry research are all part of becoming career-minded. Another step to take in this journey is to test the waters—to get some experience in areas that interest you and for which you are well suited. Employers prefer to hire people with experience, and fortunately there are several ways to gain some experience while you are in college: Engaging in experiential learning opportunities such as volunteer activities, service-learning, study abroad, internships, co-op programs, student projects and competitions, and research are all great ways to get career-based experience.

△ **Linking Classroom and Career**
This student studies computer science and works in the college computer labs, helping other students with their technology problems. Imagine what he is learning about his program of study and how his work experience relates to what he learns in his courses. Goodluz.

Experiential Learning Opportunities

Gaining experience in your field while you're in college can help you meet people who may later serve as important references for employment. Specific experiences can also teach you things you won't learn in the classroom.

Here are a number of ways to pursue this experience:

- **Volunteer activities.** Giving back to your community will benefit the community you serve and can also have tremendous personal and professional advantages. Whether you give your time to a service organization, a school, or a business, volunteering can help you develop your skill set, explore career possibilities, network, and contribute to lifelong learning. It also offers the personal satisfaction that comes when you know you are making a difference.

- **Service-learning.** Service-learning is a special category of volunteering that allows you to apply what you learn in class to actual practice. Some instructors build service-learning into their courses, but if this option isn't available, consider making that link yourself. Ask your college success instructor for help in finding a service opportunity that would enrich your classroom learning.

- **Study abroad.** Awareness of other cultures expands your thinking and your exposure to people different from you. If possible, take courses in another country so that you can learn about a different culture, experience new traditions, and practice a different pace of life. Many colleges provide short- and long-term options, so find an opportunity that works best for your schedule. Some study-abroad programs also include options for both work and service-learning experiences.

- **Internships and co-ops.** What you learn in the classroom can be applied to the real world through internships and co-op opportunities. An *internship* is a short-term, structured method of on-the-job training. As an intern, you are not likely to be paid, but you might be able to receive academic credit. Check with your academic department and your career center to find out about internships available in your major. Remember that if you have one or more internships on your résumé, you'll be a step ahead of students who ignore this valuable experience.

A *cooperative (co-op) program* allows you to alternate work experience and classes. As a co-op student, you can also have paid work assignments that provide you with an opportunity to apply what you've learned in college to the workplace.

- **Student projects and competitions.** In many fields students engage in competitions based on what they have learned in the classroom. They might compete against teams from other colleges. In the process they learn teamwork, communication, and problem-solving skills.

- **Research.** An excellent way to extend your academic learning is to work with an instructor on a directed research project. Research extends your critical-thinking skills and provides insight into a subject above and beyond your books and class notes. This experience also allows you greater exposure to instructors who can become mentors and professional advocates.

Working in College

You may find that you want or need to have a job while you're in college. Among the many benefits of holding down a job while taking classes are the following:

- Gaining professional experience

- Earning money for tuition, books, and living expenses

- Networking / making connections

- Learning more about yourself and others

- Developing key skills and attributes, such as communication, teamwork, problem solving, work ethic, and time management

Your first decision will be whether to work on campus or off. If you choose to work on campus, look for opportunities as early in the semester as you can. You might be pleasantly surprised to learn how varied on-campus opportunities are, such as tutoring in the writing or math center, being an attendant in the fitness center, or serving as a student ambassador for the admissions office or career center. Often you will see students on campus who are studying while

" Students who work on campus are more likely to graduate from college than are students who work off campus. "

they work. This is one benefit of on-campus employment. Another benefit is that the schedules are often flexible. Still another is that you might be able to connect with instructors and administrators whom you later can consult as mentors or ask for reference letters. In addition, your boss will understand that you occasionally need time off to study or take exams. Finally, students who work on campus are more likely to graduate from college than are students who work off campus; keep this fact in mind as you think about mixing college and work.

Some on-campus jobs are reserved for work-study students. The federal work-study program is a form of government-sponsored financial aid that provides part-time employment to help students with college expenses. Once you accept the work-study award on your financial aid notification, you will be sent information regarding the steps you should take for getting a job within the program. Keep in mind that your work-study award will be limited to a certain amount of money each term; once you reach your earnings limit, you can no longer work until the next term begins. Most work-study jobs are on campus, but some nonprofit organizations in your community may be able to accept work-study students as well. Generally, you will have to interview for a work-study position whether on or off campus. Check with your college's financial aid office or career center to get a list of available jobs and to get help preparing your application materials and getting ready for the interview.

An off-campus job might pay better than an on-campus one, or be closer to your home, or be in an organization where you want to continue working after you finish college. The best places to start looking for off-campus jobs are your campus career center and your financial aid office. Feel free to speak to a career counselor for suggestions.

Whether you choose to work on or off campus, keep in mind that overextending yourself can interfere with your college success and your ability to attend class, do your homework, and participate in many other valuable parts of college life, such as group study. Determine how involved you are able to be with your job, and keep your work hours within reasonable limits. Students who work in paid jobs more than fifteen or twenty hours a week have a lower chance of success in college. ■

TRY IT!

MAKING DECISIONS ▷ College Jobs and Your Career

At this point in your college experience, you probably have at least tentative plans for the major and/or the career you will pursue. If you must take a job while going to school, think about what jobs might be available on campus and in the outside community that could provide valuable experience to help you meet your goals. Look at your campus Web site and your local newspaper (either the print or the online version). Make two lists—one for on-campus jobs that you discover on the campus Web site and the other for off-campus jobs listed in the paper that relate to your intended major. Make a decision to investigate the availability of the jobs you identify.

Job Search Strategies

It may be hard to imagine yourself searching for a job—after all, you've just begun college. But we want to give you some job search strategies that can be applied to an internship or a co-op program while you are in college as well as to a career-level job once you graduate. Here are a few strategies to try:

- **Learn about the major employers in your college's geographic area.** Once you know who the major employers are, such as manufacturers, service industries, and resorts, check them out and visit their Web sites. If you like what you see, visit your career center to arrange an informational interview or a job-shadowing opportunity.

- **Scan ads.** Visit online job boards, and look at the classified ads in the local newspaper, either in print or online.

- **Check your college's student newspaper.** Employers who favor hiring college students (such as UPS) often advertise there. Be cautious about work opportunities that seem unrealistic, such as those offering big salaries for working at home or those that ask you to pay an up-front fee for a job. When in doubt, ask your career center for advice.

- **Be aware that many job openings are never posted.** Employers often find it easier to hire people who are recommended to them by current employees, friends, or the person vacating the position. Faculty members often hire students for their research labs based on performance in the classroom.

Market Yourself

Some people think that marketing yourself is what you do when you need a job, but in fact that's not the case at all. Marketing yourself is actually about developing a presence at your college and within your industry. If you can create a name and reputation for yourself, you can shape your own future. Here are two points to consider:

- **If you don't do it, no one else will.** Taking control of your own image is your responsibility. There is no one who can portray you as accurately as you. Remember to share your career goals with instructors, advisers, friends, and family—they can't help market you if they don't know you. The more others know about your professional goals, the more they are able to help you make professional connections.

- **Get an edge over your competition.** You need to stand out from your peers if you want to go far in your career. Think carefully about what you are doing to advance yourself professionally outside the classroom, such as becoming a co-op student, an intern, or a volunteer.

Build a Résumé

A good résumé is an excellent and necessary way of marketing yourself. Before you finish college, you'll need a résumé, whether it's for a part-time job, an internship, or a co-op position, or to show to an instructor who agrees to write you a letter of recommendation. There are two résumé formats: chronological and skill focused. Choose the chronological format if you have related job experience (listing your jobs and other experiences, starting with those that are the most recent). Choose the skill-focused résumé if you can group skills from a number of jobs or projects into several meaningful categories. Your career center can help you choose the format that is right for you based on your experience and future goals.

On average, employers spend seven to ten seconds screening each résumé to glean their first-round picks. Many employers also use résumé-scanning software to identify key terms and experiences that are highly prized by employers. If you are a new professional, a one-page résumé is appropriate. Add a second page only if you have truly outstanding skills or work experiences that won't fit on the first page, but consult with your career center for guidance on this point. If you are in college to get retrained and change your career, make sure to update the information on your résumé.

Write a Cover Letter

A cover letter is *more important* than a résumé and much harder to write well. When composing and sending a cover letter, think about who will receive it. Different organizations will have different requirements. Your academic adviser or career counselor can help you address your letter to the right person; so can the Internet. Never write, "To whom it may concern." Use the proper formats for date, address, and salutation. These are details that hiring managers pay attention to, and a mistake in your letter may cost you an interview. And make sure to ask someone whose writing ability you trust to proof your cover letter.

A cover letter written to explain how hiring you will benefit the organization is an excellent way of marketing yourself to a potential employer. It is important to review the organization's Web site and find out what skills and experience its current employees have. Use the cover letter to highlight your skills for every requirement of the position. Your career center can help you write a cover letter that talks about your education and your relevant experience.

Know How to Interview

The first year of college might not seem like a time to be concerned about interviews. However, students often find themselves in interview situations soon after arriving on campus. You might be looking for a position in student government, searching for an on-campus job, competing for a scholarship, choosing a summer job opportunity, or applying for an internship. Your preparation for an interview begins the moment you arrive on campus because, as a first-year student, the interview will be about you and your experience in college. Luckily, the chapters in this book have begun preparing you for the interview process.

Interview preparation. The purpose of the interview is to exchange information. The interviewer's goal is to assess your abilities and competencies. For you, the interview is an opportunity to learn more about the employer and to determine whether there is a match between your interests and abilities and the position you are applying for. By researching the organization and its employees prior to an

△ **First Impressions**
A critical step on the way to any job is the personal interview. This is your chance to put your best foot forward. Remember to be on time, dress professionally, offer a firm handshake, answer questions honestly, and smile! Jonathan Stark.

interview, you will know what questions to ask. Here's how you can get started:

1. **Start with the organization's Web site.** This is usually the single best resource. Scroll through the entire site, and research the available products and services. Note details you can use to develop good interview questions to ask and prepare relevant answers to anticipated interview questions. If the company does not have its own Web site, go to other sites, such as Hoovers (hoovers.com), that provide extensive information about organizations and industries.

2. **Review competitor Web sites.** Gather information on developments in the organization industry sector.

3. **Ask for advice.** Ask your instructor or your career center about the organization.

4. **Use your library.** Find articles in business publications and industry trade magazines.

5. **Note the employer's goals and values.** These tell you about the organizational culture.

6. **Take the research you have conducted on the organization with you to the interview.** You will want to show that you have taken the time to find out about its products and services prior to the interview.

After you've done your research, the next step is to practice interviewing *before* the actual interview. Check with your career center to find out whether you can participate in a mock interview. Many career centers also have practice interview software. InterviewStream is a popular program that allows you to record answers to interview questions asked by the computer for replay and review. Because the interview is recorded using a webcam, you can review not only your words but also your body language. Nonverbal communication is often more important than what you actually say in the interview. Even if a mock interview session is not available, the career center can offer tips on handling an interview situation.

Appropriate interview conduct. In an interview situation, any of the following might make the difference in whether you are hired for the position:

- **Dress appropriately.** First impressions matter, so always dress neatly and appropriately. You can be somewhat casual for some types of employers, but it is better to dress too professionally than too informally.

- **Arrive on time to the interview.** If your interview is off campus, determine how long it will take you to travel to the interview site before the day of your interview.

- **Follow up.** It is important to follow up any interview with a thank-you e-mail or a signed card. Many times, the person to whom you addressed your cover letter is not the person with whom you actually interview. Prior to leaving the interview, ask for the business cards of the professionals you've met so that you have their contact information. ■

TRY IT!

SETTING GOALS ▷ Planning an Exciting Future

Have you explored your institution's career center? If so, did your visit allow you to think about the relationship between your academic work and your ideal job? Thinking about your dream career can motivate you to succeed in the present. While you're making these big plans, it's always a good idea to have a backup plan that builds on your strengths and your interests, just in case the dream career doesn't happen.

Skills Employers Seek

One of the many important purposes and outcomes of your college experience is gaining a combination of knowledge and skills. Two types of skills are essential to employment and to life: content skills and transferable skills.

Content Skills

Content skills are intellectual, or "hard," skills you gain in your academic field. They include writing proficiency, computer literacy, and foreign language skills. Certain types of employers expect you to have extensive knowledge in your academic major before they will consider hiring you; for example, to get a job in accounting, you must have knowledge of QuickBooks or Microsoft Excel's advanced features. Employers will not train you in basic applications or knowledge related to your field, so remember to be prepared to speak of your qualifications during the interview process. For most college students it's sufficient to have some fundamental knowledge. You will learn on the job as you move from entry-level to advanced positions.

Transferable Skills

Transferable skills are general abilities that can be applied in a lot of settings. Some transferable skills are listed and described in Table 13.2.

Transferable skills are valuable to many kinds of employers. They give you flexibility in your career planning. For example, volunteer work, involvement in a student professional organization or club, and personal hobbies or interests can all build interpersonal awareness and teamwork, leadership, and effective communication abilities. Internships and career-related work can offer you valuable opportunities to practice these skills in the real world. ∎

Top-Ranked Skills and Qualities

Employers ranked skills and qualities that job candidates possess according to what is most important. The following abilities ranked most highly:

The ability to
- Work in a team structure
- Make decisions and solve problems
- Plan, organize, and prioritize work
- Verbally communicate with persons inside and outside the organization
- Obtain and process information
- Analyze quantitative data
- Demonstrate technical knowledge related to the job

In other words, the ideal candidate is a team player and good communicator who can make decisions, solve problems, and prioritize.

Source: National Association of Colleges and Employers, *Job Outlook 2014* (Bethlehem, PA: National Association of Colleges and Employers, 2013).

◁ **Making Connections**
Some career fairs may be specific to fields such as health care, information technology, or business. Others may be specific to the audience, such as this career fair for military veterans. Attending events like these is part of planning for your career. Career fairs give job candidates the opportunity to make a strong first impression with potential employers. © Sandy Huffaker/Corbis.

Table 13.2 ▽ Transferable Skills and Abilities

Transferable skills	Abilities
Communication	Being a clear and persuasive speaker
	Listening attentively
	Writing well
Presentation	Justifying
	Persuading
	Responding to questions and serious critiques of presentation material
Leadership	Taking charge
	Providing direction
Teamwork	Working with different people while maintaining control over some assignments
Interpersonal	Relating to others
	Motivating others to participate
	Easing conflict between coworkers
Personal traits	Showing motivation
	Recognizing the need to take action
	Being adaptable to change
	Having a strong work ethic
	Being reliable and honest
	Acting in an ethical manner
	Knowing how to plan and organize multiple tasks
	Being able to respond positively to customer concerns
Critical thinking and problem solving	Identifying problems and their solutions by combining information from different sources and considering options

△ **Celebrate!**

Before you know it, you'll be a college graduate, equipped with all the knowledge and skills you have acquired and on your way to a successful career and a bright future. © Ariel Skelley/Blend Images/Corbis.

Chapter Review

Steps to Success:
Considering Majors and Careers

○ **Understand the nature of the new economy that you will be entering.** It is global, innovative, without boundaries, ever changing, and social.

○ **Be responsible for planning your own career.** No one else is going to plan your career for you, but plenty of people on your campus are willing to help *you* do it. Think seriously about your major. You eventually have to get a degree in something, and you want to feel confident and comfortable about the major that you select.

○ **Enhance your employability by getting different kinds of work and travel experience during college.** You can get different experiences while taking classes— or better yet, consider maintaining your momentum during the summer. Continuous enrollment is a good thing. See your adviser and career center to learn about experiences that your college offers: volunteer work or service-learning, study abroad, internships and co-ops, and others.

○ **Learn which of your characteristics could and should affect your career choices.** Strive to define your interests, skills, aptitudes, personality, life goals, and work values. Talk them through with a career counselor. It's a normal thing for college students to do.

○ **Get professional help from your career center.** Advisers can help you write your résumé and cover letters, learn and practice interview skills, and much more.

○ **Keep in touch with your instructors.** Consider keeping in touch with the instructor of this course and with other instructors. Later in college you may need to ask them to write letters of reference for you as you seek employment or admission to graduate school.

○ **Make a commitment to yourself.** You may think that you are not yet ready for a high level of commitment because too many things are still uncertain about your major and your future life. That's perfectly natural. But we urge you to make a commitment to return to college next term and next year and to get as much as you can out of this life-changing experience.

○ **Be aware of what today's employers seek from new employees.** Make sure you can demonstrate both the content and transferable skills necessary for the jobs that interest you most.

Applying what you've learned . . .

Now that you have read and discussed this chapter, consider how you can apply what you have learned to your academic and personal lives. The following prompts will help you reflect on the chapter material and its relevance to you both now and in the future.

1. Sometimes the best way to learn about a career is to talk to someone who is working or teaching in that field. Set up an appointment to talk with a professor who teaches in the area in which you are interested. Find out as much as possible about the education required for a specific career in that field.

2. Choosing a major is a big decision, one that should include consideration of your personal learning style, your personality, and your goals and values. How will insights you've gained about your emotional intelligence and how you learn guide your exploration of majors and careers?

Use Your Resources

GO TO ▷ **The career center:** If you need help learning about specific jobs and careers, about preparing an effective résumé and cover letter, and about preparing for an interview.

GO TO ▷ **Academic advisers / first-year counselors:** If you need help finding supportive networks to connect academic learning to co-curricular and extracurricular learning.

GO TO ▷ **Your instructors:** If you need help connecting your academic interests to careers.

GO TO ▷ **The library:** If you need help finding information on careers.

GO TO ▷ **Upper-class students:** If you need help navigating courses and finding important resources.

GO TO ▷ **Student organizations:** If you need help finding leadership development opportunities.

GO ONLINE TO ▷ **The Occupational Information Network (O*NET) Resource Center (onetcenter.org):** If you need help getting information on occupations and skill sets and links to professional sites for selected occupations.

GO ONLINE TO ▷ **The Occupational Outlook Handbook (bls.gov/ooh/):** If you want to review the U. S. Bureau of Labor Statistics' source for up-to-date information about careers and career trends.

GO ONLINE TO ▷ **The Career Key (careerkey.org/choose-a-career/how-to -choose-a-career.html#.Vi5ZtCtBZeE) or Mapping Your Future (www.mappingyourfuture.org):** If you need help exploring careers.

GO ONLINE TO ▷ **The Riley Guide (rileyguide.com):** If you need help finding tips for interviewing and job search strategies.

NOW... How do you measure up?

1. The world economy is changing, and how it changes will probably affect job prospects.
   - ○ Agree
   - ○ Don't Know
   - ○ Disagree

2. There is no guarantee that anyone's first career choice will be permanent.
   - ○ Agree
   - ○ Don't Know
   - ○ Disagree

3. I know my strengths and interests and how they might influence my career choice.
   - ○ Agree
   - ○ Don't Know
   - ○ Disagree

4. One of the most important things college students can do in the first year is visit the campus career center.
   - ○ Agree
   - ○ Don't Know
   - ○ Disagree

How do your answers here compare to your responses to the quiz you took at the start of the chapter? Which sections of this chapter left a strong impression on you? What strategies for selecting your major and planning for your career have you started to use? Are they working? What other strategies will you commit to trying?

LaunchPad
macmillan learning

LaunchPad Solo for College Success is a great resource. Go online to master concepts using the LearningCurve study tool and much more. **macmillanhighered.com/collegesuccessmedia**

Index

A

Abstract of article, reading, 99
Academic advisers, 2, 41, 68, 216
  planning and, 11, 14
Academic articles/journals. *See*
  Scholarly articles/journals
Academic goals, 10. *See also* Goal
  setting
Academic honesty, 121–23
Academic planning, 11–14
Active class participation, 72, 75
Active reading, 89–106
  of different kinds of textbooks,
    97–100
  four-step plan for, 91–96
  improving, 101–3
Adaptability, emotional intelligence
  and, 29
ADD, 66–67
ADHD, 66–67
Adjunct instructors, 7
Advisers. *See* Academic advisers
Aerobic exercise. *See* Exercise
Age diversity on campus, 170
Alcohol use, 209, 210–11
Analysis, as level of learning,
  138, 139
Anger, managing, 25, 26
Annotations, making while reading,
  93, 94
Anorexia nervosa, 203
Anxiety
  public speaking and, 155, 156
  while taking tests and exams,
    111, 117
APA documentation style, 154
Appealing to false authority, 132
Application, as level of learning,
  138, 139
Arguments, thinking critically about,
  131–32
Artistic personality type, 222, 224
Asking questions. *See* Questions,
  asking
Assertiveness, emotional intelligence
  and, 29
Assigned reading, 57, 71
  doing for class preparation,
    73, 91
  marking, 93–94
  planning, 100, 102–3
  vocabulary in, 101–2
Assuming truth, as faulty reasoning,
  132–33
Assumptions, challenging, 130
Attention deficit disorder, 66
Attention deficit hyperactivity
  disorder, 66
Attention level. *See also* Paying
  attention improved memory
  and, 114
  study time and, 48
Audience
  public speaking and, 155–56,
    157
  writing for, 153
Aural learners
  critical listening and, 74–75
  methods for, 64
  preferences of, 60
  remembering information and, 84
Authority
  appealing to false, 132
  evaluating sources for, 149–50

B

BAC, 210–11
Bandura, Albert, 58
Bar-On, Reuven, 27
Bar-On Model of Emotional
  Intelligence, 28–29
Begging, as faulty reasoning, 132
Beliefs, challenging, 130, 169
Bias, evaluating sources for, 150
Binders, for each course, 73, 82
Binge eating disorder, 203
Birth control, 209
Block scheduling, 48, 49, 95
Blog posts, 153
Blood alcohol content (BAC), 210–11
Bloom, Benjamin, 138
Bloom's taxonomy, 138–139
Body mass index (BMI), 204
Books, as research source, 146, 148
Borrowing funds, balancing with
  working, 189–90
Bracero, Analee, 144
Brainstorming, critical thinking and,
  134
Branch mapping, 92
Breathing, stress management and,
  200
Budgeting, 180, 181–84
Bulimia, 203

C

Caffeine, stress management and, 201
Calendars, 35, 205
Campus career centers, 11, 12, 221,
  225, 231
Campus learning centers. *See*
  Learning centers
Campus library resources, 147–48
Campus organizations and groups,
  getting involved in, 4, 173
Campus tutoring centers, 46
Career centers, 11, 12, 221, 225, 231
Career fairs, 225, 233
Career planning, 215–237
  emotional intelligence and, 30
  exploring inderests for, 221–24
  getting experience and, 175, 226–28
  job search strategies, 229–31
  major connected with, 11–12, 215
  new economy and, 217–18
  personality type, 221–24
  self-assessment for, 219–20, 221, 225
  setting goals for, 8–10
  skills employers seek and, 232–33
  working in college and, 11, 225, 227
Cheating, 121–23. *See also* Plagiarism
Checkcards, 192
Choosing topic, 146
Chronological résumés, 229
Cigarette smoking, 211
Citing sources, 154
Class discussion. *See* Discussion
Classes
  getting most out of, 71–88
  preparing for, 73
  selecting, 14
  taking notes in. *See* Note taking
Class participation, 72, 75
Class schedule, 43, 47, 49
Clubs on campus, getting involved
  in, 4
Cognitive learning disabilities, 66, 67–68

Collaboration, 120

Collaboration, 120
  critical thinking and, 134
Collaborative learning teams, 56–57
College Board PROFILE form, 187
College education, advantages of, 3–4
College instructors. *See* Instructors
College librarians, assistance from,
  137, 147, 149
College library resources, 57, 147–48
College success courses, 1, 5, 30
Communication skills, 13, 143, 225
  citing sources and, 154
  offline *versus* online, 167–68, 217
  parents and, 166
  safe sex and, 208
  speaking and, 155–57
  in workplace, 175, 233
  writing and, 151–55
Community involvement, 36. *See also*
  Connecting with others
Community service, 174
Competitions, career planning and,
  227, 229
Comprehension, 138
  interactive learners and, 84
  monitoring while reading, 95
Computer literacy/skills, 12–13, 46,
  145, 225. *See also* Internet *entries*
Concentrating, while reading, 94–95
Conclusions, drawing, 131, 145
Condoms, 209
Conflict with others, 163
Connecting with others, 23, 161–78.
  See also Relationships in digital
  age, 167–68
  diversity on campus and, 169–72
  getting to know instructors, 6–7, 103
  through community service, 174
  through involvement on campus,
    173–74
  through tutors and study groups, 110
  through VARK learning styles, 63
  through working, 174–75
Content skills, sought by employers,
  232
Contraceptives, 209
Conventional personality type, 222, 224
Cooperative (co-op) education, 186,
  227
Cornell Format, for note taking, 77
Cost cutting, 182–83
Courses. *See also* Classes
  dropping, 123, 187
  elective *versus* required, 11
  online, 43, 46, 76
  required for major, 9, 14
Course schedule, 47, 49
Course syllabus, 6–7, 73, 109
Cover letter, for résumé, 230
Creation, as sixth level of learning,
  138, 139
Creativity, critical thinking and, 134,
  136
Credit cards, 191–92, 193
Credit report, obtaining, 193
Credit score, 191, 193
Critical listening, 74–75
Critical thinking, 127–42
  applying skills in, 134–37
  Bloom's taxonomy and, 138–39
  in college and life, 129
  faulty reasoning and, 132–33
  strategies for, 130
Cultural literacy, 145
Cultural views of time, 35, 37
Cyberbullying, 206–7

D

Daily planners, 44
Databases
  researching with, 137, 147, 148
  for scholarly articles, 148
Dating relationships
Deadlines, 34, 36, 43, 123. *See also*
  Time management
Debit cards, 192
Delayed gratification, 30
Delivery of speeches, 156
Depression, 199, 206, 207
Developmental arithmetic disorder, 68
Developmental writing disorder, 67
Diet. *See* Nutrition and diet
Digital footprint, 12, 225
Digital textbooks, 96
Discussion, 5
  assigned readings and, 73
  note taking from, 81
  participation in, 37
Distractions
  avoiding while studying, 48–49
  dealing with, 42
  with online exams, 120
  with online reading, 96
  procrastination and, 41
Diversity on college campus, 161,
  169–72
Drafting
  steps for, 151–52
  of summaries, 116
  of texts and e-mails, 168
Dressing appropriately for interviews,
  231
  for speeches, 157
Drinking alcohol, 209, 210–11
Dropping, course, 123, 187
Duckworth, Angela, 23
Dyslexia, 67
Dyson, May, 96

E

Earnings, future, college education
  and, 3
Eating disorders, 203
Eating healthy. *See* Nutrition and
  diet
Economic diversity on campus, 170
Economy, today's, career and, 217–18
Editing, 153
EI. *See* Emotional intelligence
Electronic calendar, 205
Electronic planners, 44
Electronic tools, for note taking, 83
E-mail, appropriate use of, 153, 167,
  193
  etiquette for, 168
Emergencies, credit card for, 191
Emotional health, 199, 206–207
Emotional intelligence,
  understanding, 17, 18, 25–30
Emotions
  effect on success, 30
  managing, 25–26
  self-awareness of, 29
  test preparation and, 111
Empathy, emotional intelligence
  and, 29
Employment after college
  job search strategies for, 229–31
  money management and, 184

Employment during college
  balancing with borrowing, 189–90
  benefits of, 174
  career planning and, 11, 225, 227
  work-study and, 185–86, 227
Encyclopedias, topic overview with, 146
Energy levels, time management and, 38–39
Engaged learning, 53–68
  benefits of, 55
  collaborative learning teams and, 56–57
  learning disabilities and, 66–68
  learning styles and, 59–65
  learning theories and, 58–59
English as a second language, 103
Enterprising personality type, 222, 224
Entertainment, cutting costs of, 183
E-readers, pros and cons of, 96
ESL, 103
Essay questions on tests/exams, 117
Evaluating sources, 137, 149–50
Evaluation, as level of learning, 138, 139
Evidence, examining, critical thinking and, 132
Exams, 107–126
  academic honesty and misconduct on, 121–23
  preparing for, 109–13
  strategies for taking, 117–20
  studying for retention and, 114–16
Exercise
  scheduling, 46
  stress management and, 199, 203
  test preparation and, 111
Expenses, budgeting for, 181–82
Experiential learning opportunities, 13, 226–28
Expressive language disorders, 68

F

Facebook, 168
Face-to-face communication *versus* online, 167–68, 217
FAFSA, 186–87, 190
Fallacies, logical, 132–33
False assumption, 132–33
False authority, appealing to, 132
False cause, 133
Family relationships, 36, 162, 165–66
Faulty reasoning, avoiding, 132–33
Federal loans, subsidized and unsubsidized, 189–90
Federal work-study, 185–86, 227
Feeling connected. *See* Connecting with others
Fifty-minute study blocks, 48
Fill-in-the-blank questions on tests/exams, 118–19
Finances, personal. *See* Money management
Financial aid, 41, 179, 185–88
Financial aid office, 186, 187
Fixed expenses, 182
Fixed mindset, 21
Flash cards, 116
Flexibility, 49, 232
  emotional intelligence and, 29
Focusing
  to improve memory, 114
  as key to success, 37
  while reading, 94
Forgetting curve, 84
Formal style of writing, 153
Free Application for Federal Student Aid, 186–87
Freewriting, 151

G

Gailliard, Amy, 72
Gardasil vaccine, 208

Gavi, Ariela, 198
Generalizations, hasty, 133
Global economy, 217
Goal setting
  assigned reading, 73, 91
  engaged learning and, 55
  exam preparation and, 113
  importance of, and methods for, 8–10
  personal budget, 184
  realistic, 23
  for study time, 48, 64
  time management and, 8, 35–36
Google, 137, 149
Google Scholar, 148
Grades, 7, 12, 123, 225
  emotional intelligence and, 30
Graduate school, planning for, 189
Grants, 185
Gratification, delayed, 30
Grit, resilience and, 23
Group discussion. *See* Discussion
Group study. *See* Study groups
Growth mindset, 21

H

Happiness, emotional intelligence and, 29
Harassment, zero-tolerance policy for, 172
Hasty generalizations, 133
Hate crimes, 172
Healthy living, 197–214
  alcohol use and, 209, 210–11
  emotional health and, 199, 206–7
  exercise, 46, 111, 199, 203
  nutrition and weight management, 199, 201–3, 204
  sexual health and, 199, 208–9
  stress management and, 199, 200–1
Highlighting, 83
  while reading, 93–94, 98
HIV (human immunodeficiency virus), 208
Holland, John, 221
Holland Personality and Career Types, 221–22
Homework, class notes for, 85
Honesty, academic, 121–23
HPV (human papillomavirus), 208
Humanities textbooks, reading, 98–99

I

Identity theft, 192, 193
Impulse control, emotional intelligence and, 29
Income, budgeting and, 181
Independence, 33
  emotional intelligence and, 29
Indra, Titus, 90
Informal style of writing, 153
Information literacy, 143–50
  choosing, narrowing, researching topic and, 146
  evaluating sources and, 149–50
  understanding, 143–44
  using library and, 147–48
Instructors
  clarifying assignment and, 153
  connecting with, 6–7, 103
  feedback from, 144
  learning styles and, 65
  learning teams and, 57
  materials provided by, 73, 76, 82
  preparing for tests with, 107, 109
  research topic and, 146
  respectful behavior toward, 37
  reviewing tests and, 119
Interactive learners, 84

Interests, personal, career and, 11, 220–24
Internet. *See also* Online *entries*
  collaboration, critical thinking and, 134
  exams on, 120
  searching on, 137, 149
  using to improve memory, 114
Internships, 226
Interpersonal skills, 233
  emotional intelligence and, 29
Interviewing, 230–31
Intrapersonal skills, emotional intelligence and, 29
Investigative personality type, 222, 224
Involvement
  in campus organizations and groups, 173
  in community, 36

J

Jobs. *See* Employment *entries*
Journals/journal articles. *See* Scholarly articles/journals
Jumping on bandwagon, 132

K

Kadison, Richard, 30
Kahneman, Daniel, 129
Key terms, vocabulary development from, 101
Key words
  in essay tests, 118
  Internet search with, 146
  in reviewing notes, 84
Kinesthetic learners, 60, 64
Kolb Learning Styles Inventory, 59
Kossick, Brent, 216

L

Larsen, Nicoleta, 34
Late payments/fees, on credit cards, 192
Leadership skills, 4, 12, 233
Learning, engaged. *See* Engaged learning
Learning, six levels of, 138–39
Learning centers
  emotional intelligence and, 28
  learning disabilities and, 171
  in libraries, 147
  tutors and, 46
Learning challenges/disabilities
  learning with, 66–68
  meeting people with, 67, 170–71
Learning styles
  engaged learning and, 59
  questionnaire to determine, 60–64
  teaching styles and, 65
  types of, 59–60
Learning teams, 56–57
Learning theories, 58–59
Lee, Frank, 162
Levels of learning, six, 138–39
Librarians, assistance from, 137, 147, 149
Library resources, 57, 147–48
Life goals, career planning and, 220
Lifelong process, career development as, 218
Listening, 71, 74–75
List format for note taking, 80
Living expenses, budgeting for, 181–82
Loans, balancing with working, 189–90
Logical fallacies, 132–33
Long-term goals, 9, 36. *See also* Goal setting

M

Magazines, researching with, 146, 148
Main idea, identifying while taking notes, 81, 84
Majors. *See also* Career planning
  choosing, 189, 215
  making decisions about, 11
  requisite courses for, 9, 14
Managing money. *See* Money management
Mapping
  mind mapping, 115–16
  while previewing, 92
Margin notes, writing while reading, 94
Marijuana, 211
Marketing yourself, 229
Marking textbooks while reading, 93–94
Marriage, during college, 164, 165–66
Marshmellow study, 30
Maslow, Abraham, 58
Matching questions on tests/exams, 119
Math course, note taking in, 82
Math exams, preparing for, 111, 112
Math textbooks, reading, 97
Media literacy, 145
Meditation, stress reduction and, 200
Meija, Gustavo, 18
Memory, improving, 84, 114
Merit scholarships, 185
Microsoft Excel, 83
Microsoft Word, 83
Mind mapping, 115–16
Mindsets, 21–22
  for future career, 218
Misconduct, academic, 121–23
MLA documentation style, 154
MLA Handbook for Writers of Research Papers, 154
Mock interviews, 231
Money management, 179–96
  balancing work and borrowing for, 189–90
  budgeting and, 180, 181–84
  financial aid and, 41, 179, 185–88
  managing credit and, 191–92, 193
Moods, emotional intelligence and, 29
Mosley, Shawn, 2
Motivation, maintaining, 17, 19, 42–43
Multiple-choice questions on tests/exams, 118
Multitasking, avoiding while studying, 48
Myers-Briggs Type Indicator, 59
MyPlate eating guidelines, 202

N

Napping, 39
  stress management and, 205
Needs
  Maslow's hierarchy of, 58
  scholarships based on, 185
  versus wants, 182
Newspapers, researching with, 146
Notes, creating for speeches, 156
Note taking, 75–86
  adjusting for different classes, 81
  electronic tools for, 83
  learning teams and, 57
  methods for, 77–80
  in quantitative courses, 82
  reviewing after, 84–86
  while listening, 71, 76
  while reading, 94
Nutrition and diet
  healthy snacks, 39, 202
  paying attention to, 199, 201–3
  stress management and, 201
  test preparation and, 111

O

Online communication, 167–68, 217
Online courses, 43, 46, 76
Online databases, research with, 147, 148
Online reading, 96
Online tests, strategies for taking, 120
Optimism, emotional intelligence and, 25, 29
Organization
  class preparation and, 73
  of schedule, 44–46
  using to improve memory, 114
Organizations on campus, getting involved in, 4, 173
Outlining
  for essay tests/exams, 117
  for note taking, 78
  for science textbooks, 98
  for speeches, 156
  studying from, 111
  while previewing, 92
  writing process and, 151, 152
Overlearning, to improve memory, 114

P

Paragraph format, for note taking, 79
Parenting, during college, 165–66
Parent Loan for Undergraduate Students, 190
Parents, relationships with, 166
Participating in class, 72, 75
Passwords
  identity theft and, 193
  online access and, 147, 168
Paying attention, 12, 48, 59, 73, 74, 114
Peer-reviewed scholarly articles/journals. See Scholarly articles/journals
Periodicals
  information time line for, 146
  researching with, 148
Personal attacks, 132
Personal bias, evaluating sources for, 150
Personal finance. See Money management
Personal identification number, debit cards and, 192
Personalities, career planning and, 11, 219–20
Personality types, 221–22, 224
Personal relationships, managing, 163–64
Personal skills, career planning and, 219
Personal traits, 233
Physical activity. See Exercise
Physical challenges/disabilities, 170–71
Physical health. See Healthy living
PIN, debit cards and, 192
Plagiarism, 108, 122, 145, 154, 155
Planners, daily or weekly, 44–45
PLUS loans, 190
Points of view. See Viewpoints
Positive attitude, 20, 22
Positive self-talk, test preparation and, 111
Posting, online, appropriate use of, 168
PowerPoint, 83, 116, 156
Pregnancy, protection against, 208, 209
Prejudice, resisting, 170
Preparation for class, 73
Presentation skills, 156, 233
Previewing, before reading, 91–92
Prewriting, 151
Prezi, 156
Primary sources, value of, 99

Priorities, setting, 26, 36, 43
Private student loans, 190
Problem solving
  critical thinking and, 134–35
  emotional intelligence and, 29
  group assignment and, 81
Procrastination, 35, 40–41, 94, 102, 123
PROFILE form, College Board, 187
Pronunciation, in speeches, 156
Publication Manual of the American Psychological Association, 154
Public speaking, 155–57
Punctuality
  for interviews, 231
  as sign of respect, 37

Q

Quantitative courses, note taking in, 82
Questions, asking
  for academic advisor, 14
  critical thinking and, 129, 130, 137
  to overcome procrastination and distractions, 40, 43
  in study groups, 57

R

Rape, protecting against, 209
Reading, active. See Active reading
Reading, assigned. See Assigned reading
Reading disabilities, 67
Reading, online, 96
Read/write learners, 60, 64
Realistic personality type, 222, 224
Reality testing
  emotional intelligence and, 29
  living expenses and, 181
Reasoning, faulty, 132–33
Reciting, to remember information, 84
Relationships. See also Connecting with others diversity on campus and, 161
  with family members, 36, 162, 165–66
  with instructors, 6–7
  personal, 163–64
Relevance of sources, 149
Reliability of sources, 149
Religious diversity on campus, 170
Remembering, as first level of learning, 138–39
Research
  experiential learning and, 227
  information literacy and, 145–46
  for interview preparation, 230
  learning teams and, 57
  online, 137
  setting aside time for, 46
  using library for, 57, 147
Research papers, 99, 144
  citing sources, 154
Resilience, 23–24, 29, 119, 163
Respect, time management and, 37
Résumé, building, 35, 216, 229–30
Reviewing, 48, 116
  while reading, 96
Reviewing notes, 84–86
Review sheets, 115, 116
Revising, 152
Rewards, for meeting goals, 43, 49
Romantic relationships, 164
Roommates, 163
Rowling, J. K., 24

S

Safe sex, communicating about, 208
SaVE legislation, 209
Savings account, establishing, 190

Scams, identity theft and, 193
Schedule of classes, 43, 47, 49
Scheduling time, 35, 39, 44–45. *See also* Time management
Schlossberg, Nancy, 59
Scholarly articles/journals evaluating, 99
  information time line for, 146
  researching with, 148
Scholarships, 185, 187
Science courses, note taking in, 82
Science exams, preparing for, 111, 112
Science textbooks, reading, 97–98
Search engines, Internet, 137, 149
Self-actualization, 58
  emotional intelligence and, 29
Self-assessment, for career planning, 219–20, 221, 225
Self-awareness, emotional, 29
Self-regard, emotional intelligence and, 29
Self-talk, positive, for test preparation, 111
Service-learning, 55, 226
Sexual assault, protecting against, 209
Sexual diversity on campus, 171
Sexual health, 199, 208–9
Sexually-transmitted infections, 208–9
Short-term goals, 8–9, 36, 55. *See also* Goal setting
Sisu, resilience and, 23
Skill-focused résumés, 229
Skills
  career planning and, 11, 219
  creative thinking and, 130
  sought by employers, 232–33
Sleep
  stress management and, 199, 205
  test preparation and, 111
Slippery slope argument, 133
SMART goals, 9–10
Smoking, and health, 211
Social activities, in campus life, 36
Social learning theory, 58–59
Social media, 4–5, 168
Social networking sites, appropriate use of, 167–68
Social personality type, 222, 224
Social responsibility, emotional intelligence and, 29
Social science textbooks, reading, 98–99
Source citation, 154
Sources
  evaluating, 137, 149–50
  list of common, 146
Speaking, 155–57
Steel, Piers, 40–41
Stereotyping, 169–70
STIs, 208–9
Stress management, 115
  emotional intelligence and, 18, 29
  exercise for, 199, 203
  healthy living and, 199, 200–1, 205
  overextension and, 41
Student loans, 189–90
Study-abroad programs, 226
Study groups, 54, 56–57, 103
  comparing notes in, 84
  preparing for exams with, 110, 111
Studying
  avoiding distractions while, 48–49
  goal setting for, 48, 64
  improving concentration during, 94–95
  maximizing time for, 38–39, 46, 48
  2-for-1 rule for, 44
  while previewing, 91
Study location, 94
Subsidized federal student loans, 189–90
Substance abuse, 199
Success
  procrastination and, 41
  setting goals for, 8–10

Suicide, 206
Summaries, writing, for test preparation, 116
Supplemental Instruction classes, 81
Syllabus, 6–7, 73, 109
Synthesis, sharing ideas and, 150

T

Taking notes. *See* Note taking
Talent, scholarships based on, 185
Teachers. *See* Instructors
Teamwork skills, 233
  learning teams, 56–57
Technology
  face-to-face social interaction and, 217
  personal budgeting, 184
  to stay fit, 205
Ten-minute rule, in research, 149
Tests, 107–126
  academic honesty amd misconduct on, 121–23
  preparing for, 57, 109–13
  strategies for taking, 117–20, 201
  studying for retention and, 114–16
Textbooks
  getting most from, 95
  reading different types of, 97–99
Texting, appropriate use of, 153
Thank-you notes, to interviewers, 231
Thesaurus, 101
Thesis statements, 151
Thinking critically. *See* Critical thinking
Time, cultural views of, 35, 37
Time management, 35–46. *See also* Procrastination
  campus activities and, 36, 173
  employment and, 35–36
  for exercise, 204
  goal setting and, 8, 35–36
  maximizing study time and, 38–39
  organizing time and tasks for, 44–46
  pitfalls of poor management, 40–43
  punctuality and, 37, 231
  for reading assignments, 100
  for reviewing notes, 86
  setting priorities for, 26, 36, 43
  stress management and, 41
  while taking tests and exams, 117, 118
  for writing process, 153
To-do list, creating, 43, 46
Topic, choosing, narrowing and researching, 146
Transcripts, 14
Transferable skills
  career planning and, 219
  sought by employers, 232–33
Transition theory, change and, 59
Transportation, cutting costs of, 183
Travel time, using wisely, 49
True/false questions on tests/exams, 119
Truth, critical thinking and, 130. *See also* Critical thinking
Turnitin's Original Check, 154, 155
Tutoring centers on campus, 46
Tutors, preparing for tests with, 110
2-for-1 study rule, 44

U

Underlining, while reading, 93–94
Understanding, as second level of learning, 138, 139
Unemployment rate, college education and, 3
Unsubsidized federal student loans, 190

V

Values, personal
  career planning and, 219
  time management and, 35
Variable expenses, 182
VARK Learning Styles Inventory, 59–64
Verbal harassment, 172
Viewpoints
  considering, critical thinking and, 131
  evaluating sources for, 150
Visual aids, for speeches, 156
Visual learners
  mapping and, 92

methods for, 60, 64
  PowerPoint and, 83
Vocabulary, developing, 101–2
Volunteering
  career planning and, 226
  connecting with others by, 174
Vonn, Emily, 108

W

Wants, *versus* needs, 182
Washington, Jalen, 54
Web sites. *See also* Internet *entries*
  career center, 225
  job interview and, 230

materials from, 82, 147
  scholarship search on, 185
  secure passwords for, 168
Weekly planning, 44–45
Weight management, 199, 201, 204
Wellness, 199–200. *See also* Healthy
  living
Wheel mapping, 92
Wikipedia, 144, 146
Word choice, in speeches, 156
Word games, for vocabulary
  development, 101, 102
Word lists, reviewing, 102
Work ethic, 175, 186
Working. *See* Employment *entries*

Workplace skills, career planning and, 175, 219
Work satisfaction, career planning
  and, 220
Work-study
  as financial aid, 185–86
  getting experience from, 227
Writing, basics of, 151–55. *See also*
  Note taking
Writing disabilities, 67–68

Z

Zisa, Jeff, 180